CW00780249

SUMMER STAR

Three time group one winner Lashed poses after winning Whakanui Stud International Stakes Te Rapa

ACKNOWLEDGMENTS

There can be no stories without storymakers. That's why every person within the wide and wonderful thoroughbred industry should be acknowledged for their contribution to this edition of the New Zealand Thoroughbred Racing Annual, the editions which preceded it and the ones to follow. Obviously they cannot be all named, but there are other individuals and organisations who have been key elements in ensuring the 2004 edition made it to print. Foremost are New Zealand Thoroughbred Racing, New Zealand Thoroughbred Marketing, Mercedes and advertisers. Mike Dillon, Dennis Ryan and Aidan Rodley have supported with editorial and there has been massive input from regular photographers Trish Dunell, Race Images, Palmerston North and Race Images, Christchurch. This year we have also welcomed on board Melbourne-based photographer Bruno Cannatelli, whose library includes every edition of the Annual. Once again Jag Graphics has excelled in design.

PUBLISHED BY
BRADFORD PUBLISHING LTD
PO BOX 116, PAEROA
PH/FAX: 07 862-6456

EDITOR
DAVID BRADFORD
bradford-publishing@xtra.co.nz

DESIGN
JAG GRAPHICS LTD
PH: 09 373-5336
FAX: 09 373-5337
www.jaggraphics.co.nz

PRINT
EVERBEST PRINTING LTD

CONTENTS

79

FROM THE EDITOR

As New Zealand becomes increasingly a part of global racing, so does the New Zealand Thoroughbred Racing Annual find itself reaching into new horizons. That's why the 33rd edition includes a significant section on racing in Hong Kong – the new, exciting and challenging home of last year's champion trainer Paul O'Sullivan; why, along with regular coverage of Kiwis in Australia, a chapter is devoted to the endeavours of three New Zealand fillies in the American Oaks.

But predominantly this edition, as always, is about New Zealand horses and horse-people. It salutes a dream season for the Te Akau racing operation headed by its principal David Ellis, talented young trainer Mark Walker and star performers King's Chapel and Distinctly Secret. It recognises the great deeds of other great horses and the people behind their greatness.

Boxing Day at Ellerslie showcases the razzle dazzle of racing, with high fashion and the meeting of the cream of the three-year-old crop in our foremost classic, the Mercedes New Zealand Derby. In 2003 racegoers got a special bonus when 21-year-old superstar of the past Bonecrusher led out the Derby field in his final public appearance. The New Zealand Thoroughbred Racing Annual marks the occasion with a 29-page tribute to a special champion. Putting "Red's" story together was a particularly pleasurable experience – hopefully readers will find it equally so.

David Bradford

AN END TO A BEGINNING

New season underway

By David Bradford

To most people August is the middle month. Winter is not yet at an end and the buds of spring are still around the corner. But in the world of New Zealand racing August heralds the beginning of a new season and traditionally the time to celebrate and remember all the excitement and glamour – and sometimes sadness – of the one just committed to the history books.

For 33 years the New Zealand Thoroughbred Racing Annual has hailed the champions and recorded the great occasions which have plucked at the heartstrings of the participants and followers of arguably the world's most pulsating leisure industry. August 2003 was the launching pad for another intriguing chapter in the history of New Zealand racing.

To begin with, the TAB and the Racing Industry Board had been merged into a single entity. Go-getting agri-businessman Guy Sargent had been elected chairman of New Zealand Thoroughbred Racing and gone – into retirement – was 12 times champion jockey Lance O'Sullivan. There was already a different feel to start of the 2003/2004 season.

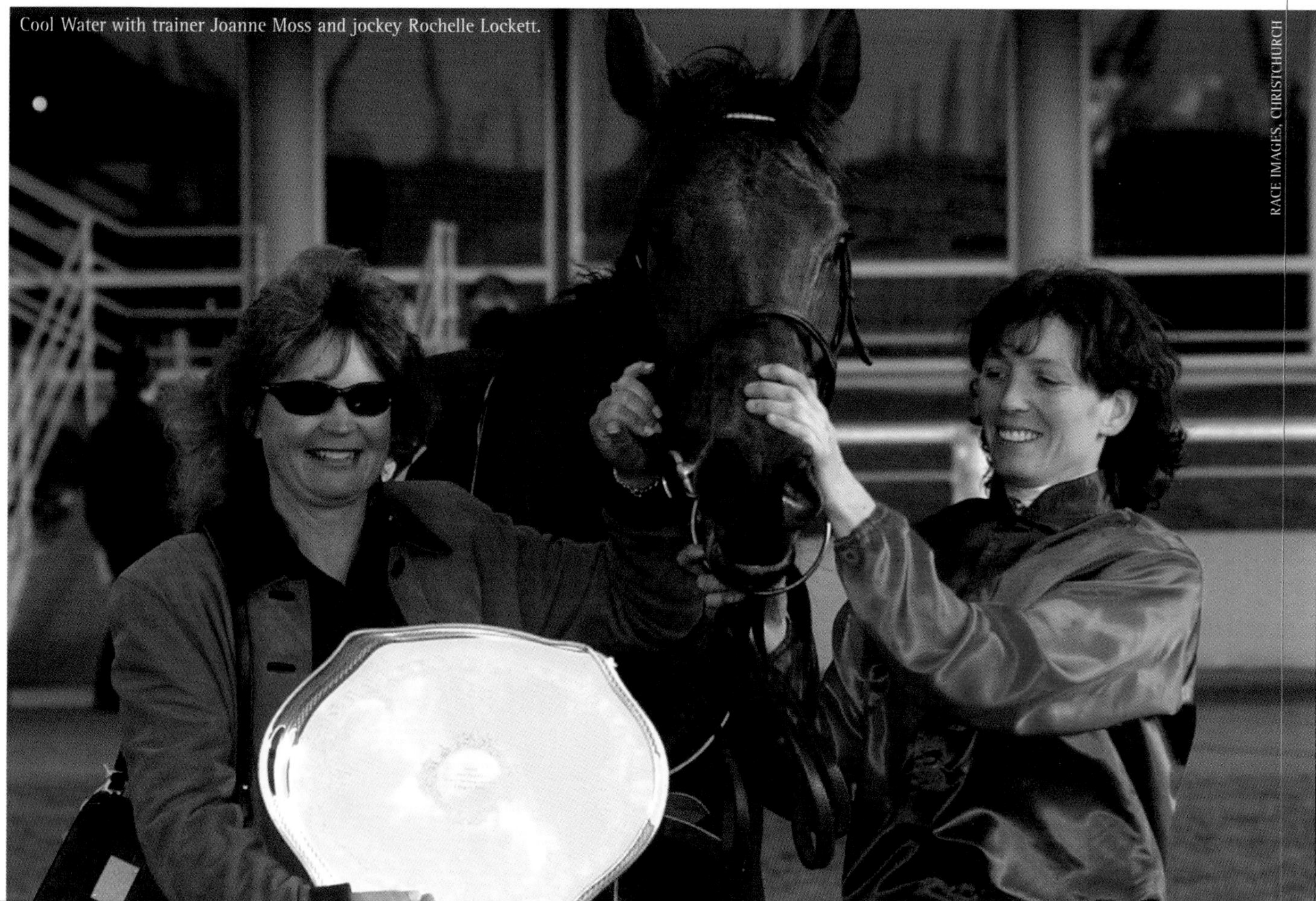

Cool Water with trainer Joanne Moss and jockey Rochelle Lockett.

RACE IMAGES, CHRISTCHURCH

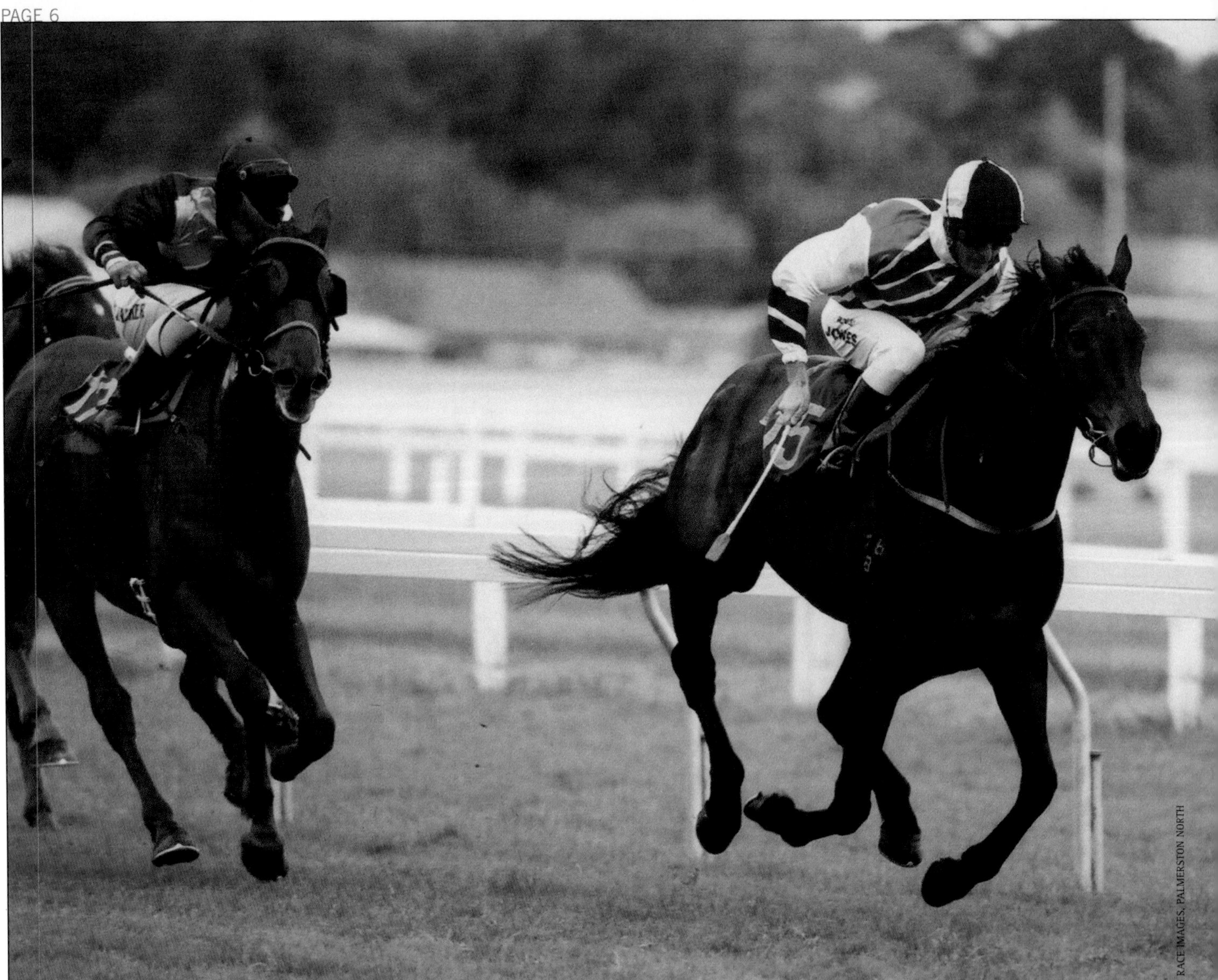

Miss Potential's dazzling win in the Mudgway Partsworld Stakes.

But none of that counted for much at the South Island's showcase winter meeting and the annual running of the Grand National Hurdles, the Grand National Steeples and the 105th Winter Cup. Awapuni trainer Lisa Latta won the Winter Cup with Tuscany Warrior, but as John Costello was to report in Blood Horse he is unlikely to be remembered with the same reverence as winners of the past like Catalogue and Soneri.

Catalogue won the race three times in the 1930s – with a Melbourne Cup in between – while Soneri in the 1940s carried 71.5kg in the second of her two wins. But the two big jumping races of 2003 were both captivating affairs.

The Grand National Hurdles was won by Cool Water in the expert hands of Rochelle Lockett at the expense of Willy Wince and Classic Spirit. The winner hailed from one of racing's outposts, Gisborne, and the win was a major triumph for his trainer Joanne Moss and the benefits of beach training. Though something of an unknown in the training ranks Moss, at 33, is not short on experience.

She was riding horses by the time she was four, graduated to showjumping and hunting, and was working for Laurie Laxon when the stable's star was Melbourne Cup winner Empire Rose. After gaining more stable experience at Coffs Harbour on the northern New South Wales coast, she spent time at a pre-training establishment in Japan.

There was a measure of Grand National nostalgia about Cool Water's win for his owners. He is raced by Mark and Shelley Treweek in partnership with Mark's parents Neil and Pauline. As a jockey Neil Treweek – now the track manager at Te Rapa – won the 1972 Grand National Hurdles on Never Give In. Earlier he had won the Homeby – Grand National – Lincoln steeples treble on Linred.

Matamata jumper Cuchulainn was the hot favourite for the Grand National Steeples after leadup wins in the Wellington Steeples and the Homeby Steeples. Ridden by Finbarr Leahy, he lived right up to expectations when holding out the globe-trotting Eric The Bee, who was making his final appearance.

Eric The Bee went as close as possible to a fairytale ending to his career which had produced wins in both the Grand

National Hurdles and Grand National Steeples and campaigns in America and Europe.

Cuchulainn, in the words of trainer Bob Autridge, "can be a tough old bugger at times", but is as genuine as they come on raceday and richly deserved the success that came his way during the winter of 2003. Nearing the end of the season he starred yet again when he won the Friday Flash Great Northern Hurdles in spectacular fashion. That triumph is recorded in detail elsewhere in this publication.

Whereas things went mainly according to plan throughout the Grand National carnival, there was a shaky start to the Hawke's Bay spring extravaganza of flat racing on August 30 when the group one $100,000 Mudgway Partsworld Stakes had to be transferred from Hastings to Wanganui because of bad weather. Befitting the status of the race, the first three home were Miss Potential, Tit For Taat and Rosina Lad.

In many ways Miss Potential is the embodiment of the despair and exhilaration which sometimes runs parallel in racing. Her incredible winning comeback run in group one company came after fracturing her near-side front knee in the Tauranga Classic. General opinion then was that she would have to be euthanased. But her Te Kauwhata owner-trainer Bill Borrie had other ideas.

An engineer by trade, Borrie constructed a special frame to support Miss Potential while the injury mended and after 15 weeks of dedicated attention by his wife Carrie the mare was once again a racehorse.

Miss Potential's Mudgway Partsworld Stakes win will always be treasured by the Borries as their most poignant moment in racing. But a lasting memory for many others will be her fifth placing against Australia's best metric milers in the 2004 Doncaster Handicap at Randwick when she went into the race on a short preparation and looked the likely winner with 100 metres to run. During the winter she proved her real class in Queensland when blitzing a strong field over 1500 metres in the $400,000 Winter Stakes.

Cool Water drives to the finish of the Grand National Hurdles.

By the time the Mudgway Partsworld Stakes had been run and won the New Zealand racing industry had gathered in Christchurch at the annual Mercedes awards dinner to declare Tit For Taat the Horse of the Year for 2002/03. A year later August signalled the same honour going the way of King's Chapel – this time the venue being Auckland and the Sky City casino.

Cuchulainn takes the last jump in front in the Grand National Steeples.

RACE IMAGES, CHRISTCHURCH

SEASON OF GLORY

New Zealand's stable of champions

By David Bradford

For Te Akau Racing Stables, the 2003/04 season gave every indication of having been crafted in heaven. In truth it was 12 months when years of hard work, careful planning, attention to detail and a lot of risk taking brought bountiful returns. The rewards were many and varied.

To begin with, resident trainer Mark Walker snared his first premiership. On the way to that achievement Te Akau had won New Zealand's richest race, provided the champion three-year-old and horse of the year and produced 12 individual two-year-old winners. In a headline-grabbing venture of a different kind it purchased the top-priced colt at the national yearling sales.

The principal of the Te Akau operation is high-profile administrator David Ellis – currently a director of New Zealand Thoroughbred Racing and past president of the Waikato Racing Club. His home base is Te Akau Stud, a 2600 acre cattle and sheep operation in the north-west Waikato which includes 600 acres for horses with facilities for pre-training, spelling and a small band of broodmares. Te Akau's racing stables are adjacent to the Matamata training complex which is obviously home to Mark Walker.

Walker teamed up with Ellis on leaving school and now, aged 32, is a partner in the operation. The pair have moulded their separate talents into an incredibly successful force in arguably New Zealand's toughest and most demanding industry. Both attribute their success to teamwork – not just between themselves but including dedicated and enthusiastic staff.

Walker concedes to a sense of achievement in winning his first training premiership – walking to the stage to collect his trophy at the Mercedes annual racing awards dinner was in no way a chore. But the premiership had not been a primary

King's Chapel powers home in New Zealand 2000 Guineas.

FOR TE AKAU

RACE IMAGES, CHRISTCHURCH

TOP: Kapsdan, one of twelve individual 2 year old winners for Te Akau, winning the group 2 Ford Wakefield Challenge Stakes at Trentham.
BOTTOM: Members of a syndicate which races a brilliant filly celebrate their win

goal at the beginning of the season. "I don't believe they are things you win," he said at season's end. "They come your way if you get things right. My goal has always been to place horses where I think they have the best chance of winning – to give their owners a chance to enjoy their racing. That's why it's important to win lesser races for lesser talented horses."

But even the phlegmatic Walker doesn't shirk from the sheer joy of winning the big ones – the classics, cups and important weight-for age races. In only the second month of the 2003/04 season he was thrust to a special high when he won the $750,000 group one Kelt Capital Stakes with Distinctly Secret. Those sorts of races are never easily won but on race morning Walker was so confident he told Ellis only bad luck could beat the horse.

Distinctly Secret vindicated that confidence when he beat Hail by three and three-quarter lengths with Irish Rover, who had beaten Mudgway Partsworld Stakes winner Miss Potential in the Glenmorgan Stakes at his previous start, third ahead of Ben Sparta. In the process of winning, Distinctly Secret was given a perfect trip by stable jockey Opie Bosson. Walker recognises Bosson as a very important cog in the Te Akau wheel and later said a lot of his pre-race confidence hinged around the fact that Bosson never panicked if things went wrong. "He just finds a way of getting out of trouble," he said.

SONJA BRADFORD

$1.1 million Danehill colt with Mark Walker at Te Akau stables.

That Kelt Capital Stakes win rocketed Distinctly Secret into favour for the Caulfield Cup, in which he finished third to Mummify, just nosed out of second by Grey Song. The merit of the performance is reflected in Mummify's time for the 2400 metres of 2:25.98 being the second-fastest on record. At his next Melbourne start Distinctly Secret finished fifth in the weight-for-age Mackinnon Stakes, which he would have won given anything like a decent run. Then, for the second time, he found the 3200 metres of the Melbourne Cup just

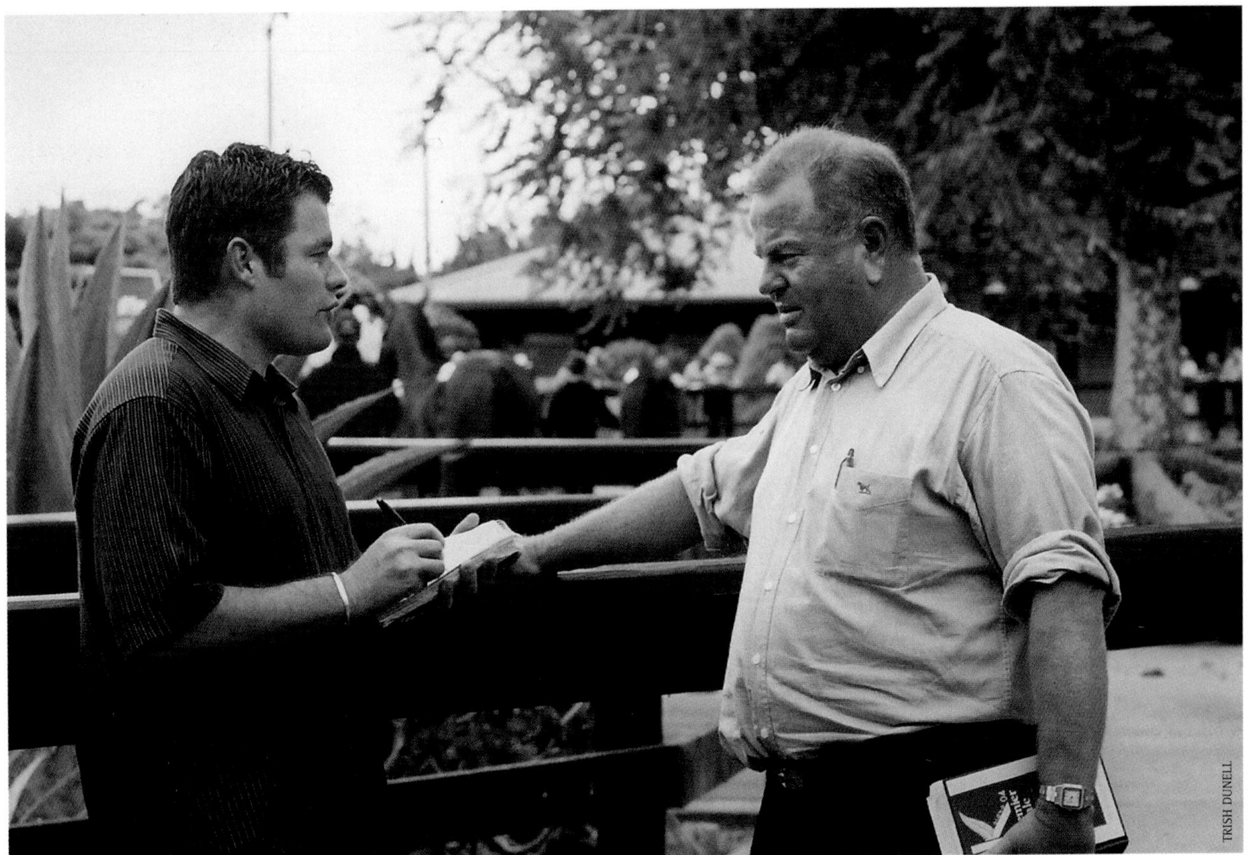
TRISH DUNELL

Waikato Times racing editor Aidan Rodley getting the facts from David Ellis.

Distinctly Secret displays his rare class as he romps away with the Kelt Capital Stakes.

beyond him.

Distinctly Secret's final race of the Melbourne spring carnival was the Sandown Classic, in which the winner Legible enjoyed a charmed rails run while Distinctly Secret was forced over extra ground and lost by a short neck. The consolation for the bad luck during the campaign was a bagful of place money.

Bad luck again dogged him during a cut-short Queensland winter campaign. The first thing that went wrong was when, on the eve of his departure, he got involved in a nail-biting battle with Irish Rover in the Lawnmaster Awapuni Gold Cup.

Track specialist Irish Rover looked all over a winner until the never-say-die Distinctly Secret refused to quit and found some extra petrol in the tank from lord knows where to force a dead-heat. Said Walker on a backward look at Queensland: "It was the sort of race he could have done without. It knocked him and I think he was still feeling it when we left." But once the Doomben Cup came around, Walker believed he had the horse spot on. The weight-for-age conditions and the distance both suited and Distinctly Secret had that "let-me-at-'em" attitude about him. Then on race eve disaster struck.

Distinctly Secret had given himself a slight nick when galloping. Enough of a cut to bandage, but nothing to worry about –

until a minor infection set in and it was too late within the rules to administer antibiotics. There was no alternative but to scratch.

Walker and Ellis don't dwell on the odd thing which went wrong during the season – they're just happy about what went right.

That was the way they looked at the season of their horse of the year King's Chapel. The three-time group one winner showed the Aussies a taste of his exceptional class when he won the Gold Coast Guineas, only to succumb to an outside barrier draw in the Doomben Ten Thousand and be almost knocked to the ground in the Stradbroke Handicap. Such was the physical buffeting jockey Glen Boss took in the Stradbroke he had to get the assistance of others to remove the saddle when he returned to the enclosure. But there were great New Zealand moments to look back on.

As a two-year-old King's Chapel had won the $500,000 Mercedes Super Bonus Classique at Te Rapa and there was a time when it looked as if he, and not stablemate Maroofity, would be the season's leading juvenile. At three it was King's Chapel who was the star, with group one wins in the New Zealand Two Thousand Guineas, the Telegraph Handicap and the Family Hotel WFA.

Each win was achieved in quite sensational fashion.

When King's Chapel went into the Couplands Bakeries Two Thousand Guineas, a question mark still hung as to whether he would manage the 1600 metres. That little detail was confidently taken care of by Opie Bosson, who dictated the pace and then sprinted his mount clear to win by two lengths. Backed up over the same distance in the Bayer Classic he finished third to Russian Pearl and Taatletail. To follow was one of the finest training feats of the season.

The Bayer Classic was run on November 27 and Walker took King's Chapel home from Levin and gave him a break from training. He was not to resume until January 17 against the hottest sprint company in the country in the ING Telegraph Handicap at Trentham. It was a huge ask of a three-year-old but he displayed his class to win from outsider Sunlaw and topweight Sedecrem – putting up the near world record time of 1:6.8.

The winning mount went to Noel Harris, substituting for Opie Bosson who couldn't make the 52kg. Harris, whose first win in the big Trentham sprint had come 21 years previously on Sharif, does have close ties with Te Akau, and not just as a lightweight rider. His partner Shannon Melton is the stable's office manager and a regular trackwork rider.

If King's Chapel had to work hard for that win, it was a different story when the Family Hotel WFA was transferred from a flood ravaged Otaki to Hastings. The big guns were all on hand for the big 1400 metre race on February 19, including Railway Handicap winner Vinaka, the wonderfully consistent and talented Sedecrem and the classy Zvezda. Ridden by visiting Australian jockey Rhys McLeod, King's Chapel was simply awesome when winning by three and a quarter lengths from Vinaka, with Sedecrem alongside in third. Mark Walker tends to plump for the Telegraph Handicap effort as being the better, but the ease with which King's Chapel disposed of Vinaka and Sedecrem was quite incredible and not everyone will agree with him.

Racing was only part of the summer excitement for Te Akau. There was also a new twist to its yearling sale activities. David Ellis and Mark Walker are meticulous when making yearling inspections pre-sale but when they fine-tune their shopping list it usually consists of entries in the middle price range, and sometimes quite lower. It therefore sent a ripple of surprise through the sales auditorium at Karaka when in the closing minutes of the premier session David Ellis bought the sales-topper for $1.1 million.

Later he was to tell how he and Mark Walker had discussed in December the merits of buying into a Danehill colt with sire potential. Later he looked over some of the champion's progeny at the Magic Millions Gold Coast Sale, but none

David Ellis and New Zealand 2000 Guineas sponsor Ray Coupland.

impressed as much as the one from Grand Echezeaux already inspected at Pencarrow Stud. He was the sixth to last lot to be offered and Ellis says the wait was pretty nerve wracking.

The overseas opposition was tackled by Ellis in the knowledge that several established clients had committed to taking shares and all ten were taken up within 48 hours. Besides his handsome looks the colt boasts a mouth-watering female pedigree. His dam Grand Echezeaux is an Australasian Oaks-winning daughter of Zabeel and a half-sister to Hong Kong Cup winner Romanee Conti, who in turn is the dam of Caulfield and Melbourne Cup winner Ethereal.

Vendor of the colt Pencarrow Stud is owned by brothers Peter and Philip Vela, who also own New Zealand Bloodstock Ltd. Not surprisingly they put their hands up for a share. The occasion also coincided with the birthday of Peter Vela's daughter Victoria, which prompted David Ellis to invite her to come up with a name. She chose Darci Brahma.

In a sense, it is two names. Darci is a corruption of DRC, representing the Domaine of Romani Conti wines while Brahma translates to creator of gods. By season's end the colt was one of 50 rising two-year-olds who had gone through Te Akau's early education programme.

Te Akau clients are a mixture of partnerships, individuals and a big number of major breeders. Horse numbers are also added to with the progeny of around 10 broodmares owned by Ellis and Walker. Many commute between Matamata and the satellite stable at Rangiora managed by Gus Clutterbuck.

A significant addition to the mix is new stable apprentice Troy Harris, the 16-year-old son of Noel. He was launched with a debut winning ride at Ruakaka on June 23.

The newest training premiership winner is in no way fazed by his success or by the scale of the operation. "It's a bit like the America's Cup," he jokes. "There's only one captain, but you're never going to win without the right crew."

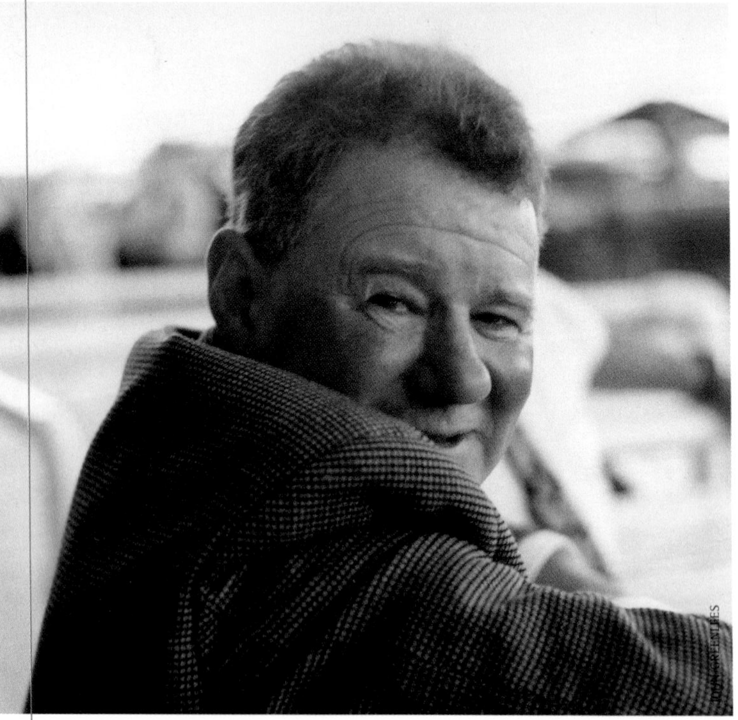

TOP LEFT: King's Chapel too good in Telegraph Handicap.
LEFT: Gus Clutterbuck, manager of Te Akau's Rangiora stable.

Opie Bosson and King's Chapel after their convincing win in the New Zealand 2000 Guineas.

RACE IMAGES, CHRISTCHURCH

WAIKA

STU

WS bred STARCRAFT - the centre of attention at Royal Randwick after his AJC Derby victory

LINDA & ALAN JONES COLLECT GOLD

Mercedes Awards Dinner

By David Bradford.
Photos by Lawrence Smith.

It was like Athens had moved to Auckland's Sky City Casino – all eyes on the gold medallists – when Alan and Linda Jones won the ultimate accolade at the 2004 Mercedes industry awards. On an occasion exclusively designed around achievers they were standouts moulded into a single shining beacon which had changed the course of New Zealand racing. Their award for outstanding contributions to racing excellence was both popular and richly deserved.

But, as with Olympic medal ceremonies, the joy and emotion of the recipients told little of what had gone on before. The self belief, the determination, the grit which turns natural talents into gold medals. Alan and Linda Jones may not have run marathons to get to the victory dais but there have been times when the trail has been equally gut-wrenching.

Alan Jones was born in England, spent most of his early years in Rhodesia and finished off his schooling in New Zealand before becoming a relatively obscure jockey. As an apprentice he rode seven winners from his first 30 rides, then failed to get a winner in his next 100 mounts. He managed a better strike rate as jumps jockey but aged 20 was walking at 72kg and there was no way he was going to be another Lester Piggott, or even a Craig Thornton of the future.

The springboard to his training career was the airstrip at Raglan and when he relocated to Paeroa most would have identified it as another dead end. Yet, something awaited the young trainer at Paeroa which was to change his life – a pretty teenage horse mad pharmacy assistant by the name of Linda Wilkinson. Together they were to batter down the male chauvinism which still lurked like a cancer on New Zealand racing until the late 1970s and embed themselves into turf history.

Snow Wilkinson, Linda's stepfather, was a Paeroa blacksmith. That was probably why when she broke a leg in a car accident as a three-year-old she was given a tiny pony as a get

Linda and Alan Jones.

well present. It was that pony, Midge, who was to ignite her love for horses and lead her to others which took her through the various stages of pony club and hunting. But it was the racehorses who trained at Paeroa which really set her adrenalin alight and introduced her to Alan Jones, first as a track rider and then marriage at age 19.

Encouraged by success in races at gymkhanas and point-to-point meetings restricted to lady riders, the young housewife asked a simple question. Why can't I become a jockey? The reply that the Rules of Racing didn't allow for it seemed to her as no answer at all. So she asked again: How come major overseas countries licence female jockeys? The first reply was totted out again. From the time Linda was a toddler no had never been a satisfactory answer. So, with the help of friends

Trainer Karen Fursdon (far right) heads up the support team for champion stayer Upestthym.

she set about changing the rules.

With the devoted support of husband Alan, human rights people, womens libbers, members of the media and some forward thinking racing folk, she finally won the right to be apprenticed to her trainer husband. She wasn't New Zealand's first female apprentice – that distinction had gone to Vivienne Kaye, who had become indentured to her father Alan Kaye. Whereas, Linda had been turned down because she was supposedly too old at 24, married and not strong enough, the New Zealand Racing Conference (then the ruling body) ran out of arguments against an unmarried 15-year-old.

But when Linda, by now mother of daughter Clare, began her professional riding career in August 1978, not even she could have envisaged the impact she would have on Australasian racing. She was the leading apprentice for the season with 49 wins, won four races in a single day, became the first female to win against the male professionals in Australia, and was the first female to ride against the professionals at Doomben, Randwick, Rosehill, Morphetville, Flemington, Ascot Park (Perth) and Canberra.

Her great talent, good looks and vivacious personality made her a media hit and the darling of racegoers on both sides of the Tasman. She broke down social and gendre barriers and opened the way to the many fine female riders who are now so much an integral part of the New Zealand racing. She continues to be one of New Zealand's great racing ambassadors. But if Linda's late blossoming career reached meteroic heights, husband Alan never dwelt in the shadows. He pursued the cause of female jockeys. Two standouts to whom he became boss and mentor were Catherine Treymane and Linda Ballantyne.

Ballantyne retired with 539 winners, 30 of them overseas. Treymane, now training had 479 wins, 130 overseas.

He rapidly established himself as a master trainer and when Pomp And Glory won the Easter Handicap last April he completed a clean sweep of Ellerslie's feature races – highlighted with two Auckland Cups, a New Zealand Derby and a Railway Handicap. No doubt spurred on by the battles with bureauracy over Linda's jockeys licence he has taken a keen interest in administration and eventually was to serve on the board of New Zealand Thoroughbred Racing – the replacement body for the former enemy, the New Zealand Racing Conference.

One of the nicest twists to this happy story mix of young love, fame and glory and rags-to-riches is a speedy mare named Alynda – named for the two heroes. Alynda's first contribution was winning New Zealand's richest sprint race, the Railway Handicap. Her legacy has been a family dynasty which in no small way has contributed to the couple's financial security.

Keeping up with the Joneses isn't easy, but at least Alynda has had a good crack at it.

MERCEDES AWARDS

OUTSTANDING CONTRIBUTION TO RACING EXCELLENCE	**ALAN AND LINDA JONES**
HORSE OF THE YEAR	**KING'S CHAPEL**
OWNER OF THE YEAR	**SIR PATRICK & LADY HOGAN**
DEWAR STALLION	**ZABEEL**
MERCEDES BROODMARE	**FLYING FLOOZIE**
DUNSTAN TRAINER	**MARK WALKER**
NEWCOMER TRAINER	**IAN GEORGE**
FILLY OF THE YEAR	**TAATLETAIL**
WEIGHT-FOR-AGE CHAMPION	**LASHED**
CHAMPION TWO-YEAR-OLD	**KEENINSKY**
CHAMPION THREE-YEAR-OLD	**KING'S CHAPEL**
CHAMPION SPRINTER/MILER	**KING'S CHAPEL**
JOCKEY OF THE YEAR	**LEITH INNES**
CHAMPION APPRENTICE	**MICHAEL WALKER**
JUMPS JOCKEY	**MICHELLE HOPKINS**
GROSVENOR STALLION	**VOLKSRAAD**
BREEDER OF THE YEAR	**SIR PATRICK & LADY HOGAN**
CHAMPION JUMPER	**CUCHULAINN**
CHAMPION STAYER	**UPSETTHYM**
MEDIA CONTRIBUTION	**BARRY LICHTER**

Michael Walker.

David Ellis receives the Horse of the Year award won by King's Chapel from Mercedes managing director Ernie Ward.

Sir Patrick and Lady Hogan.

Leith Innes.

Michelle Hopkins with NZTR director Graeme Sanders.

The Mercedes-Benz E-Class

Suspension that can change as quickly as the road does.

▸ The optional Airmatic suspension in the E-Class is capable of controlling each wheel's reaction to bumps, potholes and corrugations individually.

▸ So, if you find yourself driving on four different road surfaces at the same time, the E-Class will remain composed. (If this sounds a bit far-fetched, think about your last trip on a New Zealand country road.)

▸ What's more, Airmatic suspension allows the driver to react to changing road conditions. Which means that the E-Class suspension can change from the feel of a luxury saloon to that of a sports car at the press of a button.

▸ More cleverly still, you'll find that Airmatic lowers the car imperceptibly at speed to improve both fuel consumption and handling.

Of course, it's far better to experience this from behind the wheel of the E-Class.

▸ To arrange a test drive, call 0800 320 230 for the location of your nearest Mercedes-Benz showroom.

▸ Or for further details on all our cars, please visit our website at www.mercedes-benz.co.nz

Mercedes-Benz

WRC/3799

LASHED LASHES OUT IN ZABEEL CLASSIC

Ellerslie's Weight-for-a-Age Feature

By David Bradford

Sometimes the best laid plans of mice and men go awry. But long range plans worked to perfection when Sir Patrick Hogan set himself to win the group one $150,000 Zabeel Classic – a race for which, supported by other shareholders in the champion sire, he was the principal sponsor.

It was perhaps an irony that the horse who won the event for him was not a product of his famous Cambridge Stud, but an Australian-bred he bought for what has become the bargain basement price of $80,000. In many ways the purchase was more of a barter than an outright sale. Central to the deal was colourful transtasman trainer Graeme Rogerson.

Originally Rogerson had bought Lashed as a yearling for former Melbourne Crown Casino boss Lloyd Williams and she had already won two races when she was offered to Sir Patrick, who turned the situation into a business opportunity. He agreed to buy the filly on behalf of himself and wife Justine with two provisos. One of these conditions was that Lashed should carry Sir Patrick's colours and not those of the Rogerson stable. The other stipulation was that Rogerson agreed to buy some of the Cambridge Stud draft at the Sydney Easter Sales – the reason for Sir Patrick being in Australia in the first place. Both conditions were met.

Lashed was to become one of Australia's leading three-year-old fillies, placing second in the VRC Oaks but failing to snare a group one win. After her busy three-year-old programme she had only a couple of Australian races as a four-year-old before coming to New Zealand on December 22 and joining Rogerson's New Zealand training partner Stephen Autridge at Tuhikaramea, near Hamilton.

Throughout her Australian campaigns Lashed had been plagued by back problems and regular swimming had been part of her therapeutic programme. But after arriving at her New Zealand base she missed her daily swim on one occasion and according to Autridge seemed so much more free in her action. As a result he cut the swimming entirely from her training routine.

Neglected by the punters at odds of 15 to 1, Lashed was ridden with utmost confidence by Opie Bosson in the Zabeel Classic and unwound a dazzling finish after being at the rear of the 12-horse field to beat Penny Gem by a length and a half. Penny Gem had looked all over a winner when she ran past tiring pacemaker St Reims, but was overwhelmed by Lashed's late burst. Waikato Cup winner El Duce was a brave third. Highly rated three-year-old Philamor, who had disappointed an army of admirers in the Derby, raced on the outside of the leaders for much of the way and finished sixth.

Before the summer was through Lashed was to prove the

AUCKLAND RACING CLUB

Sir Patrick Hogan presents the Zabeel Classic trophy to Lashed's co-trainer Stephen Austridge.

Lashed too good in Zabeel Classic.

weight-for-age star, adding another two group wins. The first of these came in the Whakanui Stud International at Te Rapa, again over 2000 metres, on February 7. Once again Penny Gem was the bridesmaid after Lashed collared her in the last gasp to win by half a head. Veteran galloper Kaapstad Way was a length and a quarter away third ahead of the remainder, who had been well whipped.

This time Sir Patrick was not winning his own race. The group two event he sponsored earlier in the day – the Cambridge Stud Sir Tristram Fillies Classic – had been won by the Rogerson/Autridge trained Taatletail. However, the second group one win beside Lashed's name on retirement as a broodmare was probably of greater value than the $62,500 winning stake.

And things only got better for Lashed in New Zealand.

In wretched conditions at Ellerslie on February 28, she beat Deebee Belle and Hail in the New Zealand Stakes after looking a 100 to 1 chance with 50 metres to run. An ecstatic Sir Patrick rushed from the stands to greet the mare and was soaking wet by the time the winner's stall was reached. Rider Opie Bosson was hailed as a hero and was engaged as Lashed's jockey for a Sydney autumn campaign mainly targeting the Ranvet Stakes. But the rare burst of summer form in New Zealand was her lot for the season.

Over previous years Sir Patrick had won Auckland and Wellington Cups and a Railway Handicap and watched as Surround, whom he'd leased out, become the champion filly of Australia. But these days racing has taken on a greater lustre as he withheld numerous richly bred fillies from sale in anticipation of racing them himself before they were consigned to the Cambridge Stud broodmare band.

He confesses to an adrenaline rush every time he sees his emerald green colours with yellow spots on the racetrack and regards the warm fuzzies as no more than a just reward for the hard work he and his wife put into making Cambridge Stud the best-known breeding operation in Australasia. But he is also quick to point out that racing is no more than the fun part of his life. The core activity will always be breeding.

For the past 23 years Cambridge Stud has been leading vendor at the national yearling sales. Sir Patrick has no intention of easing up until the total reaches 25 years – and with drafts spearheaded by Zabeel and Stravinsky and paddocks of mares with mouth-watering pedigrees that goal would seem nothing else but a foregone conclusion.

TORLESSE TRIUMPHS AT RICCARTON

New Zealand Cup

By David Bradford

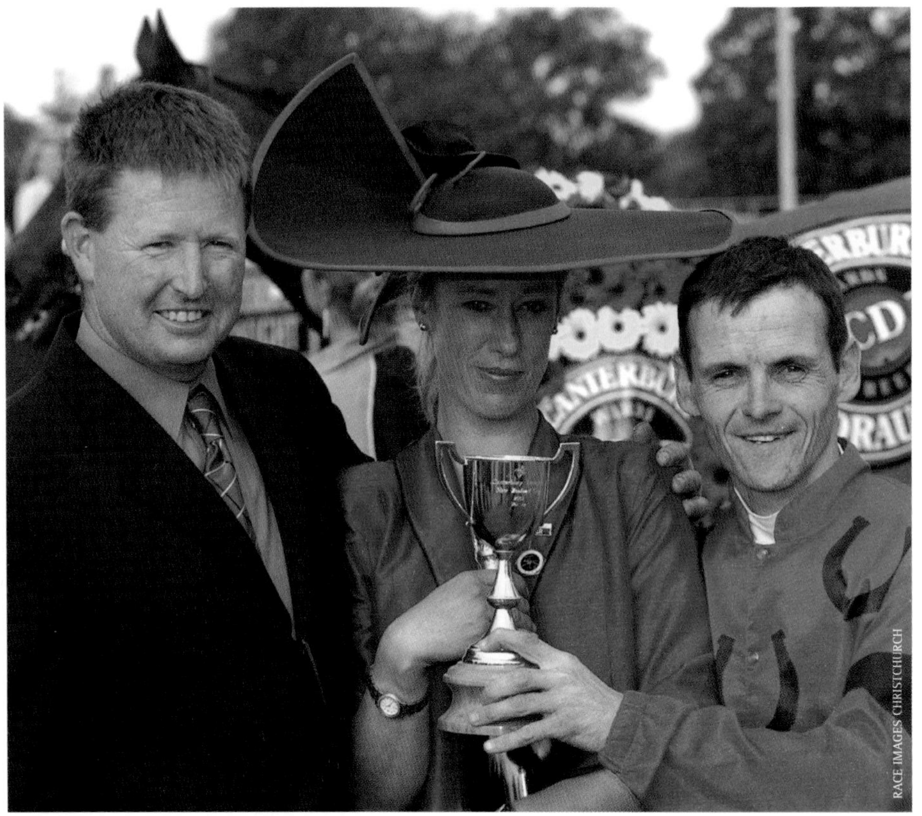

Mandy Brown flanked by husband Matt and jockey Terry Moseley.

Fatherly advice can be pretty handy at times – even if it comes from your father-in-law. Just ask Mandy Brown, trainer of 2003 New Zealand Cup winner Torlesse. Mandy Brown first saw Torlesse as a two-year-old offered at a ready-to-run sale. She didn't like his plain looks and fancied his shonky knees even less. Husband Matt was also unimpressed. But Matt's father Ken was on an entirely different wavelength. Ken had fallen in love with the horse's pedigree.

He was by Volksraad from the group one winner of 12 races in Seamist. Trained in the South Island by John Parsons, Seamist made numerous North Island raids where wins included the Awapuni Gold Cup, the Auckland Stakes at Ellerslie and the Japan/New Zealand Trophy at Tauranga. As a three-year-old she had run second in the One Thousand Guineas to Jennifer Rush.

After Mandy and Matt had taken all that into consideration they took another look at the video of Torlesse's breeze-up. They were suitably impressed and negotiated his purchase for $50,000 after he had been passed in at auction. It proved to be a good piece of business because the New Zealand Cup provided him with his 12th win and took his earnings to $432,000.

Following an impressive three-year-old season Torlesse was campaigned in Australia where he was a winner in Melbourne but then encountered degenerative foot problems. These were finally overcome by the fitting of special bar shoes which allowed an increased blood flow and took pressure off the eroding pedal bone. Later his career was further threatened by a pinched nerve in a shoulder.

Following a lengthy spell, and free of problems, he went into the New Zealand Cup as a six-year-old and after racing at the tail of the field most of the way powered home to win decisively by two lengths from fellow South Islander Cabella. Galway Lass, trained by Paul O'Sullivan and ridden by Michael Walker, started favourite and finished third. There was a gap to the others who were headed by Soldier Blue.

The win was a triumph for the extended Brown family which races Torlesse under the banner of the Ngapuke Stables Syndicate. The group comprises Mandy Brown, husband Matt and his parents Ken and Veronica plus his brother Robin and Robin's wife Vicky. Usually they have around 12 horses trained by Mandy near Rangiora.

After a five-year grounding with her aunt Jan Hay, Mandy Brown began her training career as a 21-year-old. She had been in the business 13 years when Torlesse provided her with her greatest triumph. Jockey Terry Moseley was also recording his most important win. After struggling as a young rider in the North Island, Moseley shifted south and was third behind Jamie Bullard and Paul Richards on the list of South Island-based jockeys in the 2002/03 season. The 2003/04 season continued to be kind to him.

Torlesse powers home for victory.

RACE IMAGES CHRISTCHURCH

DEADHEAT

Counties Cup baffles cameras

By David Bradford

Punters and jockeys alike were confused at the finish of the Eagle Technology Counties Cup. Judge Andrew O'Toole, with his electronic aids, avoided the confusion but neither was he able to declare a winner. Instead he called a dead-heat between Leica Guv and Penny Gem.

The pair went into the race with very different form credentials. Leica Guv had been struggling to find form against good company after winning the New Zealand Derby two seasons earlier, but the previous month Penny Gem had won the group one Avery Ford Captain Cook Stakes at Trentham. In that weight-for-age race over 1600 metres she had taken a photo decision over Marie Claire.

Penny Gem started second favourite behind Sunray while Leica Guv was despised in the betting in the 16-horse field and only Crown Prince and Cyclades were less fancied.

Not surprisingly Leica Guv set the pace, but instead of fighting former South African jockey Eddie de Klerk he settled kindly and was allowed to ease eight lengths clear coming to the home turn. It was a clever piece of riding and the key factor in almost stealing an outright win. Afterwards Penny Gem's rider Michael Coleman was to say his mount was in front one stride before the winning post and one stride past. On the line he didn't know – his doubts confirmed by the camera.

Leica Guv was trained for his New Zealand Derby win by three-time Australian equestrian Olympian Jeff McVean. In the new season he had taken his elder daughter Emma-Lee on board as his training partner and it was Emma-Lee who celebrated her first training success at Pukekohe while her father was supervising younger daughter Katie at showjumping events at Hawera.

Hopes were high that Leica Guv was on the comeback trail but as the season unfolded further that did not prove the case.

The day's other star attraction was the $60,000 Auckland Thoroughbred Breeders Stakes, which again fell to the stable of Trevor and Stephen McKee after twice winning the event with Sunline. This time the winner was the three-year-old filly Pay My Bail, who started favourite and took a long neck decision over the classy Miss Potential. Afterwards Trevor McKee, who races the filly in partnership with Thayne Green, declared the big summer mission for Pay My Bail would be the group one Railway Stakes at Ellerslie. In that race she beat all except Vinaka.

Notable among the winners in the supporting races on Counties Cup Day was Pomp And Glory, who in the autumn stepped up to group one level and won New Zealand's most famous metric mile, the Easter Handicap at Ellerslie.

Pay My Bail holding out Miss Potential in Auckland Throughbred Breeders Stakes.

Penny Gem (outer) and Leica Guv locked in battle at the finish of The Counties Cup.

TRISH DUNELL

One cup, two jockeys.

Riders Eddie de Klerk (Leica Guv) and Michael Coleman (Penny Gem) share the laurels.

DOUBLE DOUBLE FOR CUP STARS

Te Rapa and Avondale features

By David Bradford
Photos by Trish Dunell

Twin results such as provided last season by two of New Zealand's warrior racehorses, El Duce and Regal Krona, are a racing rarity. Their odds-beating efforts came with successive wins in the Waikato and Avondale Cups and earned both an elite place in the history of both races.

These two staying races are northern focal points of late spring and early summer racing and are often looked upon as pointers to the Auckland Cup, though in recent times neither event has been a reliable indicator.

El Duce and Regal Krona have more than a few things in common. Neither is very big physically but both make up for that with natural ability and an appealing will to win when at peak fitness. Both boast husband-and-wife trainers – in the case of El Duce Donna and Dean Logan and in the case of Regal Krona Roger and Sheryl McGlade. When they achieved their repeat wins both were eight-year-olds.

Regal Krona won the 2002 New Zealand Bloodstock Avondale Cup from Deebee Belle and Ebony Honor. In the Auckland Cup a few weeks later Regal Krona ran last but Ebony Honor was a close and unlucky third behind Bodie and Oarsman.

Twelve months later Regal Krona's winning jockey of 2002, Michael Coleman, as regular rider for the Michael Moroney/Andrew Scott stable, switched to The Mighty Lions and talented young rider Andrew Calder was given the chance to bring Regal Krona home first after being a tail-ender on the home turn. In a blanket finish the winning margin over The Mighty Lions was a short head with a long head to Bel Air. El Duce was sixth. Come the Auckland Cup and The Mighty Lions ran fourth, Regal Krona 12th and Bel Air and El Duce were not in the field.

This second Avondale Cup was a notable triumph for the

McGlades who before their marriage had met with significant success when training on their own accounts. Early in his career Roger McGlade won the Auckland Cup with Stylish Dude and nine races with Regal Krona's sire Krona. Among Krona's notable wins were the New Zealand Two Thousand Guineas, the Bayer Classic and in Australia the Tulloch Stakes. As Sheryl Douglas, his wife put her imprint on New Zealand racing by winning the Great Northern Hurdles with Clem and the Grand National Steeples with Just Jojo. Jumpers continue to be the first love of Sheryl McGlade and she has been a key figure in promoting the cause of jumps racing and encouraging young riders.

In the autumn Regal Krona went within an ace of picking up another important cup when he lost a photo decision to Royal Secret in the $80,000 Hawke's Bay Cup. Royal Secret, under 52kg and receiving 3kg from Regal Krona, owed her win to a masterly ride along the rails by Noel Harris whereas Michael Coleman had been forced to go wide on Regal Krona. With 100 metres to run Regal Krona looked the certain winner, but in the end went under gallantly by a short head.

In 2002 El Duce won his way into the hearts of punters with successive wins in the Waikato Cup and Ellerslie's Queen Elizabeth Handicap – efforts which saw him run as

Regal Krona (blue and white colours) surges to the front in the Avondale Cup which he went on to win by two lengths.

unplaced favourite in the Auckland Cup. All-in-all it was a remarkable comeback for a horse who had suffered life-threatening injuries while racing in Singapore. El Duce's rider in the 2002 Waikato Cup – and also in major races in Singapore – was Catherine Treymane. In retirement she was replaced by Australian Rhys McLeod during one of the Melbourne jockey's several forays into New Zealand racing during the season.

McLeod sent El Duce clear rounding the home turn to beat My Governess by three-quarters of a length with Bel Air turning in another honest effort to be a similar distance back third. Old adversary Regal Krona was sixth. My Governess trained on to finish third behind Upsetthym and Galway Lass in the Auckland Cup. El Duce's best effort at the Ellerslie summer carnival was third behind Lashed and Penny Gem in the $150,000 Zabeel Classic.

At eight years Regal Krona and El Duce can be classified as oldtimers and their repeat wins in two such keenly sought after races put the final seal on their class. Regal Krona became only the third horse to win back-to-back Avondale Cups since the race was switched from the spring to the summer in 1970. The others were Happy Union who won for Te Rapa trainer Bill Winder in 1977 and '78 and the Jim Gibbs trained Maurine in 1988 and '89. In the case of El Duce it was necessary to go back to the 1960s to High Mark to find the previous back-to-back winner of the Waikato Cup. In the twenty years before that only Foxwyn and Deceptive had achieved the feat.

The other star at the Waikato Cup and Avondale Cup meetings was Philamor. His wins in the Hamilton and Avondale Guineas made him favourite for the NZ Derby and stamped him as a young galloper of great class. Things did not go well for him in the Derby but that in no way dimmed his great future.

El Duce romps home for his second Waikato Times Cup win.

Philamor in regal pose.

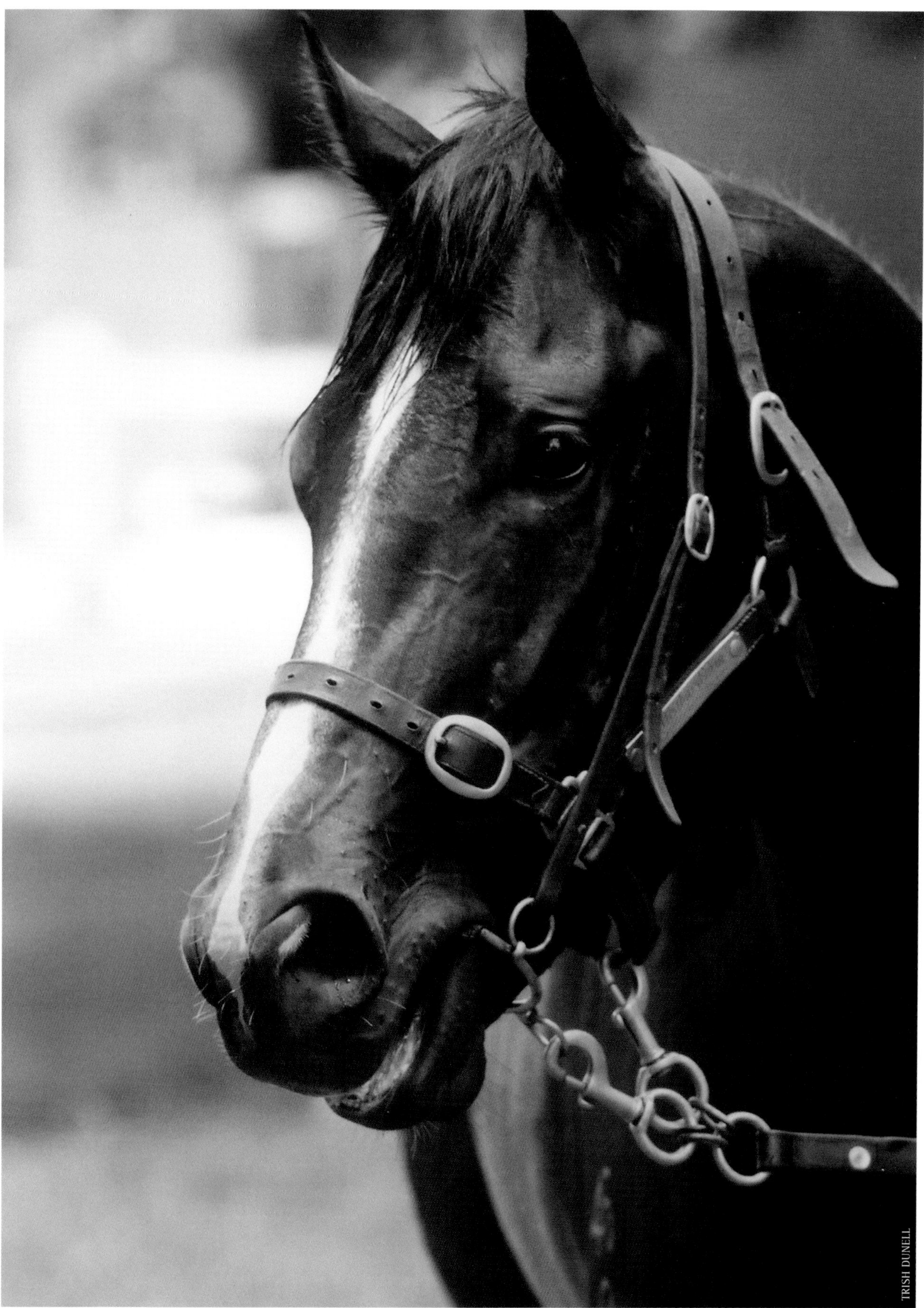

TRISH DUNELL

Falkirk looking chipper after winning the first race of Waikato Cup Day.

HOWIE AND LORAINNE STRIKE GOLD

Manawatu Cup action

By David Bradford

The Manawatu Racing Club's big day of December racing belonged to the husband and wife Otaki training team of Howie and Lorraine Mathews and owners Peter and Nancy Izett of Taupo, who collected both group races on the programme – the Z1 Motoring Manawatu Cup and the Higgins Challenge Stakes.

Bought as a weanling by Peter Izett, Manawatu Cup winner Rising Heights grew to be a big rangy fellow who, from an early stage, gave promise of ability above his physical and mental maturity. He won his early races from the Takanini stable of Frank and Craig Ritchie, but was transferred to Otaki when Mathews returned to New Zealand after a working stint in Japan. His Manawatu Cup win, at the expense of Corrupted and Galway Lass, came after a good ride by Darryl Bradley.

Doyle, who was recording his tenth win at his 60th start when taking out the Higgins Challenge Stakes, was selected as a yearling by Mathews who told his longtime client and friend that some careful blacksmithing would overcome problems of a slightly clubbed foot. Taking on board Mathews' advice, the Izetts secured the youngster for $17,000.

In the autumn Doyle was to hit the headlines again when he won the group three Thompson Handicap, a long established Wellington Racing Club metric mile run in 2004 at Otaki. It was a thoroughly deserved win considering Doyle had finished second in the race on three earlier occasions.

Doyle's willingness to give of his best and his matey attitude has endeared him to Mathews. "If I could clone him I'd be the happiest man in the world," he said after the Thompson win. In many ways Doyle does no more than mirror the attitudes and work ethic of his trainer.

Mathews' first schoolboy job came in 1969, working for Matamata training legend Dave O'Sullivan. His career as a jockey ended with 80 wins and he was not long out of his teens when he branched out as a trainer. The big break came when he became private trainer to Matamata owner Hec Tapper. On one occasion in the 1970s he trained and rode three winners for Tapper at Te Awamutu. But an even better day for the pair was winning the Wellington Cup with Big Gamble.

The biggest win so far for Mathews as a public trainer is the Brisbane Cup with Coshking – a horse who also placed second in the Sydney Cup. Taking employment at a pre-training establishment in Japan was the result of a marriage breakup and the need to save some money and make a fresh start. Moving with every step of that fresh start has been his former partner, now wife, Lorraine. The couple train out of a complex which was once part of Ashford Park stud and have become a formidable force on the central districts scene.

Manawatu Cup winner Rising Heights with trainers Howie and Lorraine Mathews and jockey Darryl Bradley.

STARLET JOCKEY WINS BIGGEST CUP

Auckland Cup Carnival

By David Bradford

Racing carnivals around the world have a habit of throwing up unexpected stars and that was certainly the case with the Auckland Racing Club's four-day summer carnival, stretching from Boxing Day through to January 2.

All the pre-carnival hype had justifiably been centred on the Mercedes New Zealand Derby, which besides its status as the country's most important classic was also charged with titillating leadup form. Because of this the Lion Red Auckland Cup – New Zealand's most important race for stayers – was left a little in the shadows. But a five-year-old mare and an English-born apprentice not long out of her teens were to rewrite the early script.

Upsetthym and Gemma Sliz, in company with trainer Karen Fursdon and a battalion of owners and supporters, stole the show. Stepping up to open class, Upsetthym plunged her way into Auckland Cup contention on Boxing Day with a resounding win over 2400 metres in the group two NZ Herald Queen Elizabeth Handicap. The $100,000 race was by far the biggest win for both trainer and jockey. But Fursdon saw Upsetthym's win as no more than the mare's just deserts. Earlier in the year she had actually made a Melbourne Cup entry for the mare. but a losing battle with heavy tracks through the winter and early spring saw Melbourne plans scrapped and the Auckland Cup become the prime target.

In the Queen Elizabeth, Upsetthym enjoyed a good passage in a slowly run race and powered home to win by a length and a quarter from outsider Lafleur, with another little fancied runner in 2001 New Zealand Derby winner Leica Guv a long head further back. Asgoodas was almost in line fourth with the favourite Sunray, unsuited by the lack of pace, eighth.

Traditionally the Queen Elizabeth Handicap sets the scene for the Auckland Cup. Things were no different in 2003. Rider Leith Innes urged punters to stick with Sunray, who he was certain would lap up the 3200 metres on New Year's Day, while Sunray's trainer Paul O'Sullivan said don't forget about Galway Lass. Six days before the Queen Elizabeth, Galway Lass had finished third behind Rising Heights and Corrupted in the Manawatu Cup and already boasted a placing at 3200 metres in the New Zealand Cup. Many had also identified the run of My Governess in the Queen Elizabeth as that of an improver.

But the horse whose name was on almost everyone's lips was Upsetthym. To most her Boxing Day run had signalled

AUCKLAND RACING CLUB

Spoils of victory...Gemma with Cup and her La-z-boy chair.

Upsetthym home for the money.

her as the next Auckland Cup winner. But there was not the same confidence about her 22-year-old rider coping with the white hot intensity of a group one race worth three hundred and fifty thousand dollars. Karen Fursdon, however, had no doubts. She said the tiny blonde had turned in a perfect ride in the Queen Elizabeth and had prior claims to the Cup ride not only because of the Boxing Day win but because of all the hard work she had put in during the mare's preparation.

Outwardly Sliz handled the pressure well but she took some insurance. On Cup eve she sought out retired 12-times champion jockey Lance O'Sullivan for advice on tactics. The advice O'Sullivan gave may well have cost his brother Paul victory with Galway Lass and another Auckland Cup win for Wexford Stables, stables which Lance himself now runs. But it was vintage O'Sullivan counselling. Afterwards Lance O'Sullivan was to say, "I gave her the same advice as dad [icon trainer Dave O'Sullivan] gave me when I rode in my first group one race. He said just treat it like a 2000 metre maiden at Thames – keep your cool and be patient. And that's just what Gemma did. She was brilliant. I couldn't have ridden the race better myself."

On the day Gemma Sliz was certainly a cool dude. In virtually a carbon copy of her Queen Elizabeth ride she guided Upsetthym to a length and a quarter win over Galway Lass, with My Governess another length back third and just shading The Mighty Lions. Few Auckland Cup winners have been greeted with a more emotional return to scale. The public reaction was enthusiastic but the syndicate of winning owners was lost in ecstasy as they rejoiced in an impossible dream coming true.

The ownership of Upsetthym has its origins at Cambridge Stud where she was bred by Rhythm from the Zabeel mare Set Up. Because of a leg injury she was not offered for sale as a yearling and that fact, plus some family links, eventually saw her find her way into Karen Fursdon's Matamata stable. The catalyst was longstanding Cambridge Stud employee Peter Stanaway, who as a youngster had ridden trackwork for Karen's trainer father Norm Crawford.

It was through Stanaway that Karen approached Cambridge Stud proprietor Sir Patrick Hogan about the availability of fillies to lease. She was invited to inspect the then unnamed Upsetthym, who revealed herself to be a little backward in maturity but importantly giving no indication that her earlier injury would affect her racing prospects. As Karen was

TRISH DUNELL

AUCKLAND RACING CLUB

SONIA BRADFORD

TOP: Ultimate winner Upsetthym leaving the parade ring for the Auckland Cup.
MIDDLE: Karen Fursdon.
BOTTOM: Part-owers Ron and Lesley Hodge (left) and friends Pat and Bubs Allen pose beside the freshly painted Auckland Cup statue, bearing Upsetthym's colours.

to subsequently relate, her father had once told her that if a scar moves with the skin not to worry about it.

During her racing career Upsetthym remains leased from Cambridge Stud, but once she is retired she goes into the ownership of the syndicate. The Pepsi syndicate comprises 10 shares and its members, beginning with Karen Fursdon, are spread far and wide. Two shares are held by the Charlie Harris syndicate of Whangarei, comprising Dave Reid, Grant Adams, Gary Boucher, Nook Jones and John Fairley. Other shares are held by Dave and Janet D'Abo of Te Aroha, Graham and Lyn Birchall of Matamata, Bob and Charmaine Fleming of Mt Maunganui, Ron and Lesley Hodge of Tauranga, Brian and Mo Campbell of Ngatea and expat Kiwi, now living in Brisbane, Steve Hawkes. And when Upsetthym races they tend to take along family and friends.

The development of Upsetthym to star status put a focus on Karen Fursdon's training skills and also her loyalty to a relatively inexperienced apprentice making her way in an adopted country 12,000 miles from home. However, the fairytale run for Gemma Sliz came to an end in the Prime Minister's Cup in Queensland in May when she received a substantial fine and suspension for causing interference. For the remainder of that campaign hugely experienced international jockey Greg Childs became a permanent replacement.

The mare's big Queensland target was the Brisbane Cup in which, given every possible chance by Childs, she finished third, an effort which fully justified the trip.

Horses have had an overwhelming influence on Karen Fursdon's life. As a youngster she worked around her father's stable and rode in point-to-point races. On leaving school she worked as a receptionist for a local veterinary practice and then moved to Melbourne where she was employed in the pedigree department of Wrightson Bloodstock. She was 28 when she went into a training partnership with her father and brother Kevin. A year later she married Kevin Fursdon. The couple have three sons – Jason, Benjamin and Nicholas, aged 18, 16 and 12.

Norm Crawford withdrew from the training partnership in 1992 and Kevin in 1998. Since then Karen has been operating solo. Norm Crawford was a specially dab hand with jumpers, while one of his star sprinters, So Modest, won the Concorde Handicap at Avondale and the Telegraph Handicap at Trentham. Though he tried, the Auckland Cup eluded him. But that wasn't upsetting him on New Year's Day.

ORPHAN FOAL SUPREME

Mercedes New Zealand Derby

By David Bradford

Punters may have been caught on the wrong foot when Cut The Cake won the Mercedes New Zealand Derby but the story behind the winner is riddled with romance. It is a story made of stuff befitting a Dick Francis novel and proving beyond doubt that the greatest certainty of racing will always be the uncertainty.

For the record, Cut The Cake won New Zealand's premier classic by a long head from the faster finishing second favourite Mount Street, with Masai a long neck away third ahead of Waitoki Dream and Terrain. Third favourite Russian Pearl, the Bayer Classic winner, was eighth and the favourite Philamor 11th. Cut the Cake had been neglected in the betting, starting sixth favourite and paying $17.

Philamor, an attractive son of English Two Thousand Guineas winner Generous, owed his support to a brilliant start

AUCKLAND RACING CLUB

Cut The Cake (rails) holding Mount Street at bay.

IN PREMIER CLASSIC

to his career, which before the Derby had yielded a second and three consecutive wins from just four starts. Most significantly, those wins included the Waikato Guineas and the Avondale Guineas. But things went horribly wrong in the Derby. He drew wide, was forced over extra ground on the first turn and, unsettled, got into a duel out front with the equally unsettled Maroofity.

That should have made things easier for Mount Street, whose leadup form had also been highly impressive and whose co-trainer Colin Jillings – an old hand at winning classics – did little to mask his confidence pre-race. But things went awry when in a skirmish at the start he lost a shoe and part of a hoof. In the circumstances his effort for second was quite remarkable – but not remarkable enough to overhaul Cut The Cake.

Classic wins tend to push an extra jet of adrenaline and see those most closely connected to the victor give modesty the heave-ho and wear their hearts on their sleeves. The Cut The Cake camp was certainly no exception. For them all it was a fairytale result.

The fickle hand of fate has been a constant companion of Cut The Cake and it stretches to the syndicate of owners.

Eight months before the Derby, high-profile syndicator Paul Moroney owned Cut The Cake outright and had him listed for sale on a website. It was because of that website sales pitch that on Derby day Paul Moroney had seven partners. One of them was long-standing friend and semi-retired Matamata businessman Noel Jaggaer. The others, fairly widely spread, were Auckland property developer Tim Manning, Sky City gaming manager Helen Clelland, airport engineer Graham Breingan, retired Tauranga farmer Neal Anderson, Hamilton electrician Dave Hewitt and past president of the Victoria Racing Club Andrew Ramsden. Also sharing in the excitement were co-trainers Mike Moroney and Andrew Scott, plus jockey Michael Coleman.

Of that trio none was more excited than Scott, whose season had got off to a bad start when he had been forced to scratch Penny Gem from the Kelt Capital Stakes when he admitted to stewards he had broken the Rules of Racing by administering an injection to the mare on raceday. When Scott was subsequently charged it was ruled the offence didn't warrant a disqualification or suspension and he was fined. The episode, however, had put him under serious strain as he

AUCKLAND RACING CLUB

Paul Moroney and Mercedes chief Ernie Ward.

continued with the daily management of the New Zealand sector of Mike Moroney's transtasman operation.

Winning the Derby was like taking a monkey from his back – especially so because he had been such an integral part of a successful long-range plan which was formulated when the winner was only two. The Derby tilt looked to be on track when Cut The Cake finished fourth in the Bonecrusher Prelude won by Russian Pearl and after some impressive efforts in training Scott believed he was going into the race as a genuine chance. But Scott still had work to do on raceday.

In a media interview following the race, Scott said: "He's a hot-headed horse and once he gets upset he stays upset. That's why I've been kicking dust out the back all day, walking, walking and walking him. I travelled up with him and have stayed with him all day."

Mike Moroney, though absolutely delighted with the stable's success, took in the occasion with a slightly more benign reaction. It wasn't exactly old hat but he had done it before – with Great Command in the 1996 New Zealand Derby and Second Coming in the 1997 Victoria Derby. Michael Coleman declared the win the high point of his career – above his Auckland and Wellington Cup wins. As an apprentice he had lost the winning mount on Tidal Light to Grant Cooksley because of a suspension. In Cut The Cake's year it was

A triumphant Michael Coleman.

Cooksley, second on Mount Street, the one telling the what-might-have-been story.

But Paul Moroney's Derby story was most intriguing of all. With a maternal grandparent who had bred 1960 Melbourne Cup winner Hi Jinx and a best schoolmate by the name of Paul O'Sullivan, it was almost pre-ordained Paul Moroney would gravitate into the racing business. He first started spending weekends and school holidays around Dave O'Sullivan's Matamata stables when aged 10 and on joining the workforce was a racing reporter on both the New Zealand Herald and Waikato Times, was part of a radio racing programme and also did a spot of TV.

In 1985, with friend Berri Schroder, he established Vision Bloodstock, but five years later branched out on his own under the banner of Paul Moroney Bloodstock. He has become one of the most respected operators in the business, with his syndicating activities almost predominantly centred around the stable of brother Mike.

Before the 2004 New Zealand Derby he had bought 14 group one winners at auction. Cut The Cake was the first he had bred – and bred with considerable reluctance. He begins the Cut The Cake saga by telling how he went to the 1991 National Yearling Sales with a buying order for a Japanese client. For $135,000 he bought him a Sir Tristram – She Might Hula colt later to be named Yamanin Vital. The horse won four staying races in Japan and was also group two placed before returning to New Zealand in the new ownership of Brian and Lorraine Anderton's White Robe Lodge Stud.

Moroney's first step into the tricky business of breeding came when he syndicated a Straight Strike filly named Icing On The Cake, who suffered a tendon problem after winning her first start. Taking her to a mixed bloodstock sale as a one-tenth owner, he put in an opening bid of $1000 to get things rolling and became the 100 percent owner when no more bids were forthcoming.

Not wanting to outlay too much of his hard-earned on stallion fees he cut a 50/50 deal and arranged a mating with Kashani which produced a filly named Good Cake. She didn't have much scope but managed to win an $8000 race at Trentham which carried a $75,000 bonus. Next up he bred her to Ball Park, a horse with whom his brother Mike had won an Easter Handicap and an Avondale Cup. The foal was born dead. By this time Yamanin Vital was back in New Zealand, so believing it might be a date with destiny Paul dispatched his broodmare band of one off to the South Island.

It was a decision based on sentiment and matching types rather than one of perceived magical cross-overs of bloodlines. It also became an exercise in patience. Icing On The Cake failed to get in foal to her first mating with Yamanin Vital and slipped the foal the following year.

The third mating brought good and bad news. Icing On The Cake suffered fatal internal damage when delivering a big colt who had to be raised by a Clydesdale mare. It was this spindly orphaned thoroughbred foal with the out-sized foster mum who was to win the blue riband of the New Zealand turf.

A special reward for Andrew Scott.

MATATAMATA STABLE RULES SUPREME

Derby Day at Ellerslie

By David Bradford

On an occasion of high fashion and equally glitzy racing, the Matamata stable of Mike Moroney and Andrew Scott reigned supreme at Ellerslie on Boxing Day. Not only did it collar the ultimate event, the Mercedes New Zealand Derby, but also the $150,000 Mercedes Prelude Classic and the $50,000 weight-for-age King's Plate. The only big ones to escape were the New Zealand Herald Queen Elizabeth Handicap and the Eight Carat Stakes.

Clean Sweep's win in the Mercedes Prelude over Summer Nymph and Iflooxcouldkill, was the third for the stable in four runnings of the race after earlier successes with Dance Class and Flying Class. The filly's three Wellington owners, Graeme Duff, Max Brown and Lib Petagna, who were seeing her race for the first time, proved to be a very vocal cheer group.

After running last in her debut run in November, Clean Sweep had put herself in the frame as a serious contender for the rich Ellerslie event by winning stylishly at Otaki on Bayer Classic day.

Winner of the King's Plate was Ubiquitous – the lone three-year-old in the field. After being a two-year-old winner in New Zealand he was transferred to Mike Moroney's Melbourne operation with a tilt at the Victoria Derby in mind. And although he failed to measure up in that campaign, he blossomed in condition on his return home. The winning ride went to Australian jockey Rhys McLeod, quite regularly seen on Moroney horses in Melbourne.

It was evergreen Kiwi jockey Noel Harris, whose career began in 1970, who was giving the victory salute after Kainui Belle's win in the group two $100,000 Eight Carat Classic. The win gave Harris his 100th group victory. Earlier in the season, when also ridden by Harris, Kainui Belle had won the Wellington Guineas and the Eulogy Stakes and finished second to Taatletail in the One Thousand Guineas.

Taatletail provided the shock of the Eight Carat Classic, starting favourite and being unplaced. Rider Michael Walker was of the opinion she had failed to cope with the right-handed way of racing and that opinion was vindicated when, back to racing the reverse the way at Te Rapa, she won the Sir Tristram Fillies Classic.

AUCKLAND RACING CLUB

Clean Sweep snares Mercedes Prelude over Summer Nymph.

FASHION
Mercedes
FASHION IN THE FIELD
FINALIST
079
253
FASHIONS IN THE FIELD
028

in the field

AUCKLAND RACING CLUB

GREAT TRAINING FEAT LANDS RICHEST SPRINT

Sky City Railway Stakes

By David Bradford

Matamata's Jim Gibbs ranks as one of New Zealand's finest trainers of the last half century. Yet he stepped aside and gave the job of training Vinaka for the Sky City Railway Stakes to Paul O'Sullivan. It was a move which surprised O'Sullivan as much as the rest of the racing fraternity. But Gibbs had his reasons.

Unquestionably a sprinter of rare class, Vinaka had won Trentham's group one Telegraph Handicap in 2002, his three-year-old season, and on that occasion winning rider Lance O'Sullivan had quickly declared the horse to be one of the slickest sprinters he had thrown a leg across. The 12-time champion jockey also reiterated that only a wide barrier draw had cost Vinaka the Railway Stakes a few weeks earlier when third to Sound The Alarm and Super Impressive.

Gibbs was only being told what he already knew. But problems lay ahead. First he had to nurse Vinaka through a leg fracture. Then signs appeared that the horse might become a bleeder. And that's why Gibbs turned to Paul O'Sullivan. Always one to seek answers to problems, O'Sullivan had discovered from research that changed training regimes could be a huge help with this particular one.

That's what he did with Vinaka. He got the horse fit with interval training over 400 metres and having four gallons of blood taken from him every fortnight.

When Vinaka paraded for New Zealand's richest and most famous sprint at Ellerslie on New Year's Day it is doubtful if there was a fitter horse in the land. With Lance O'Sullivan in retirement, the five-year-old was in the hands of Opie Bosson, who guided him to a remarkable win over the speedy and brave three-year-old filly Pay My Bail, with former Australian sprinter Tully Dane making ground for third.

At the trophy presentation O'Sullivan described Vinaka's win as having provided him with his proudest moment in racing. "To prepare a winner like this for such a master horseman is something unreal," he said. Considering O'Sullivan had been co-trainer of Horlicks, winner of the Japan Cup when it was the world's richest race, it was some statement. Another statement of equal significance was forthcoming from Gibbs, who in partnership with wife Ann was both owner and breeder of the winner.

"This horse," he said, "could not have won from my stable." It was a bald statement of fact and one which O'Sullivan saw as the ultimate accolade. For Gibbs it was nearing time to quit his picturesque Parkvale Farm training complex, situated

Vinaka and Pay My Bail down to it in the Railway Stakes

Buckle My Shoe with happy owners Lance and Bridget O'Sullivan.

Bridgette O'Sullivan (left) and Julia Naismith of NZ Bloodstock Ltd.

on State Highway 27 between Matamata and Te Poi, and set up a new and smaller boutique operation nearer the Matamata township. The new Gibbs property is named for the most famous of his many topline gallopers – Doriemus.

Gibbs bought Doriemus cheaply, developed him to a level of great promise, and retained a 10 percent share when he sold him to clients of Lee Freedman's Melbourne stable. It was a case of having his cake and eating it too when he went to Flemington to see Doriemus follow up his Caulfield Cup win by adding the holy grail of Australasian racing, the Melbourne Cup. These days Doriemus lives in retirement with the Gibbses.

The following day's racing, the last of the carnival, was dominated by the group one Zabeel Classic, the New Zealand Bloodstock Royal Stakes and the Jerry Clayton BMW Trophy, both at group two level, and the group three Westbury Stud Eclipse Stakes. Lashed's win in the Zabeel Classic is mentioned elsewhere and reference has also been made of Pomp And Glory's win in the BMW Trophy.

The Royal Stakes was over 2000 metres at set weights for three-year-old fillies. Not surprisingly, Kainui Belle was the solid favourite but after a rocky run she had to settle for second behind fifth favourite Buckle My Shoe.

Once again the successful trainer was Paul O'Sullivan. This time the owner was Bridgette O'Sullivan, not only wife of Lance O'Sullivan but also Ellerslie's goodwill ambassador. Lance also had special raceday duties as a presenter and comments person for Trackside TV. The only thing which briefly dampened the enthusiasm in the O'Sullivan camp was an inquiry into interference in which Buckle My Shoe and Kainui Belle were involved. Once that was over they showed the excitement of first-timers. And justifiably so.

The O'Sullivan clan had gone to Ellerslie hoping for no more than a fifth placing to encourage a tilt at the New Zealand Oaks at Trentham later in the month. This in itself was something of a strange mission as Buckle My Shoe had been bought in Australia as a potential speedster.

By Rory's Jester, a great source of two-year-old speed, Buckle My Shoe had been paid for with proceeds of a $100,000 payout on a Lance O'Sullivan-owned broodmare killed in an electrical storm. She proved to be an early duffer in trackwork and it was November of her three-year-old season before she quit maiden ranks. Then, with the application of blinkers and longer training tasks, she started to give some genuine signs of encouragement.

Alinsky wins Eclipse Stakes.

In the Royal Stakes, Buckle My Shoe powered home under stable rider Leith Innes to win by three-quarters of a length from Kainui Belle, with Eftee One almost in line next. But later in the month in the ING Life New Zealand Oaks, Buckle My Shoe was 12th, 10 lengths behind the winner Wharite Princess.

In the Eclipse Stakes for two-year-olds over 1200 metres, the winner Alinsky was certainly bred for the job, being by the season's champion sire of two-year-olds, Stravinsky, from the Railway Handicap winner Alynda. Once again it was a family affair.

He was bred by owners Alan and Linda Jones who race him in partnership with daughter Clare. Alan Jones does the training in partnership with Brett McDonald and the winning mount went to stable rider Lynsey Hofmann.

The other big winner on the day was Judy Tankard of Cambridge, wife of bloodstock agent and former stipendiary steward Ginger Tankard and mother of trainer Bryce Tankard. She won a $47,000 A Class Mercedes, the first prize in a special competition promoted by the Auckland Racing Club and Mercedes in conjunction with Sunday News and Friday Flash. The Joneses and the Tankards were to figure on the same card again in June when Ginger Tankard negotiated the sale of Alinsky to Hong Kong.

Ann Gibbs receives Sky City Railway Stakes Trophy.

Opie Bosson brings Vinaka back to scale.

Buckle My Shoe wins for Bridgette O'Sullivan.

CAMBRIDGE STUD. WE'RE K

CAMBRIDGE STUD IS WITHOUT DOUBT THE SOUTHERN H

OCTAGONAL
Multiple Gr.1 winning Champion and sire

MOUAWAD
Multiple Gr.1 winner

SIR TRISTRAM
Champion Gr.1 Sire

CHAMPAGNE
Multiple Gr.1 winner

LUCKY OWNERS
International Gr.1 winner

DON EDUARDO
Gr.1 Derby winner and Sire

Octagonal, bred raised and sold by Cambridge Stud, was a champion of the turf with 10 wins at Group 1 level. He remains Australasia's second greatest-ever money earner (A$5.8m in prize-money). He has become a great sire in his own right as the sire of multiple Group 1 winning champion galloper **Lonhro**. Racehorses bred by Cambridge Stud's Sir Patrick and Justine Lady Hogan have amassed more than 56 individual Group 1 victories, the finest jewels in the racing world's crown. Other notable Group 1 winners bred or sold by Cambridge Stud include: **Mouawad, Don Eduardo**, **Grosvenor**, **Surround**, **Tristarc**, **Gurners Lane**, **Dr. Grace** and **Kaapstad** etc.

Yearlings sold by Sir Patrick and Justine Lady Hogan, over the past two decades at the New Zealand National Yearling Sale Series have produced over 25 Individual Group 1 Winners.

Cambridge Stud sold the highest priced yearling ever in Australasian sales history, the superbly bred Don Eduardo (Zabeel-Diamond Lover colt, sold for $NZ3.6 million, at Karaka, Feb 2000) who went on to acheive Group 1 status winning the AJC Derby before being retired to stud in New Zealand.

WN IN THE RIGHT CIRCLES

HERE'S GREATEST NURSERY OF ELITE GROUP 1 WINNERS.

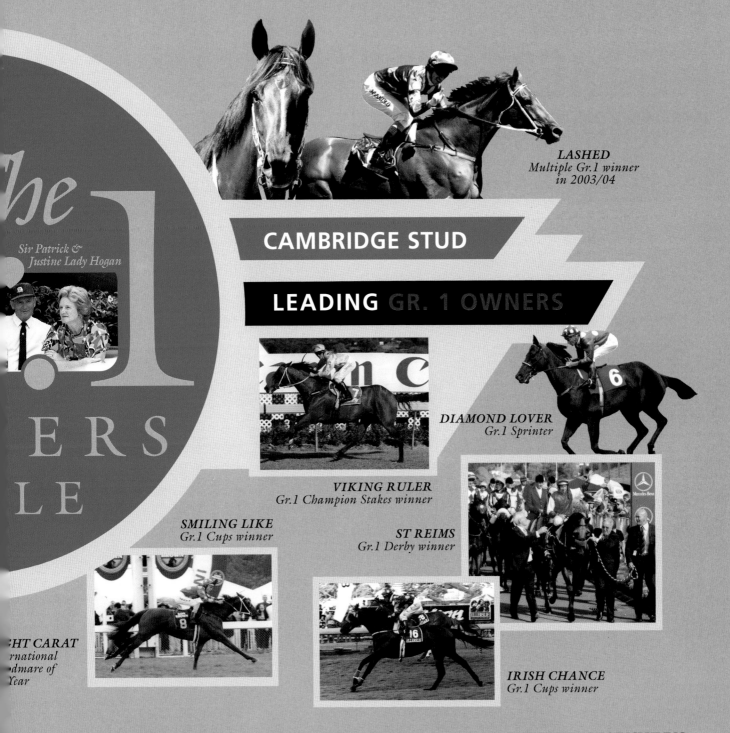

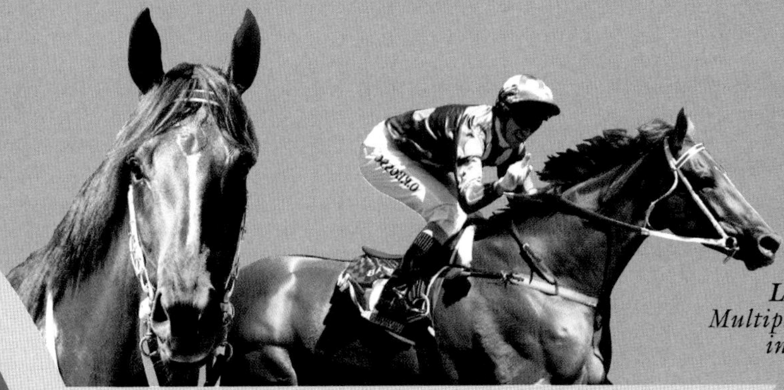

LASHED
Multiple Gr.1 winner in 2003/04

he 1

Sir Patrick & Justine Lady Hogan

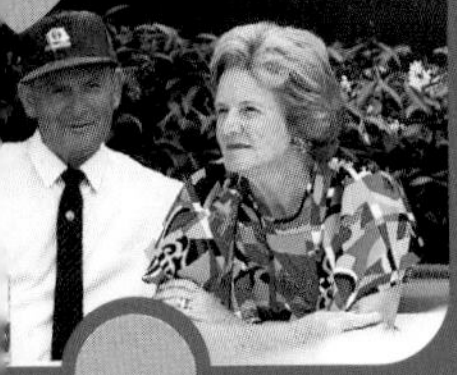

ERS

LE

CAMBRIDGE STUD

LEADING GR. 1 OWNERS

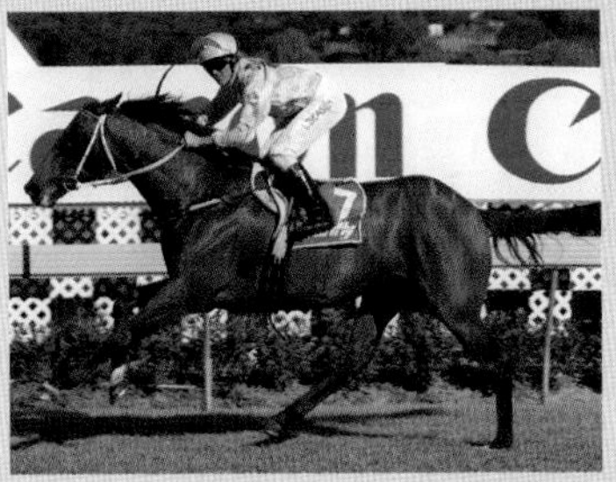

VIKING RULER
Gr.1 Champion Stakes winner

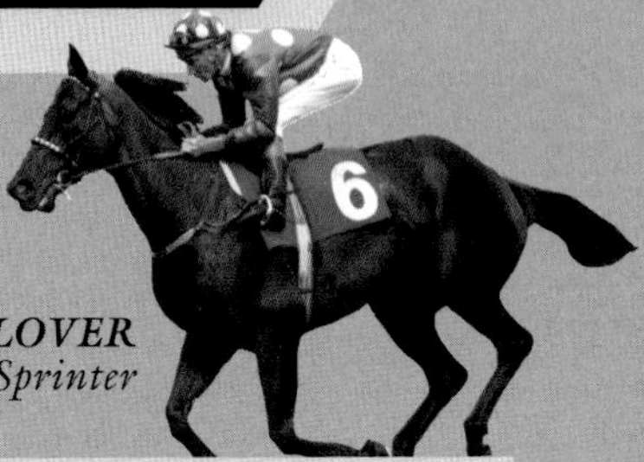

DIAMOND LOVER
Gr.1 Sprinter

SMILING LIKE
Gr.1 Cups winner

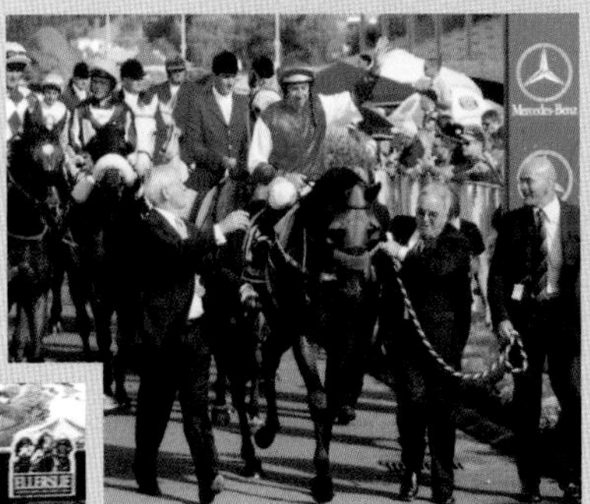

ST REIMS
Gr.1 Derby winner

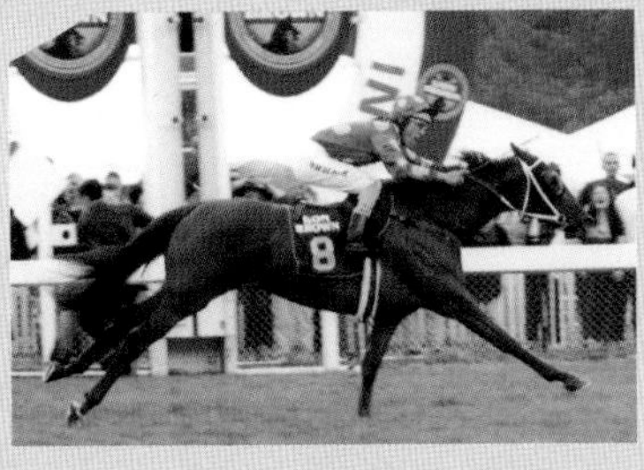

HT CARAT
rnational
dmare of
Year

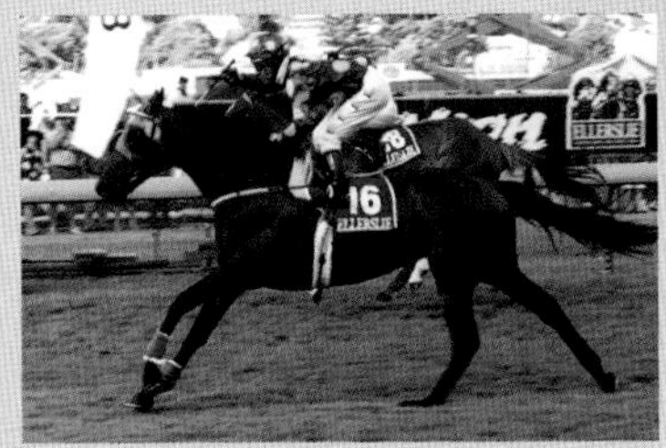

IRISH CHANCE
Gr.1 Cups winner

CAMBRIDGE STUD HAS ENJOYED MANY HIGHLIGHTS AS OWNERS OF HIGH-CLASS GROUP 1 WINNERS INCLUDING:

Lashed - Three-time **Gr. 1** winner in New Zealand in the 2003-04 racing season. These wins were achieved against the best horses in New Zealand in the **Gr. 1** Zabeel Classic (2000m) at Ellerslie, the **Gr. 1** Whakanui Stud International Stakes (2000m) at Te Rapa and the **Gr. 1** New Zealand Stakes (2000m) at Ellerslie. Smiling Like - Winner of the 2001 Wellington Cup, **Gr. 1**, 2000 New Zealand Cup, Gr. 2.

Irish Chance - Winner of the 1999 Auckland Cup, **Gr. 1**. St Reims - Winner of the 2002 Mercedes NZ Derby, **Gr. 1**. Viking Ruler - Winner of the 2001 AJC Spring Champion Stakes, **Gr. 1**. Diamond Lover - Winner of the 1987 ARC Railway H. **Gr. 1**. Kempinsky - Winner of the 2003 MVRC AAMI Vase, Gr. 2. Runner-Up in the 2003 VRC Derby, **Gr. 1**.

CAMBRIDGE STUD

PO BOX 108 CAMBRIDGE NEW ZEALAND. PHONE: 64 7 827 7887 FAX: 64 7 827 7886 EMAIL: cambridgestud@clear.net.nz WEB: www.cambridgestud.co.nz

FORMER ROGUE REDEEMS HIMSELF AT TRENTHAM

Lion Brown Wellington Cup

By David Bradford

Punters took a drubbing in the Lion Brown Wellington Cup when on an easy track the favourite Galway Lass ran last, the second favourite The Mighty Lions fifth and the third favourite Rising Heights 17th and the only runner ahead of Galway Lass. Well, to be precise, most punters were stung but not all. The owners of winner Cluden Creek had a hefty TAB fixed-odds payout to go with the $156,250 first prizemoney. They had bet $3000 at $20 odds, whereas on raceday the tote dividend was $11.35. Their former rogue horse had repaid their patience handsomely.

RACE IMAGES, PALMERSTON NORTH

Cluden Creek wins The Lion Brown Wellington Cup from Bel Air and Ebony Honor.

One of the ironic twists to the result was that Michael Walker, who had won the Marton Cup on Cluden Creek in his final leadup race to the Wellington Cup, turned the mount down in favour of riding Galway Lass. It was a decision which provided Andrew Calder with the biggest thrill in his promising career. But that bad luck – good luck scenario was only a small part of the wider background to Cluden Creek's thoroughly deserved win at the expense of outsider Bel Air and consistent 3200 metre place-getter Ebony Honor.

Early in his career, Cluden Creek didn't want to be anyone's friend, let alone be a racehorse. That's why his South Island breeders – former All Black Neil Purvis and rugby mate Barrie Barber – sent him north to get sorted out by Waverley's John Boon. It was to become an inspired move and one also appreciated by their racing partner Mrs Ali Macdonald.

Purvis and Barber knew Boon well through racing their seven-time winner Cautious Cluden from his stable during the 1990s. The "Cluden" part of both horses' names comes from Purvis' 12,500 hectare Cluden Station in Central Otago, but it wasn't just sentiment which saw Cluden Creek trekking north. He was being placed in the hands of a highly skilled horseman with a big reputation for converting the wayward.

After the Wellington Cup Boon admitted he had gone into the race with a fair amount of confidence, but that his early association with the horse had been somewhat rocky. "He was a bolshie type," he said, "a real thug who would try and walk over the top of you early on. He didn't show much ability and then one day I took him to the trials at Wanganui, put blinkers and a tongue strap on and he won. It was his last chance of a reprieve – I had almost decided not to go on with him."

Following a couple of moderate race runs, Cluden Creek turned the corner and started making steady improvement. By the time he got to the Wellington Cup he'd had 21 starts for five wins, the Marton Cup the most important.

Boon was in just his first season as a public trainer, but he was by no means a new chum. As a youngster he rode at pony club and to hunts and did an eight-month stint working for well-known Taranaki racing identity Kevin Gray.

Then came some overseas experience. He did a two-year course at the Queensland Agricultural College, graduating with a diploma in farm management and horse husbandry. Following that he went to England for six months, working for noted jumps trainer Stan Mellor. Strong New Zealand influences in his career have been the late Noel Eales, John Wheeler and Kevin Gray. All three have been clients since he set up his breaking-in and pre-training establishment in the mid-1980s. Before becoming a public trainer he held owner-trainer and permit-to-train licences. His first win was with the jumper Kangaroo in 1989 and the Wellington Cup was his 44th.

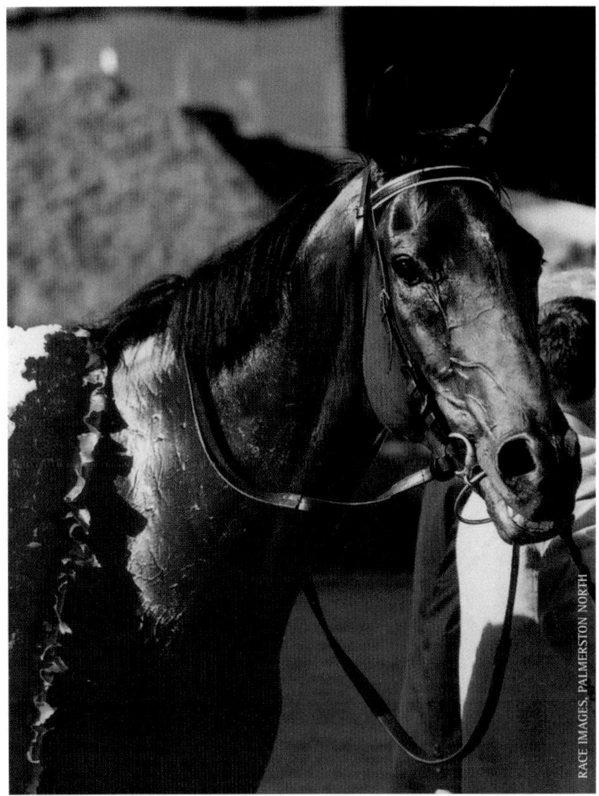

Cluden Creek with the victory laurels.

Chasing group one glory at Trentham was not quite a new experience. On New Year's Day he had saddled My Governess to finish third behind Upsetthym in the Lion Red Auckland Cup. Setbacks prevented both horses from racing in the autumn. But for the Cluden Creek camp the Wellington Cup was an event to be long remembered and savoured – even before it got under way.

They were about 40 in number and clustered along a line of open car boots laden with most of the serious joys of living. Overhead a large banner proclaimed "Camp Cluden" and as the day merged into evening camp followers grew in numbers as the principals shared their greatest day in racing. The big three all had different tales to tell.

Neil Purvis told how there would have been no Wellington Cup win if he hadn't been given Cluden Creek's dam and decided to mate her with Yamanin Vital – sire also of the New Zealand Derby winner Cut The Cake. Barrie Barber, a fisherman from Karitane, north of Dunedin, had a few more racing tales to tell. People who have been president of the Waikouaiti Racing Club and have raced enough thoroughbreds and standardbreds to win 100 races generally do. Ali Macdonald had to settle for a first time lucky story. She had never even been on a racecourse until Cluden Creek came along.

STABLEMATES FIGHT IT OUT TO THE FINISH

Trentham's Thorndon Mile

By David Bradford

Trentham has long been a happy hunting ground for Colin Jillings and his training partner Richard Yuill and punters had almost taken it for granted they would win the 2004 Thorndon Mile as they had the highly talented and consistent Sedecrem engaged. As it turned out, the punters were right on one count and wrong on another. The winner was trained by the Jillings/Yuill combination – but it was their second representative Sir Kinloch, with Sedecrem second.

On the middle day of the meeting Sir Kinloch had won quite convincingly against a six-horse field over 1400 metres, but there was a huge jump in class to the Thorndon and punters didn't want any part of him. So whereas he paid a modest $3.35 in the Royal NZ RSA 1400, he paid only a fraction below $30 when beating Sedecrem by a neck.

Much of the credit for the win was due to a heady ride by Lee Rutherford. One of Rutherford's skills is getting her mounts to settle in prominent positions in the running. That's how she rode Sir Kinloch, rating him perfectly in front, while Hayden Tinsley was late on the scene with Sedecrem. The finish was something of a nail-biter and outsider Elendil was almost in line third ahead of Lashed and Travellin' Man. Second favourite Marie Clare and third favourite Silky Red Boxer were the last two home.

While Sedecrem's army of supporters and the group of friends who race him may have considered themselves unlucky, Sir Kinloch's win was a just reward for owner-breeder Herbie Dyke, who races him with sons Steven and Simon. Earlier in the horse's career an offer of $750,000 had been refused for the horse. At the time Herbie Dyke had said: "Why sell. I don't need the money – I would much rather have the fun of racing him." A prominent figure in the motor industry, Dyke has always seen racing as the best game in town to play. He has also put in many years in administration, being a former president of the Waikato Racing Club and vice-president of the New Zealand Racing Conference.

The Thorndon Mile was Dyke's 98th win as an owner, with eight of them provided by Sir Kinloch's dam Ivory. But that contribution was chicken feed compared with the contribution of Kalgoorlie, one of his early gallopers raced from the Te Awamutu stable of the late Bill Sanders. An exceptional sprinter who won 25 times, Kalgoorlie began racing at two, lasted until he was nine and regularly stepped up to the plate to take on all-comers.

Tinsley may have walked away convinced Sedecrem would have won in two more strides but it's being in front at the winning post that counts and that was the contract Rutherford and the gallant grey fulfilled.

LEFT: Sir Kinloch wins the Thorndon Mile from stablemate Sedecrem and Elendil. RIGHT: Jubilant Lee Rutherford brings Sir Kinloch back to scale.

WHARITE PRINCESS WINS IN FAMOUS SILKS

New Zealand Oaks

By David Bradford

RACE IMAGES PALMERSTON NORTH

Wharite Princess too good in the New Zealand Oaks.

The result of the ING Insurance New Zealand Oaks was bathed in a mixture of nostalgia and the unabashed exuberance of a jockey and a trainer winning the time-honoured classic for the first time. Even more central to the occasion was a lightly raced filly by the name of Wharite Princess, whose reputation was already such that she started second favourite.

The first show of emotion came from jockey Bruce Herd, who greeted the winning post with a flamboyant flourish of the whip – perhaps more accurately flourishes. His jubilation had its roots in events which had taken place on the very same day twelve months previously. On that occasion he was the declared rider for Bramble Rose, but was injured at the barri-

Wharite Princess

er in an earlier race on the programme and was forced to watch replacement jockey Opie Bosson take the win. He felt fate had robbed and cheated him.

But Wharite Princess's win was much more than a simple payback. The special thing about his first New Zealand Oaks win was that the winner was trained by his partner Lisa Latta, already carrying their first baby (safely born in April and named Joshua Thomas). And then there was the little matter of a smashed ankle that could just as easily have provided a Bramble Rose scenario.

Between the runnings of the 2003 and 2004 New Zealand Oaks, Herd had so badly broken an ankle doctors predicted he would be away from riding for 12 months. His first objective was to prove them wrong, but while his bones mended well his weight ballooned to a scary 62kg. At the end of six months, however, he was trim, fit and ready for action.

The action came in his first comeback ride when he rode Wharite Princess (half a kilogram overweight) to a debut win on November 14, 2003. Two placings and another win followed before she was to go into the New Zealand Oaks with Herd wearing the same purple livery made famous by one of the greatest fillies ever to win the race – the 1977 winner La Mer.

It was Latta's own link with La Mer which made her first group one win as a trainer so very special for her. La Mer was trained by the late Malcolm Smith, for whom Latta worked for 13 years and trained in partnership with for 18 months before his death. It was Smith's widow Barbara who suggested Lisa should register the colours as her own. That dated back just over four years.

When Latta joined Smith as a 17-year-old she may have been a new chum at racing but she was an old hand with horses. Born into a South Island family heavily involved in breaking in horses and rodeos, she was riding by the time she could walk. She did pony club and eventing and on the rodeo circuit she was the national barrel racing champion at age 16.

Herd placed Wharite Princess midfield for most of the running, but took the daughter of His Royal Highness up to the leaders on the point of the home turn and she raced away to win by a length from the outsider Filante Etoile. There was half a length to Midnight Kiss and another length and a quarter to French Lady. The favourite Kainui Belle was seventh. Kainui Belle's rider Noel Harris said he was unsure whether she was troubled by the distance or was simply feeling the effects of recent racing.

Following the Oaks Wharite Princess was given time to overcome what Latta described as a couple of niggling problems and didn't race again during the season.

BIG PAY DAY FOR JOHN SARGENT

Mercedes Bonus Classique

By Dennis Ryan

If you were to ask Matamata trainer John Sargent for an example of the vagaries of this racing game, chances are he would have a one-word reply: Successor. Cut back to early 2003. Sargent, 12 months into his resurrected New Zealand career after four good years in Malaysia, is making heavy weather of redeveloping his client base and getting results.

The Select Colts section of the Karaka yearling sale is an obvious trawling ground for a trainer looking for likely spec material, something he can sign for and entice fresh clientele into. But after trying here and there within the restrictions of his budget, Sargent is running out of chances as that particular section of the catalogue starts to run thin.

Ten lots from the end he finally beats off the opposition and puts his name to Rich Hill Stud's bay colt by Bahhare from Betty Doolin at $21,000. The purchase could have been seen as a bit of backscratching, given that his existing clientele included Rich Hill, but was actually more to do with a touch of inside knowledge from the stud's two-year-old team member called Clifton telling him that the Bahhare stock 'don't go too badly'.

That factor might have been soundly based, but it was no aid when it came to finding someone to pay the bills on his fresh purchase. After drawing blanks Sargent was left to carry the can, with his name the only one in the owner's section of the racebook when the youngster, by this stage named Successor, appeared in the black with gold shamrocks stable colours as a spring two-year-old.

An early trial win was tempered by a midfield finish on his raceday debut, but second placings in his next two starts, one of them behind early season star Clifton Prince in the Wellesley Stakes at Trentham, had Successor looking more the part. He saved his first win for Avondale Cup day in early December when the stake attached to the race was bolstered by a $50,000 Mercedes bonus for which the Karaka sales graduate was eligible – thank you very much.

John Sargent.

Another placing behind Clifton Prince followed in the males' Mercedes Super Bonus Prelude at Awapuni, making the nuggety bay one of the leading contendors for the big one, the $500,000 Mercedes Classique at Te Rapa on January 31.

Successor's formline was not reflected in the nearly 30-to-one odds he was showing for the country's richest two-year-old race, but that mattered not one iota as he splashed

Successor ploughs through the wet to win the Mercedes Super Bonus Classique.

through the unseasonal track conditions and accompanying rain for a four-length win over leading fillies Iflooxcouldkill and Kapsdan.

For Sargent, this was the payday to beat them all. As the horse's owner and co-trainer, he was able to pocket the lion's share of the $263,750 winner's purse, having to part only with commissions to visiting Australian jockey Rhys Mcleod and to his training partner at the time, Karl Allpress.

"It couldn't have come at a better time," he now acknowledges, "and no, I didn't mind not having to share too much of it around."

Successor didn't line up again as a two-year-old and with his late July sale to Hong Kong, that is where his future lies. And as if a total of $365,000, comprising actual race stakes and bonuses under the Mercedes-Benz Super Bonus Series, was not enough to make Sargent smile, the 'healthy six-figure' payout from the sale had him literally laughing all the way to the bank.

Successor's big Te Rapa win was the partnership's tenth for the season, already by that stage three ahead of their tally from the whole of the previous season which had been their first full term since setting up shop in Matamata in early 2002. With subsequent performers such as the multiple winners Tickle and Sheka, the stable was close to a top-20 premiership slot with 24 wins as the season drew to a close.

The 2004-05 racing season would see one significant change at Ladbrook Park Stables with the decision by long-time associate Karl Allpress to strike out on his own. He had been with Sargent for 11 years, beginning in Awapuni as foreman and then assistant trainer in Malaysia before entering a full training partnership in Matamata two years ago.

The mutual and amicable agreement between the two will see Allpress operate with a permit to train licence on the property he and his jockey wife Lisa bought last year. Another change in their lives was the 'small matter' of the couple's first baby, due in the spring.

For Sargent, however, it's business as usual, or in fact more busy than ever, from his base in the 40-box barn he leases from the Matamata Racing Club. After experiencing a fluctuation in numbers over the past two years, he is now in the happy position of having a full team and an ever-expanding clientele.

Stable supporters who have been him with from his days in the lower North Island such as Jim Barlow, Bill Gleeson, Dave Bennett, Peter Gillespie, Andrew Meehan and his older brother, NZTR chairman Guy Sargent, are now joined by such names as the Duchess of Bedford and studmasters Garry Chittick and John Thompson.

Another pleasing sign of his growing popularity is the recent signing up of a three-filly syndication package comprising 20 individual shares, with some of those shares split in turn amongst multiple members.

"When I returned from Malaysia I got good support from many of my original clients, but breaking new ground hasn't been easy," says Sargent. "There has been a noticeable improvement in that respect lately, especially as the team has begun to fire, so there's plenty to look forward to in the season ahead."

BONECRUSHER

LEGENDARY Bonecrusher made his final public appearance on a racetrack at Ellerslie on Boxing Day – leading out the field for the New Zealand Derby. If he had forgotten his own triumph in the blue riband event of New Zealand racing in 1985 he certainly didn't show it

BONECRUSHER

INTRODUCTION

Compiled by David Bradford. New Zealand photos supplied by Race Images, Palmerston North and from Mitchell family files.

Twenty-one and looking as fit as the two-year-olds who had raced earlier in the day, he made it abundantly clear to former jockey partner Gary Stewart he would rather be in thick of things, teaching the modern day brats a thing or two, rather than settling for a sprint past the stands.

The vintage Bonecrusher attitude brought back so many fond memories for Stewart, who had made a special trip from Australia for the occasion. But it wasn't only Stewart who reflected with moisture-filled eyes. As so often throughout his illustrious career, Bonecrusher had once again plucked at the heartstrings of thousands of fans who refused to allow the embers of adoration to die.

Bonecrusher is one of a small but select band of champions who, in blissful and pampered retirement, have assumed the greater mantle of legend. This segment of the 2004 New Zealand Thoroughbred Racing Annual is devoted to his legend.

I like to claim I have close associations with Bonecrusher; and not simply because I was one of the original shareholders when his sire Pag-Asa was bought out of Neville Begg's Sydney stable and sent to Dave O'Sullivan in lofty hopes of winning the Railway Handicap.

No, it's more about family ties – a 50-year link with the Ritchie family for starters. And not too much less for Peter and Shirley Mitchell, dating back to when Peter attended Ellerslie trackwork with his owner-trainer father Gordon and wife-to-be Shirley was a stablehand for Merv Ritchie, father of Bonecrusher's trainer Frank. Those associations enriched the pleasure derived from personally witnessing so many of Bonecrusher's great wins, including the never-to-be-forgotten Cox Plate win over Waverley Star. Yet I never wrote about those deeds because they came at a time when I was taking a 20-year sabbatical from journalism.

That is why others will provide most of the words in this tribute to a great horse and the people behind him who set the scene for famous Melbourne racecaller Bill Collins to declare in the last gasp of a frenetic commentary on the 1986 Cox Plate, ". . . and Bonecrusher races into equine immortality."

That 1986 Cox Plate – the race of the century – could have been a good point in Bonecrusher's career to begin this tribute. But by then he was already a champion. Instead I have gone back a year and allowed long-standing Sydney colleague Bill Casey to write the prologue, as it was he who first drew a parallel with Phar Lap and sparked a cult following in Australia.

Bill's prologue is exactly the way he wrote it for his paper. And that theme will be followed by other selected articles written by New Zealand and Australian journalists, highlighting not only the highs but also the lows of "Red", the champion with the bruising name.

A moment of reflection Gary Stewart and Sharlene Mitchell about to lead Bonecrusher on to Ellerslie the last time.

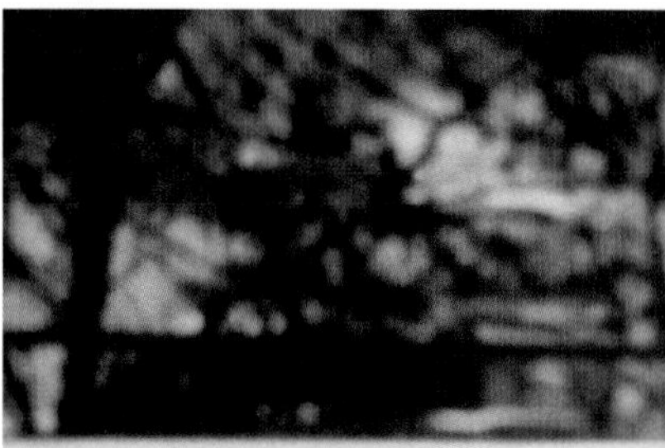

PROLOGUE

In racing matters Sydneysiders hold dear to the opinions of Bill Casey. They have been doing so for around 40 years when he moved up from Melbourne with pretty sassy credentials. In the spring of 1962 New Zealand trainer Archie McGregor befriended him and told him he was the only Aussie reporter he wanted to talk to. That proved more than a little important to Casey – and his Melbourne Age readers – as McGregor trained Even Stevens to win the Caulfield and Melbourne Cups that year and three other cup races to boot. Sydneysiders like people with that sort of edge and when he likened Bonecrusher to Phar Lap they listened.

They got the message in a Wednesday column boldly headed "FLYING KIWI A BONECRUSHER" with a sub-heading declaring "Saddling Up To Be Another Phar Lap".

And this is what Bill Casey wrote:

The girl was serious about it.

New Zealanders are very serious about two things – horses and, of course, Australians.

"You're an Aussie," the cabbie said at the New Zealand international air terminal, except you don't call him a cabbie because he doesn't like that.

It's an Australian word, cab. In New Zealand it's a taxi and he's a taxi driver. I told him I was indeed an Australian.

"Why did the Russian boat sink?" he said.

"I believe there's an inquiry," I started out.

"The Aussies sabotaged it because they didn't want to go back to Australia."

He laughed fit to split his cabbie's, I mean taxi driver's hat.

It is a fairly long drive from the airport to Auckland. He had time to tell eight anti-Australian jokes.

But the extraordinary side of all this is that they really like us. They just give us a little hurry up to take some of the wind out of our sails. There is no better host in the world than a New Zealander in his own beautiful country. He cannot do enough for you. I went over there last week to see a new boom racehorse, a three-year-old with the unlikely name of Bonecrusher, run in the Air New Zealand Stakes, their most important weight-for-age event.

Bonecrusher and Sharlene Mitchell in relaxed mode.

Anyway that serious girl I was going to tell you about – the one on the Auckland Racing Club staff – was talking very, very seriously to me about Bonecrusher the day before the race. "There was a man here some time ago," she said, obviously quite awed by what she was about to tell me. "He was one of those people who claim they can predict the future. He said that this year a horse would establish himself as another Phar Lap. The horse would be the same colour as Phar Lap, a gelding like Phar Lap, would have the same markings as Phar Lap and go to Australia like Phar Lap and win everything."

She looked me straight in the face as she added, "They say that horse could be Bonecrusher." I have been tipped by some outstanding men like Dave The Dasher,

A 100.000 fans applaud Bonecrusher as he leads out the Melbourne Cup field.

Hard Luck Hal and First Race Flareghty, but that's the best story that's ever gone with the tip.

The next day Bonecrusher, answering the girl's description right down to Phar Lap's famous black marks on the rump, even if he had a bit of growing to do to match Phar Lap's size, was bowling along in fourth place on the turn among a field of champion New Zealand horses in the big race. What happened next was awesome.

The chestnut gelding did what Tulloch and Kingston Town used to do at their very best. He accelerated so quickly he simply left his rivals standing. Only real champions, four or two-legged, can do that.

Bill Casey ended his column by telling readers he had told a Kiwi friend that in a couple of weeks Bonecrusher would win the AJC Derby carrying a spare pair of racing plates under one leg. On that Sydney raid Bonecrusher was to put his first indelible imprint on Australian turf history and people in pubs indeed did start making comparisons with Phar Lap. The legend, triggered by Casey and fuelled by Bonecrusher himself, was on its way.

What is known for certain is that from an early stage he stamped himself as a horse apart and his owner Peter Mitchell and trainer Frank Ritchie were always totally committed to not only giving him the chance to maximise his potential but also to safeguarding his wellbeing.

The starting point in the Bonecrusher story is King Country farmer Bill Punch. Brought up on the family farm at Raetihi, he inherited his love of racing from his father Emmet and his first job, before returning to the land, was on the formguide Best Bets. In January 2003 he achieved his biggest win as an owner when, in partnership with wife Bev, he won the Wellington Cup with his homebred Oarsman.

IN THE BEGINNING

Buckling down to win the 1988 Air New Zealand Stakes.

Oarsman resulted from a selective, but unfashionable, matching of bloodlines and being also the breeder of Bonecrusher it could be claimed that Bill Punch has the magic touch. But the truth is that Bill Punch mated his broodmare Imitation with Pag-Asa mainly because he held a share in the stallion. Punch had been among a party of Waikato breeders when bloodstock agent Owen Larsen negotiated the purchase of Pag-Asa out of Neville Begg's Randwick stable. The horse had fashionable bloodlines and good looks. He also had a good turn of foot, but often failed to run out his races – later found to be due to heart irregularities.

While the mating of Pag-Asa, a son of Kaoru Star, and Imitation, a daughter of Oakville, may have largely been one of expediency that was not the way an Auckland breeding buff by the name of Harold Hampton saw it. He dug deep into the ancestry of sire and dam and came up with the conclusion it was mating made in heaven.

By his own admission Peter Mitchell has always been a keen gambler. And like all serious gamblers he likes to have the odds in his favour. That's why when he set out to buy himself a yearling colt he sought Harold Hampton's advice, asking him to scour the catalogue for the best pedigree at a Dalgety yearling sale in Hamilton. No one can say Hampton didn't get the pedigree right – he was just one foal too soon. The colt Mitchell bought for $3500, and later named Super Brat, proved to be a moderate but he was showing enough promise at the time of the Wrightson Waikato sales the following year for Mitchell to go back and buy his brother for $3250 – and the rest is history.

The loose threads of Bonecrusher's beginnings which magically wove their way into a single cord of greatness are difficult to isolate in any sort of regular order. Certainly he was a super horse because he was a super athlete. But whether he was a super athlete because of a special mixture of genes, an unyielding will to win, or fluke of nature no one will ever know for sure.

This begs the question as to why one was a moderate performer and the other a champion. Hampton would say that what he termed as properly planned matings were not an absolute guarantee but provided one chance in four of a superior result. But as his critics would say that didn't explain why Nellie Melba's sister couldn't sing a note and Johnny Weismuller's brother couldn't stay afloat. Horse breeding will never be an exact science and that's why people like Bill Punch can breed champions and knockabout blokes like Peter Mitchell can afford to buy them. It's also why people like the late Harold Hampton will devote endless time and energy into seeking magic genetic crosses.

The 15th edition of the New Zealand Racing Annual, the first of 12 edited by Mike Dillon, records part of an interview with Hampton. In it Hampton refutes suggestions of being a theorist. "I work things out as a priest does," he says. "On evidence. My findings are principles of breeding, not theories on breeding." Hampton then goes on to explain the desirability, or as he put it, the multiplication, on both sides of a horse's pedigree of their strongest ancestor. In other words determining which is the strongest ancestral influence in a horse's pedigree and looking for a multiplication of that influence on both sides of the pedigree. The greater the number of times it appears the better.

He insisted this was line-breeding, not in-breeding. "In-breeding is bad," he said, "and line-breeding is good. The bad part is breeding too close. You must keep your last three generations clear of common ancestors." Hampton found more sceptics than followers, but Peter Mitchell has never regretted sitting down and listening to

Storming home to win 1985 Bayer Classic.

Australian Prime Minister Bob Hawke shares a joke with Peter Mitchell, Frank Ritchie and Jim Cassidy at Canberra.

the small, unfashionably dressed, slightly hawkish-looking man who believed he knew the pathway to champions.

Peter Mitchell inherited his love of racing from his father Gordon, an earth-moving contractor who during the 1950s and 1960s trained his own gallopers at Ellerslie, including two open class performers in Way In and Misere. As a youngster Peter Mitchell contemplated becoming a jockey, but that was ruled out by increasing weight. For a time he worked in his father's business, spent some time in Australia, and went into business on his own account early in the 1970s when he bought a billiard saloon in Ellerslie. It was that initial business venture and some successful gambling which were the beginnings of his present financial security.

Frank Ritchie was always going to be in the racing game. Racing folk appeared on both sides of his own family tree and his father Merv had been a top jumps rider before becoming a successful trainer. Frank began a jockey apprenticeship with his father but wasn't built for the job and when he became overweight switched to a training partnership. Following his marriage to Colleen he branched out on his own account but struggled financially to the extent he was about to quit when Bonecrusher said take a second look at me. Life for Frank, Colleen and sons Shaune and Craig was to change dramatically. In the case of Shaune that meant leaving school aged 18 to become Bonecrusher's permanent strapper and travelling companion – which in the eyes of Australians was nothing less than the rebirth of the Tommy Woodcock and Phar Lap pairing.

Bonecrusher had acquired his name as a result of injuries received when he came off second best in a fight with a concrete fence post. He had a strong chestnut colour, somewhat angular frame, fairly ordinary hindquarters but an eye-catching powerful forequarter – plus an aura of self-determination. Quite incredibly he came

Strolling through the business centre of Melbourne.

to hand quickly enough to run in the first two-year-old race of the season, finishing fourth in the Kindergarten Plate at Avondale on August 31, 1984. His second race was in the Terrific Maiden at Ellerslie, named for a former star of the Merv Ritchie stable, and appropriately Bonecrusher was an easy winner by two and a quarter lengths.

The odyssey was under way. There would be another 41 starts, another 17 wins, five seconds, 11 thirds and four fourths for almost $3 million in stakes. In all those races – except for when suspension or illness intervened – he was ridden by Gary Stewart, a jockey who literally came back from the dead to make his own lasting imprint on Australasian racing.

The following season, on the eve of the AJC Derby, Stewart was to recall his reaction to Bonecrusher's debut fourth in a revealing interview with Australian racing

writer Steve Crawley. But what was most revealing of all for Aussie readers was Stewart's Lazarus-like return to riding after being clinically dead. Crawley wrote:

When the field trots out for the $500,000 Fosters AJC Derby at Randwick on Saturday, spare a thought for the jockey in the cream and brown silks.

Gary Stewart, just 23, has already viewed horse racing from both sides of the fence. A few years ago, Stewart was paying through the gate to cheer his equine heroes from the grandstand. Well, "cheer" might be the wrong word in this case. Gary had to be content to keep his emotions within. Any sudden movement would hurt like hell, legacy of a trackwork smash which left him with a fractured skull and seemingly little future.

Gary backed his biggest winner when he finally woke up after that horrendous fall – doctors had pronounced him clinically dead as he lay on the turf. But they brought him back to live another day ... and four years on he is packing as much as is humanely possible into every 24 hours. All thanks to this chestnut galloping machine he partners: this freak called Bonecrusher.

"As soon as the specialists gave me the thumbs up," says Stewart, "I quietly went about getting myself fit again." He played tennis. He took long walks. Sometimes he would duck out to Frank Ritchie's stables just to be around horses. Then six months later along came Bonecrusher. Gary recalls:

"I took one look at him and knew. I knew straight away. Red finished fourth under me in his first race. When I came back to the enclosure I told Frank he was going to be a super three-year-old."

Gary has landed just over 100 winners in his interrupted career, not a great number by any standard. Tom's Dice, the second-best horse he has ever ridden, wouldn't get within cooee of the hot Derby favourite.

Before Steve Crawley did that interview Stewart and Bonecrusher had already got through one brief Australian campaign. Establishing his class by winning the Eclipse Stakes at Ellerslie – deservedly being promoted from second after severe interference from Star Board – Bonecrusher was aimed at the Golden Slipper. He had not been entered for the race but there was a backdoor way of getting into the field.

The Bramble Classic at Kembla Grange, on Sydney's south coast, was a qualifying race and if the winner was not an original entry the Illawarra Turf Club paid the $20,000 late fee. However, Bonecrusher didn't settle in well in his new surroundings and finished fifth, about three lengths from the winner. It was a very different horse who presented himself to Australian racegoers a year later.

Bonecrusher's incredible three-year-old season is mainly remembered for his wins in the New Zealand and AJC Derbies, but also included were victories in the Bayer Classic, the Avondale Guineas and over the older horses at weight-for-age in the Air New Zealand Stakes, the Cambridge Stud Stakes and Sydney's Tancred Stakes.

The season had commenced on a distinctly low-key note as wins eluded Bonecrusher in his first four starts. First up on September 14 he finished only third over 1200m against moderate company at Hastings. He was third again in the Guineas Trial at Ellerslie on October 5, and a week later was second in the Great Northern Guineas, behind Honour Bright and Hot Ice. But in that race he was hampered for room in the last 100 metres and looked unlucky to go under by a long head and a neck.

The following month he went to Riccarton for the Two Thousand Guineas, which saw Random Chance and Field Dancer locked together in a photo finish, with Bonecrusher in a gap in third place, two and a quarter lengths back. Gary Stewart blamed the defeat on Bonecrusher's lack of recent racing. It was a long time before he had to offer excuses again.

CLASSIC GLORY

When the Bayer Classic came around, Stewart was under suspension and Peter Mitchell fetched in Jim Cassidy from Sydney. Fellow Sydneysider Peter Cook was on hand to ride French Polish and the visiting riders provided the quinella. Bonecrusher took charge early in the run home and Cassidy reported an easy day at the office. "He was travelling beautifully all the way – I got him out at the 600m so he could keep up his momentum."

Winning the 1986 Australian Derby at Randwick.

In the Avondale Guineas Bonecrusher was stepping up from 1600 metres to 2000 metres and was on trial to see if he was a genuine Derby prospect. If the Bayer Classic win had been something of a run of the mill affair, the Avondale Guineas verged on the bizarre.

As the Sunday Star's Barry Lichter wrote:

What a fantastic dress rehearsal for the New Zealand Derby. Today's Avondale Guineas provided one of the most exciting finishes in years and threw up any number of prospects for the big Boxing Day classic at Ellerslie. Bonecrusher, called in third by the judge, got the nod after racing three and four wide. Hot Ice showed he could run out a middle distance when a nose back second. Flight Bijou, two noses from the winner, turned in an incredible effort after being run off the track on the home bend. Field Dancer sat parked three wide and bulldozed home to be only a neck back fourth. So tense was the finish no one in the birdcage knew who had won. Colin Jillings leaned coolly against the rail, convinced Hot Ice had only run second even though he had the judge's call. Dave O'Sullivan sweated out the photo declaring Flight Bijou a certainty beaten after losing three or four lengths in the first turn shemozzle. Frank Ritchie walked around nervously hoping Bonecrusher might get second, never dreaming he had won the race.

With the final placings promoting Bonecrusher from third to first, Lichter went on to record how Frank Ritchie had jumped two feet in the air. These days Ritchie says Lichter wasn't playing proper attention – it was at least four feet, he claims. The phlegmatic Stewart said in race postmortems he was always sure he had got up.

After Bonecrusher's decisive Derby win over Flight Bijou and Random Chance, Lichter in his roundup piece in the Sunday Star told of pre-race precautions and some scary moments 300 metres from the finish. He wrote:

It was verging on cloak and dagger stuff around the stable of Frank Ritchie on Christmas night. Just like in the movies, an all-night around-the-clock guard was put on Derby favourite Bonecrusher – not to keep out the nobblers, but to make sure he got his beauty sleep before the $200,000 race the next day.

In what Ritchie now considers a lucky omen, the only visitor to Bonecrusher's box was a bewildered white rabbit which strayed from a neighbour's hutch. Ritchie, son Shaune and friends took turns on watch, bedded down outside the horse's stall to make sure he wasn't disturbed by Christmas night revellers. "He's a curious creature who'll get up for a look if anyone goes past his box at night," said Ritchie. "I just wanted him watched to make sure he got his rest."

It all paid off when the chestnut, rested and refreshed, shut out his Derby rivals with a dazzling home turn sprint. In just 100 metres Bonecrusher swept to the leaders and dashed away to a two-length break. Then just for a couple of heart-stopping moments Bonecrusher lost some of his momentum by running around – rider Gary Stewart later said the horse had shied at a big yellow infield tent. That allowed favourite Flight Bijou to get within range before Bonecrusher recovered and held on to win by three-quarters of a length.

Following his Derby win Bonecrusher was given a short break. He then twice tackled the older horses at weight-for-age before embarking on his Australian autumn campaign.

Frank Ritchie was somewhat fearful Bonecrusher may have been a little above himself in condition for the Cambridge Stud Stakes and after consultation with Gary Stewart it was decided to ride for luck against the rails. The plan worked to perfection and Bonecrusher powered home from the rear for a comprehensive win. It was a case of more of the same in the Air New Zealand Stakes.

In the prologue to this tribute, Sydney's Bill Casey referred to likenesses to Phar Lap. It was another Australian, Tony Arrold, who seized on comments by leading Kiwi trainer Dave O'Sullivan that Bonecrusher was in the same three-year-old league as the mighty Kingston Town. Writing in The Australian, Australia's national daily, Arrold quoted O'Sullivan as saying:

"The most astonishing thing about him is his acceleration. And he has shown he can do that up to 2400 metres. I know that because it was my horse, Flight Bijou, he beat in the New Zealand Derby – and Bonecrusher had that won 400 metres out when he left them standing.

"I remember seeing Kingston Town in Sydney as a three-year-old when he left them standing in the Rosehill Guineas,

Famous strapper Shanne Ritchie and Trainer Frank Ritchie with their all-time favourite racehorse.

Tancred Stakes, the Derby and the Sydney Cup. This fellow has that same brand of acceleration. He's very, very good."

It was to this background that Bonecrusher crossed the Tasman for the second time.

The Australians had been ready and waiting for Bonecrusher. But they had not been prepared for him stealing the show on such a precious occasion as Golden Slipper Day. Despite Bounding Away's great Slipper win, it was Bonecrusher who grabbed the biggest headlines with his incredible win in the Tancred Stakes. Sydney racing writer Stephen Brassel was unstinting in superlatives when he wrote:

Kiwi superstar Bonecrusher put up one of the most sensational performances ever seen on an Australian racecourse to win yesterday's Tancred Stakes at Rosehill. And he was immediately declared the greatest horse to cross the Tasman since Phar Lap.

With 200 metres to go the commentator said he'd need wings to win and Bonecrusher took flight. Ridden the ultimate in patient races by his jockey Gary Stewart, Bonecrusher came from last with a scintillating finish to win. Such was the quality of Bonecrusher's performance Stewart had time to ease the gelding up in the last 50 metres of the race.

Brassel was not the only Aussie to pile on the accolades.

Keith Robins, longtime chief racing writer for Sydney's Daily Telegraph used the words phenomenal and fantastic. Bart Cummings said it was a sensational win and it would take an outstanding galloper to beat him in the Derby. Neville Begg, bemused as to how Pag-Asa could sire such a top galloper, said it would take a freak to beat him in upcoming races. Les Bridge was one of many who made comparisons with Kingston Town.

Prime Minister Bob Hawke reserved his accolades for Gary Stewart. "He's cool, calm and collected and good at getting the best out of what's under him," said the most influential man in Ozidom. "He should be captain of the Australian cricket team."

The AJC Derby looked to be a mere formality and a legion of new Australian fans made him an odds-on favourite. Not going with the flow was Tommy Smith – probably a bit miffed by Bonecrusher raining on Bounding Away's Golden Slipper party. He said Bonecrusher was no certainty and favoured the Les Bridge-trained Drawn. The main concern for Frank Ritchie was that in the past Bonecrusher had enjoyed at least a two-week break between races – in the Derby he was backing up after seven days.

In retrospect Frank Ritchie acknowledges the Tancred Stakes run did sap some of Bonecrusher's energy. That made his win in the AJC Derby, from an impossible position on the home turn, all the more remarkable. Pulling the last drop of energy out of a seemingly empty tank, Bonecrusher managed to take a half length win over Handy Proverb with 50 to 1 shot Agent Provocative a long head away third. The win took Bonecrusher's bankroll past the million dollar mark – a first for a New Zealand thoroughbred.

To say Bonecrusher had won the hearts of Australians was an understatement and one newspaper heading read: MILLIONAIRE OZ-CRUSHER ... Move over, Phar Lap. Steve Crawley said it all on behalf of Aussie racegoers in an article headed simply THANKS CHAMP. The talented wordsmith wrote:

He winged his way out of Sydney early this morning. Tucked away ingloriously in one of those wooden crates, he could have been any old horse New Zealand-bound. But he wasn't. He was Bonecrusher.

And with him went our respect, our hearts and well over 600,000 inconsequential Aussie dollars. Julius Caesar would have loved the warrior within Bonecrusher. Just as we did. As Big Julie often boasted: He came, he saw and he conquered. All in 14 sensational days.

This chestnut is but three years old. If he never wins another race, heaven forbid, he still will have served his purpose in life. Since the days of Banjo Paterson turf writers have been accused of degrading the word champion. It has got to the stage where many subconsciously steer clear of the description, seemingly to conform. Even with Bonecrusher.

To me a champion is a thoroughbred who leaves you with a lump in your throat, a tear in your eye and a dollar in your pocket. Which makes Bonecrusher a champion in my book from his flaring nostrils to the tip of his bloody red tail. As far as I'm concerned, they didn't need a plane to transport him across the Tasman. He could have just as easily have walked.

Bravery won the Cox Plate for Bonecrusher in the spring of 1986. Only weeks later the same bravery saved his life when struck down with life-threatening sickness on the eve of the Japan Cup. If Bonecrusher, a sprightly 21-year-old at the time of writing, had a say in the matter he could be excused for declaring the outcome of the Japan challenge was the one which mattered most. Siding with Bonecrusher on that

issue would unquestionably be owner Peter Mitchell, wife Shirley and daughter Sharlene, along with trainer Frank Ritchie and members of his family as well as regular jockey Gary Stewart. To all those people Bonecrusher was – and continues to be – more than a champion racehorse. He is a permanent and precious part of their lives.

Rank and file racegoers, however, tend to know and love Bonecrusher for his remarkable raceday deeds. And on Cox Plate Day 1986 he gave a new meaning to courage and racing excellence. His gut-wrenching battle with Waverley Star provoked a level of emotion probably unmatched on any racetrack in the world. The adrenaline rush which had obviously overtaken both horses in their desperate bid to gain ascendancy spilled from Moonee Valley's historic track, across the lawns, into the packed stands and invaded the tear ducts of young and old. When it was all over – when Bonecrusher in one last frantic lunge became the winner – there was not a dry eye in sight, with mine as moist as any.

Even before the running of the epic 1986 edition I harboured fond memories of the Cox Plate, memories which dated back to 1967 when enmeshed in the jubilant response to the very handsome Tobin Bronze winning the event for a second time just a week after taking the Caulfield Cup. It was Tobin Bronze's last race in Australia before going to America for the Laurel International and then stud duties on retirement. He could not have had a more rapturous farewell. Not a soul seemed to take any notice of the fact that the horse I had backed had run second. That horse was Terrific, trained by Frank Ritchie's father Merv.

Nineteen years later I was to become an unwitting accessory to perhaps Australasia's best ever race promotion and one which put the Ritchie family centre stage. I was in Perth on business when I received a phone call a day before the Caulfield Cup and eight days out from the Cox Plate from Moonee Valley CEO Ian McEwen. The call was on an unrelated matter but in the course of conversation McEwen declared Bonecrusher to be an unbeatable certainty in the Cox Plate.

"Better not tell Dave O'Sullivan that," I said, knowing the huge opinion O'Sullivan had of Waverley Star.

The race of the centurey was cleverly crafted by ex-pat kiwi Ian McEwen. It was over to Bonecrusher and Waverley Star to play out the script.

"Not in the same class," retorted McEwen, famous for black and white answers to everything.

"Well," I responded, "I think you would have some difficulty in convincing O'Sullivan of that."

I finished the call off by saying "See ya next Thursday". That was day my wife Sonia and I were going to stay with Ian and Jo McEwen for the remainder of the Melbourne spring carnival, an arrangement of 12 months standing.

When I did hit Melbourne, McEwen had switched horses. He had cleverly become a Waverley Star supporter to balance attention on the race and had Moonee Valley's promotions consultants, headed by Gary Gray, saturating all aspects of Melbourne media with "Race of the Century" hype. It was going to be a two-horse war the like of which Australia had never before seen. Sports-mad Melburnians lapped up the rhetoric like kids let loose in a candy store.

By race morning McEwen, himself a former New Zealand racing writer, had that "clever bugger me" look that goes with people who know they have done a good job. "Just hope that horse of yours doesn't let us down," he said, referring to Waverley Star and obviously personally back on the Bonecrusher bandwagon. As crowds thronged on course you could only admire his entrepreneurial genius.

While McEwen had written a special script for Bonecrusher and Waverley Star, another had been written for Sonia and me. Exactly 12 months earlier, Sonia and I had been married in the grounds of the old Cox family homestead – home to the McEwens. With the ceremony over we had walked through the carpark to the members stand, backed the first winner and sat down to the committee luncheon. On our first anniversary we were not sure about the winner of the first race, but knew lunch again awaited while two sets of very close friends readied themselves to win the weight-for-age championship of Australasia. It was soon to turn into a bubbly occasion.

As Sonia and I stepped through the garden gate into the carpark a woman descended on us with two flutes of champagne with a strawberry floating on top of both. "Happy anniversary," said the stranger. "We watched your wedding over the fence last year," she explained. "We always park in the same spot on Cox Plate Day." After that it didn't seem possible that anything else during the day could surprise, or move us, more. But, of course, something did. The Cox Plate.

A squillion words have been written about how Ian McEwen's Race of the Century unfolded. But Jack Elliott, the legendary former chief racing writer of Melbourne's Herald told it as well as any. He wrote:

Bonecrusher proved himself one of the world's great racehorses this afternoon when he scored over Waverley Star in a sensational finish to the W.S. Cox Plate. It must have been one of the most exciting race finishes on any Australian track in the last 50 years.

The two champions, Bonecrusher and Waverley Star, brought the Moonee Valley crowd to their feet, screaming and yelling as the horses charged past the 700 metre mark. Most of the racegoers, even the professionals, put down their glasses, yelling and waving their arms as first one horse, then the other, took the upper hand. The race turned into a two-horse war after the 13 runners were sorted out.

Bonecrusher and Waverley Star made their runs together, hitting the front at the 700 metre mark with the rest of the field burnt off. First it was Waverley Star being called the winner, two strides later it was Bonecrusher. So it went on until they hit the line with Bonecrusher the victor. He started 9-10 and the official margin was a neck from Waverley Star, 3-1, with The Filbert, 80-1, three lengths away third.

Among other articles, Keith Robins from Sydney referred to the hysteria the two horses had evoked, of people screaming their lungs out and how no horse in the world could beat Bonecrusher at his pet distance of 2400 metres.

Shane Templeton described how Bart Cummings had

Peter Mitchell (left) and Frank Ritchie with portrait of a champion.

declared it was the best race he had ever seen and Bob Hoysted said it deserved to be a deadheat. Peter McFarline of The Sun made the pertinent point that for the first time, and possibly the last, in ballyhooed racing advertising, Bonecrusher and Waverley Star had put on a show far and away above the hopes and claims of their most optimistic publicists.

Winning the 1988 Air New Zealand Stakes from subsequent Japan Cup winner Horlicks against the rails.

Keith Robins had chosen the word hysteria well. The simple truth was that the amphitheatre created by the saucer-like Moonee Valley racetrack and its enclosed environs actually was overtaken by hysteria. Like everyone else I was caught up in its web and at some point found myself chanting "go, go, go, go." I hadn't had a bet, intending to be a neutral observer. I guess I yelled because I didn't want the magical theatre unfolding before my eyes to come to an end. I was pleased for Frank Ritchie, sorry for Dave O'Sullivan – over the moon about being there when history was made.

Ian McEwen had traded his "clever bugger me" look for one of benevolent thanks to the media, who gathered by the score after the last race in the committee area. It was while I was in their midst that Bill Whittaker, with whom I had forged a lasting friendship during the 1960 Interdominion Trotting Championships in Sydney, sidled up to me with the sort of studied look that hardly matched the glass of beer in his hand.

"One of the young blokes has just asked me if this is the greatest race I've seen," he said. "Before I tell you what I said, what would you have told them?"

I had already pondered that question. "Bill, if I'd been asked that question when I walked on to the track today," I replied, "I would have said the night Caduceus won the Interdom final at Harold Park." Bill's calculating expression suggested I was on the right track. "Yeah," he said. "Hot favourite, off 36yds, crowd of 50,000 they reckoned – health and safety wouldn't allow it these days. Then the protest from the Apmat mob. Christ, that protest was like putting a time bomb in the joint – if they'd taken the race off Caduceus and given it to Apmat the stewards would have been lynched, Harold Park demolished."

It was my turn to say yeah. "Yeah, it was some night," I said. "But I reckon today beats it – maybe we were young and impressionable in 1960."

"Reckon so," said Bill. "Least that's what I told the young blokes – today was the greatest. Better have another beer then, seeing our lives have just been changed." And that's what Bonecrusher did. He changed people's lives.

JAPAN CUP FEVER

The Japan Cup was always a feverish affair. Being the richest race in the world in 1986, it had been a target for Bonecrusher since the autumn of his three-year-old season. Everything looked on track during an undefeated spring in Melbourne where he won the Underwood Stakes, the Caulfield Stakes and dramatically won the Cox Plate at the expense of fellow Japan Cup rival Waverley Star. He had become one of the most discussed racehorses in the world and there was generally universal acceptance of the confidence in the Bonecrusher camp. He had travelled well, worked well – then the wheels fell off, as Mike Dillon explained in the 1987 edition of the Racing Annual:

Even the first words were ominous. "Look Dad, he's left some of his overnight feed."

It was 7.00am at Tokyo racecourse, Thursday, November 20, and New Zealand's bid to win the $2.3 million Japan Cup for the first time had just been dealt a crippling blow from which it would not recover. The speaker was Shaune Ritchie, strapper to New Zealand's equine giant Bonecrusher, the horse to whom most had already conceded defeat in the Japan Cup. But as trainer Frank Ritchie and owner Peter Mitchell stepped into the horse box, silhouetted by a brilliant Tokyo daybreak, Bonecrusher looked more like a broken down cart horse than a thoroughbred about to do battle with some of the world's best. The head that had shut out Australasia's best threatened to bury itself in the straw.

Bonecrusher was suffering from a bacterial infection so severe he could hardly walk, let alone continue a race preparation. It was a huge disappointment, after everything looked to be on target. The smiles had been there for all to see when a week after arrival in Tokyo he had completed a rousing semi-final trial.

Ritchie could hardly contain his delight. "He's ready to jump clean through his bridle," he said. Gary Stewart agreed. "He's never worked better," he said. Bonecrusher's final gallop was to have been on that fateful Thursday, but that plan, and many others, were halted in a stride when the camp arrived at the champ's box.

Three Japan Racing Association vets were quickly on the scene examining a very distressed Bonecrusher. Two related problems emerged. Firstly a language barrier between the Japanese vets and Frank Ritchie and the desire of the Japanese trio to begin treatment immediately. Bonecrusher had quickly become a hero in Japan. He was the shortest pre-post Japan Cup favourite on record after Waverley Star's runaway win in the Fuji Stakes a week earlier. Under the rules all medication had to cease by 3.00pm on that very day – the reason for the Japanese vets wanting to take urgent action. Frankie was adamant he wanted no medication administered until he knew its composition.

Shirley Mitchell with cherished painting of the race of the century.

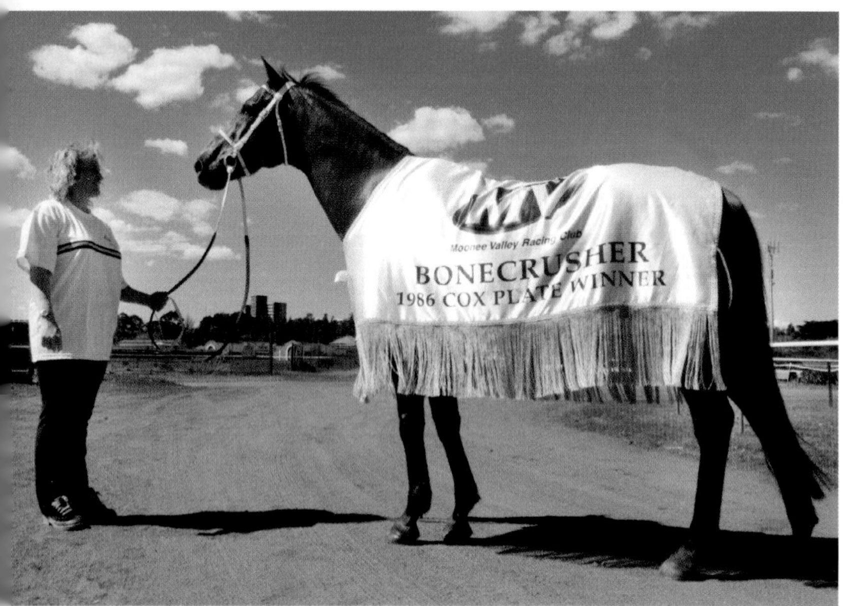

Sporting the Cox Plate rug.

The stalemate came to an end with the appearance of visiting Woodville vet Kem Keene, in Japan after his wife had won a free trip to the Japan Cup in a radio competition. Keene gave the okay to the drugs the Japanese wanted to use and Bonecrusher's life was at least out of danger in 36 hours. Ritchie had nothing but praise for the assistance given by the Japan Racing Association and its veterinary surgeons. "They were fantastic," he said. "Before I came here I'd heard from several people that the veterinary standard in Japan is as high as anywhere in the world and now I know that for myself. They just couldn't do enough for us."

It will forever remain a mystery how Bonecrusher contracted the infection, but Kem Keene's guess is that it was from the air. Said Keene: "When a horse goes to a foreign country, as distinct from Australia, it comes into contact with a whole new range of infections it has never struck before. Therefore a horse has no level of immunity at all if it's struck by an infection. The effects can be very severe. The bug Bonecrusher had was, I'd say, very virulent as well. So virulent that if he hadn't been treated as quickly as he was he could have well died."

Bonecrusher was down but not out. After a month's quarantine in Melbourne he arrived back in New Zealand mid-January and on February 10 announced to the world he was back when finishing third over 1400 metres in the Lion Brown Sprint at Te Rapa. His first serious autumn mission was the Australian Cup over 2000 metres at Flemington and in a final leadup run easily beat a moderate field over 1600 metres at Avondale. The Australian Cup was to prove an absolutely gut-wrenching affair and to this day Frank Ritchie believes it was the race which took the first edge off his greatness. It was a race of great controversy with allegations of unfair gang-riding tactics. The race created a media frenzy and the massive scrapbooks belonging to the Mitchell family recording Bonecrusher's wondrous deeds include numerous colourful accounts of the occasion. The one which follows carries no byline, but its author paints an accurate and poignant picture of what transpired:

For the few seconds it takes a champion racehorse to negotiate the home bend at Flemington and the next 200 metres, Bonecrusher must have felt Australia an inhospitable place.

And the thoughts of jockey Gary Stewart, trainer Frank Ritchie, strapper and constant companion Shaune Ritchie and owner Peter Mitchell, had they spoken, would never have won a "G" rating. At that stage of the $250,000 Australian Cup, the Bonecrusher script had gone terribly wrong.

The other champion and the only horse with a conceivable chance of bringing down a legend, At Talaq, had taken a run between horses – courtesy of stablemate

Sir Lustrious – and sprinted two lengths clear. He did the same thing in another race last November (the Melbourne Cup) *and held on all the way down Flemington's relentless straight to become part of racing lore. As his rump began to fade from sight, the New Zealanders found themselves swamped in the backwash of tiring horses. In short they had nowhere to go and much to prove.*

That they found somewhere to go and proved much will long be remembered. Not since 1955 has another New Zealander (Rising Fast) been the recipient of so much affection from Melbourne's racegoers. Not since 1960, when Tulloch made his heroic comeback from a life-threatening illness, has a horse attracted so much pre-race attention. An hour before the Australian Cup, the fans clustered around Bonecrusher's No 52 stall. There was in fact a human traffic jam around an area normally inhabited only by owners, trainers and strappers. And another 100 metres away, At Talaq stood quietly in his stall. Around him the admirers could be counted on the fingers of two hands.

Perhaps the scarcity of racebooks was the reason. You could sniff the Bonecrusher aura without an official guide. Despite the improbability of miracles, the 1987 Australian Cup was, in its own way, as unforgettable as the 1986 W.S. Cox Plate. All the plans of the seemingly invincible Colin Hayes stable came to fruition – except the bob-of-a-head finish.

At Talaq was two lengths in front by the time Bonecrusher was extricated to make his run, and the grand stayer seemed to be going better. But with the crowd roaring, and young Stewart wielding the whip in his left hand like a flagellist in another setting, the script reverted to the original. So it was an Australian Cup for legend and folklore. Not a remake of the Cox Plate but a masterpiece of its own.

And forget not At Talaq. Like Waverley Star, he becomes the year's nomination for best supporting act.

Following the Australian Cup the plan was for Bonecrusher to go to Sydney for the Rawson Stakes and Tancred Stakes. On the eve of the Rawson Stakes Gary Stewart was hospitalised with appendicitis. With Shane Dye the substitute rider, Bonecrusher was a lacklustre and shock third behind Myocard and Waverley Star. When he disappointed in subsequent training he was sent to New Zealand for a spell. He was to be away from racing for 11 months.

Things didn't go well for Bonecrusher following his aborted Sydney autumn. He suffered muscular problems and much of his exercise was done on farmland at a pre-training establishment. If there was hint of any excitement in his life it came with rounding up cattle. But in the long run country life was therapeutic and he returned to health. His fans had been waiting patiently but the racing establishment was rocked when his selected comeback race was in the South Island – over 1600 metres at Wingatui. The Otago Racing Club had a promotional gem placed in their laps and were understandably ecstatic. Frank Ritchie and Peter Mitchell had fingers crossed.

Bonecrusher, in keeping with his reputation, came up with a late finishing burst to take a narrow win. The second race of this fresh campaign was a bid to win his second Air New Zealand Stakes. It was time to start plucking at heartstrings again. Mike

The gut-wrenching win over Melbourne Cup victor At Talaq was not a re-make of The Cox plate. The Australian Cup was a masterpiece of its own.

Last to first in the Cambridge International Stakes.

Dillon, who had repositioned himself as racing editor of Sunday News, captured the emotion with a story headed BONEY'S BURNING! and carrying the kicker line "Amazing run just tears Frank apart". He wrote:

Champion Bonecrusher reduced trainer Frank Ritchie to tears with his world-beating last-to-first victory in yesterday's Air New Zealand Stakes at Ellerslie. Tears streamed down Ritchie's face as Bonecrusher returned to one of the greatest receptions at Ellerslie of modern times. "Yes, I'm crying and I'll probably cry again," he said. "Who wouldn't after what we have just seen."

What Ritchie and the large crowd at Ellerslie had seen was Bonecrusher once again do the impossible in coming from last on the home turn and down a red-hot weight-for-age field. "Can you believe it," said an incredulous Ritchie. "He couldn't possibly win on the turn. I had written him off." So had everyone else.

Pre-race plans to have Bonecrusher handy to the pace had to be scrapped when the gelding missed the start. "He was unsettled in the barrier and lost a length," said rider Gary Stewart. "He was no hope," said owner Peter Mitchell, who had also written off his chances on the home turn.

The finish Bonecrusher turned in ranked with his greatest performances in the Tancred Stakes and Cox Plate. "In many ways that was his greatest ever performance," said Ritchie, "because things were against him coming into the race. If there was ever an element of doubt in some minds about him coming back to his best form then it has been removed by that effort. He's an absolute freak and champion. And, what a sensational ride!"

That short head win over subsequent Japan Cup winner Horlicks clinched a return to Melbourne for a clash with reigning Australian champion Vo Rogue in the $500,000 Bi-Centennial Australian Cup. Unfortunately that race failed to live up to the media hype and sadly spawned the heading in the New Zealand Herald "FIZZER OF TWO CENTURIES" when almost rank outsider Dandy Andy beat Vo Rogue with Bonecrusher a distant third.

The opportunity for redemption came at Ellerslie shortly after Bonecrusher's return home. With Peter Tims substituting for Gary Stewart he started favourite for the $200,000 Television New Zealand Stakes, but lost narrowly to Horlicks. The defeat came as a shock to the Bonecrusher camp but Peter Mitchell was quick off the mark in offering congratulations to Horlicks' trainer Dave O'Sullivan. It was payback time for O'Sullivan's graciousness after Waverley Star lost the famous Cox Plate battle.

Frank Ritchie says one of his most treasured moments in racing will always be the sportsmanship displayed by Dave O'Sullivan in the pandemonium which immediately followed the 1986 Cox Plate when he embraced him and said well done. As Ritchie explains they had both so desperately wanted to win the same race – and a couple of times in the straight it looked as if it could be O'Sullivan's. "I don't think Dave will ever know how much his congratulations meant to me," Ritchie has said so many times since.

For his part, Dave O'Sullivan has always shrugged it off as simple act of courtesy and giving credit where credit was due. He admits, however, there have been plenty of times when replaying the famous tape he's been guilty of adding a "bugger Bonecrusher" to Bill Collins' famous commentary. But he also concedes there was more than a little compensation when winning the other big race both camps so badly wanted – the Japan Cup.

Following the Television New Zealand Stakes there was an addition to Bonecrusher's late autumn campaign. It was the Queen Elizabeth Stakes at Canberra – a race programmed to coincide with the Queen's visit to open Australia's new Parliament House. The race was immediately billed as a matchup with the champion Australian three-year-old Beau Zam, trained by Bart Cummings. Two things went wrong. Gary Stewart had to forgo the ride with an injured knee and on the day Bonecrusher was disadvantaged by a rain-affected track in which Beau Zam revelled. After a keen duel, Beau Zam won by a head, but replacement rider Jim Cassidy asserted that had the track been firm Bonecrusher would have won by three lengths.

Bonecrusher may not have got the win but Ritchie and Mitchell got to meet the Queen and play golf with Australian Prime Minister Bob Hawke. So it wasn't all bad.

The champion's racing days were getting closer to their end, but some lofty goals still remained. In the spring he finished third to Our Poetic Prince and Horlicks in the Cox Plate and then journeyed to Tokyo for another Japan Cup bid. He arrived in Japan in good condition, but only managed eighth, probably unsuited by the slow early pace. But there were also signs his halcyon days were probably behind him. The following year a tendon injury brought about his retirement.

His new temporary home for the next couple of years was Puketutu Island, the home too, of former brewery magnate and philanthropist, Sir Henry Kelliher, and also where former champion pacer Cardigan Bay had lived in retirement. Barry Lichter accompanied Bonecrusher on the ride from the Ritchie stables and filed the following report:

"Well that's it. It's all over . . ."

With those few words ended one of the most exciting eras in New Zealand racing history. The speaker is strapper Shaune Ritchie. He's on the main road out of Takanini heading for Puketutu Island where the champion galloper Bonecrusher today begins retirement. The 20 minute car ride to Mangere goes by in almost total silence. Owner Peter Mitchell is at the wheel, lost in thought. Ritchie at his side with a faraway look in his eyes. The Crusher rolls along behind, weaving about in his float and whinnying loudly as the unfamiliar route unfolds.

Big Red turns round and squeals, as if to say "Hey, you missed the airport turnoff back there." But his globetrotting days are over. And so is the five and a half year roller-coaster ride enjoyed by his connections. After surviving a near fatal lung infection in Japan, the Crusher has finally succumbed to a minor tendon injury. How cruel that such a small piece of sinew attaching his leg muscle to the bone should rob the champion's many fans of what promised to be his greatest comeback.

The Crusher's flanks flash red in the sun as he thunders off the float. Mitchell, trainer Frank Ritchie and their wives Shirley and Colleen gather to watch a ritual that has been played out so many times before. It's Red, strutting round his new paddock dragging young Ritchie by the lead rope. But as he flares his nostrils, scenting the air, Bonecrusher knows something is up.

He gives Ritchie one last nudge and nestles his head close to the boy. Not a word is spoken but you know they're saying goodbye. Half an hour later and the Crusher team is still saying its farewells. Mitchell poses one last time with the big chestnut. It's hard to walk away.

Bonecrusher's stay at Puketutu Island only lasted as long as it took Peter Mitchell to buy and set up his own retirement home at Takanini within walking distance of the Ritchie stables. No horse could have had more love and affection showered on him. He still receives Christmas and birthday cards – he even has his own website.

On the eve of his Cox Plate win New Zealand's then Minister of Overseas Trade Mike Moore appointed him a sporting ambassador. Peter Mitchell has never allowed him to shirk his civic duties since. Over the years he's made numerous promotional visits to Australia, leading out fields for icon Australian races like the Melbourne Cup and Cox Plate and many others of lesser renown. He's also made numerous appearances around New Zealand racetracks, the Mitchells always keen to share their great champion with his adoring fans.

EPILOGUE

Bonecrusher made an art form out of achieving the impossible. But his epic win in the 1986 Cox Plate will always stand apart.

His level of fitness is remarkable. Though 21 on his final public appearance, when he led out the 2003 New Zealand Derby field at Ellerslie he looked as majestic and as keen as the contestants. New Zealand has had many champions, but Bonecrusher is unquestionably among the upper echelon and one the Aussies have always shared with us along with Phar Lap.

This tribute to Red – as he was always known around the Ritchie stable – was never meant to be a chronicle of his great racing achievements. It was always intended as a salute to a legend, not only crafted by the great horse himself, but by a media which wallowed in recording his every breathing moment. It was the media which ensured Bonecrusher made the progression from champion to legend. It is for that reason this tribute has been written around so many of their stories.

Just recently on a winter's day at a trials meeting on a country track I asked Shaune Ritchie – who as an 18-year-old lad had been likened to Phar Lap's youthful strapper Tommy Woodcock – if he remembered the day Bonecrusher was delivered to Puketutu Island.

"How could you forget," he said. "I left school to become his strapper and it plunged me – just a kid – into a champagne life. I got to travel, meet the most famous trainers in the world, be amongst some of the best horses in the world. That day I knew the champagne life was over – a fresh start had to be made somewhere."

Ritchie said that day he stood with Bonecrusher in his first moment of retirement he had no idea at all what the future held. "Then I got lucky," he said. "I went to work for John Dunlop in England for 18 months and he treated me like a son. I got to travel with horses to Italy, Germany, France, Ireland and Scotland. He took a big interest in me, I think, because one of his own boys, Harry, had been so well looked after when working for Dave O'Sullivan in New Zealand and Colin Hayes in Australia. So maybe I have a lot to thank those two people for, too. But without Bonecrusher I would never have met John Dunlop in Japan."

These days Shaune Ritchie, who first trained in partnership with his father, trains on his own account at Cambridge after also spending time based in Sydney. Like all trainers he's waiting for a champion to come along – but while hope may spring eternal he knows better than most his life is unlikely to include another Red.

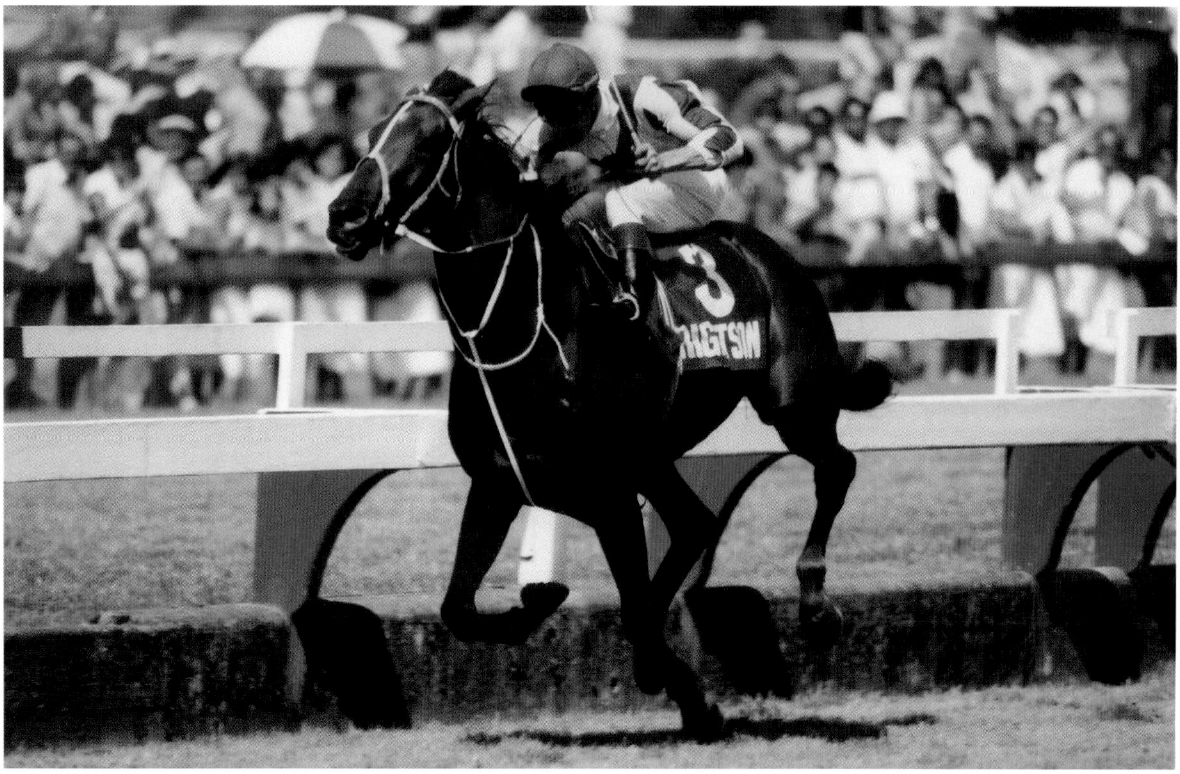

A champion in full flight.

Frank Ritchie remains a high-profile trainer at Takanini, in partnership with Shaune's younger brother Craig. Inside 12 months Frank will move to a new complex at Cambridge. The Mitchell family remain dedicated to pampering Bonecrusher, while watching their cream and brown racing silks being carried by horses of a lesser creed. Gary Stewart resides in Australia.

In a traditional epilogue this should spell the finish. But it is not. In the same context as "My Way" became Frank Sinatra's signature song, Bonecrusher's signature race was the 1986 Cox Plate. Those of us privileged to be there that unforgettable day have our own special memories. As distinct from simply the race, Steve Crawley's memories stretch over the entire day and no one has ever described it better. His final word on the Race Of The Century follows in an article headed: FROM DAWN TO ETERNITY.

EPSOM AT DAWN. A couple of minutes past six and your watch tells you the sun is up. But your eyes, confronted with fog and mist, a couple of hundred trackwork riders with no names, and even less familiar thoroughbreds, tell a different story. Horses here, horses there, horses everywhere. Its hypnotic . . . it leaves you in a trance.

Ten past six and Gary Stewart, a jockey, steers Bonecrusher, a horse, down the stable lane towards the track. Out of the corner of his eye Stewart sees another jockey, this one named Lance O'Sullivan. Stewart turns and his eyes and those of O'Sullivan's meet. Stewart begins to nod "Good morning", but O'Sullivan turns away

Still a New Zealand Derby star aged 21.

before the action is complete. For two young men destined to be so close for the best part of this miserable day, they seem so very distant.

Jockey O'Sullivan, along with his dad, Dave, and older brother, Paul, co-trainers of a horse named Our Waverley Star, are bunking across the road with the Meagher family. John Meagher trained What A Nuisance to beat the O'Sullivans' Koiro Corrie May by a whisker in last year's Melbourne Cup. When Dave O'Sullivan walked into the Meagher home for the first time this spring, he was greeted by a framed photo of his old grey mare's narrow defeat at Flemington. He didn't say a word, walking straight to the bathroom, grabbing a towel, walking back to the foyer and gently hanging it over the photo. Nobody likes finishing runner-up.

Down the road and to the left Peter Mitchell, Bonecrusher's owner, is locked away in a rented room, watching videos of past W.S. Cox Plates, the race with a $750,000 stake and regarded as the equine championship of Australasia. Mitchell has something of a name as a card player in New Zealand. He plays horse racing as he does poker – for keeps.

Time's the worry. Tick, tock. Clip Clop. Two twenty-five and the crowd at Moonee Valley approaches 25,000. Bonecrusher and Our Waverley Star are further apart now than they will be at any other stage during the next 40-odd minutes – five metres, if that. Bonecrusher is waiting in stall 102, Our Waverley Star No 99. For the 1986 Cox Plate they are to carry the same weights, saddle cloth numbers two and three and start from barriers 10 and 12 respectively. Only a couple of points separate them in the betting ring.

Through the fog and mist you can almost sense that the Valley is about to carve out another legend. Not one like Phar Lap's, who won this great race twice in the thirties. Not one like Ajax's, or Gunsynd's. Not even one like Kingston Town's. For this legend will belong to two horses and to two jockeys when the only thing missing at the Valley is sunshine.

At the winning post a couple of minutes to three, Gary Stewart and Lance O'Sullivan see the whites in one another's eyes. Daylight is a poor third. Bart Cummings says: "The greatest race I've ever had the pleasure of witnessing anywhere in the world." Bob Hoysted says: "They were both winners, only Bonecrusher got the money."

He did, too. Saw the post and lunged as a flag racer would do on a beach. Won by a whisker. A tape of a New Zealand pop singer's rendition of the "Bonecrusher" song blares over the course. And so many people follow both horses back to the stripping stalls it must embarrass the makers of the Phar Lap movie. Your day at the track ends as it began . . . in a trance.

Monogamy has never been part of Bonecrusher's makeup. Ask him who is the most loving woman in the world and, had the power of speech been another of his gifts, he would say, "Both of them – Shirley and Sharlene." That's the way it is with Red. Never do things by halves.

Shirley Mitchell, wife of owner Peter Mitchell, and daughter Sharlene are probably seen by the macho Bonecrusher as his slave girls. They pander to his every need, put up with his likes and dislikes, simply love him to bits. Ten minutes in the company of Shirley and Sharlene and you know there's not a bachelor bloke around who has it better than Red.

Both women have a store of Red stories – special moments with the champion which will never be erased from their memories.

For instance their recollections of the AJC Derby differs greatly from the one usually found in the historical records. Recalls Shirley: "Sharlene had been riding at some equestrian event and we got home just in time to listen on the radio. When he started making his run from the back we started shouting our heads off like a couple of mad things. We made so much noise we couldn't hear the announcer and when it was over we were just looking at one another – we didn't know if he had won or lost."

It is Shirley who has faithfully fed Bonecrusher throughout his lengthy retirement on the Mitchell's 10-acre lifestyle block at Takanini, just down the road from the training tracks. Skilled horsewoman as she is, Shirley never takes risks. "He can be a bit of a bugger at times. I'm careful of his back feet – it's not that he's bad, he's just full of himself and can let fly. He puts on a real act when he changes paddocks – tears around, stands on his hind feet and boxes the air with his front feet."

Shirley also admits the great one can be a bit of a brat. "He likes to get his own way and will get quite angry if you reprimand him. I've learned not to growl at him – just tell him quietly he's being a goat and to behave himself."

Sharlene has been the one who has ridden Bonecrusher most in retirement. Early on she decided to convert him into a dressage horse. That proved below Red's dignity. Dressage instruction came to an end one day during the brief time Bonecrusher was living at Puketutu Island.

"He just didn't want to know anything at all about dressage," says Sharlene when recounting the events which led to Red becoming a missing person. "I was changing his head collar for a bridle when he slipped away from me and was off. I just assumed he'd go back to his paddock and mates. But he wasn't there. I hunted everywhere, but he had just disappeared. Vanished. After half an hour I found some clues – hoof marks in the stable courtyard which led to the only box with an open door. He was inside hiding from me."

Dressage lessons may have become a thing of the past by the time Bonecrusher got to his present home but Sharlene continued to be very much a part of Red's life. She accompanied him on almost all of his nine or ten promotional visits to Australia. To lift his fitness levels for these appearances, and others in New Zealand, she exercised him at the Takanini training complex. Some of the more bizarre events where they have appeared together include taking part in city street parades in Melbourne and Sydney and being the surprise guest at a formal rugby league luncheon attended by Prime Minister Helen Clark in Wellington.

Says Sharlene: "There were 600 guests and there was a prize for the person who could guess who the surprise celebrity was. The clue was a carrot on every plate. The horse float pulled up outside the Town Hall and Red took everything in his stride until he got inside and felt the give in the special flooring that had been put down for him. What was worse, it was slippery. Frank [Ritchie] and I were terrified he'd slip and panic. I felt sick at what could happen and I know Frank was feeling the same way.

"But I think that was also the time I fully realised just how clever he is. Frank said let's do this one step at a time' and that's what we did – well, two steps at a time really. Frank and I were on each side of him. He would take two steps, stop, look at both of us in turn and seem to say 'okay, so far so good' and then take two more steps, stop, and go through the same routine. He was incredible. If he had panicked it could so easily have been a broken leg. Once outside he just stepped back on to the float as if it was all part of the day."

Horses who hobnob with Australian and New Zealand prime ministers, like to play hide-and-seek, have a postage stamp printed in their honour, hold the title of sporting ambassador and win the odd race or two tend to be like that. Legendary.

A special postage stamp in his honour.

Bonecrusher

(Pag-Asa – Imitation) Chestnut gelding, bred 1982
44 STARTS, 18 WINS, 5 SECONDS, 11 THIRDS. EARNINGS: $2,888,085

Given the status of official sporting ambassador by the New Zealand government of the day, Bonecrusher captured the imagination of the whole country - not just race fans - with his mighty performances during the 1980s. The illness that prevented him from running in the 1986 Japan Cup made headline news. Was it his catchy name that appealed so widely? Or his likeable character that touched our hearts? Undoubtedly they added to his image, but it was his outstanding courage in a series of fighting finishes in major races that really set Bonecrusher apart from other horses. When racing buffs reminisce about great races, Bonecrusher's 1986 WS Cox Plate always comes up. That stride-for-stride battle with Waverley Star down the Moonee Valley straight is still capable of bringing out goose bumps. There has never been a worthier winner of the New Zealand Horse of the Year Award than Bonecrusher, a true champion.

26

YEARLING SALES REACH BIG EXPECTATIONS

2004 Series at Karaka

The 2004 edition of the National Yearling Sales at Karaka was for the most part like all thoroughbred auctions. Well conformed stock of quality pedigree met the aspirations of their vendors – values slumped when the basic criteria were not met.

There was, however, much for selling agents New Zealand Bloodstock to rejoice about.

First, rigorous marketing of the sale produced a strong international buying bench, which had to go head-to-head with a robust force of Kiwi buyers. This was one of the keys to the strength of the competition also for middle-range stock. Secondly, vendors were prepared to meet the market and provide a healthy clearance rate. In this atmosphere there was an increase in aggregate, average and median prices.

The aggregate for the premier session was $44,782,000, compared with $34,209,500 the previous year. But in analysing this 31 percent difference, account has to be taken of the fact that the 2004 total came from 400 lots sold, while in 2003 there were only 353. The 2004 average of $111,955 represented a 17 percent increase over the previous year and an eight percent rise in the median price saw a lift from $67,000 to $75,000.

For the 23rd successive year Cambridge Stud headed the vendor list, the 46 lots it sold fetching $7,402,500. The runner-up slot went to Windsor Park Stud, which sells solely in New Zealand.

Pencarrow Stud, operated by New Zealand Bloodstock's principals Peter and Philip Vela, had the distinction of providing both the top and third top colts. Their sales-topper was an outstanding colt by Danehill from Grand Echezeaux who fell to the local bid of Te Akau Racing at $1.1 million. A daughter of champion sire Zabeel, Grand Echezeaux is an Australasian Oaks winner and belongs to the immediate family of Hong Kong Cup winner Romanee Conti and her Melbourne and Caulfield Cup winning daughter Ethereal.

The second top lot was another quality son of Danehill, offered by Curraghmore Stud. From the imported Shirley Heights mare Push A Venture, he claimed close relationship to the seven-time European group one winner Rock Of Gibraltar and fetched $1 million. He was bought by the British Bloodstock Agency's Adrian Nicoll – making his first visit to New Zealand since 1983 – and was destined to enter the Australian stable of Tony McEvoy.

Pencarrow's third placed colt was by Quest For Fame from Chimeara, a two-time winning daughter of Danehill and the Australasian Oaks winner Tristalove, who fetched $750,000.

Heading the fillies was a stunning daughter of Zabeel from Waihora's Lass, the group winner of 11 races. She was offered on behalf of Haunui Stud and prominent breeder Marie Leicester.

Apart from Nicoll, well-known figures on the international sales scene included Demi O'Byrne, of Coolmore Ireland, Richard O'Gorman, Grant Pritchard-Gordon and Hubie De Burgh. But it was Graeme Rogerson's transtasman racing operation which was the leading buyer with an outlay of $3,202,500 for 27 lots. New Zealand Bloodstock, as agent, accounted for 20 lots worth $2,912,000 and David Ellis, Te Akau Racing's principal, secured 28 lots for $2,912,000.

The selected session of the sale – the second tier – saw a return to mixing the colts and fillies together. The move was popular with both vendors and buyers and, as with the premier session, there were increases in aggregate, average and median. The top price was $190,000 for a colt by Cape Cross from the Danehill mare Gardenia, while the average was $30,331. South Korea was a new face on the buying bench, accounting for 22 sales.

Lot	Col	Sex	Breeding	Purchaser	Location	Price
1	B	C	Cape Cross / Hairini	Rogerson Bloodstock	Hamilton	$80,000.00
2	B	C	Montjeu / Hanalei	Mr David Ellis	Ngaruawahia	$60,000.00
3	B	C	O'Reilly / Herbaceous	New Zealand Bloodstock Ltd	Hong Kong	$80,000.00
4	B	F	Zabeel / Hit	Mr Peter Moody	Victoria	$50,000.00
5	BG	C	Stravinsky / Horlicks	Mr Tony Bott	Australia	$240,000.00
6	B	C	Montjeu / Howkudai	Mrs Donna Logan	Ruakaka	$150,000.00
7	BR	C	Kaapstad / Human Touch	Psd $45,000 Res $60,000		$0.00
8	B	C	O'Reilly / Icy Calm	Newlands Thoroughbreds	Victoria	$55,000.00
9	B	C	Stravinsky / Improviste	Mr John Salanitri	Victoria	$365,000.00
10	BR	C	O'Reilly / Initial Offering	Anzac Lodge	Cambridge	$35,000.00
11	B	F	Montjeu / In My Time	Mr Robert Priscott	Te Awamutu	$55,000.00
12	BR	F	Octagonal / Instantly	Mr Garry Barlow	Palmerston North	$30,000.00
13	C	C	Stravinsky / In the Vain	Dominion Bloodstock	South Africa	$120,000.00
14	D	F	Zabeel / Intrim	Mr Peter Walker	Auckland	$60,000.00
15	B	C	Montjeu / Iridescent	Mr Demi O'Byrne	Ireland	$62,500.00
16	BR	C	Redoute's Choice / Ishkala	Withdrawn		$0.00
17	B	F	Zabeel / Jacqwin	Bba Ireland	Ireland	$410,000.00
18	B	C	Quest for Fame / Jallas	Mr Richard Dee	Cambridge	$50,000.00
19	B	C	Pins / Jelignite Jen	Mr Tony Pike	Cambridge	$57,500.00
20	BR	F	Cape Cross / Jen's Halo	Mr David Ellis	Ngaruawahia	$42,500.00
21	B	C	Pins / Jet Show	Mr Bruce Elkington	Victoria	$50,000.00
22	B	C	Grand Lodge / Joan Barry	Withdrawn		$0.00
23	B	C	Generous / Joe's Girl	Robert Roulston Bloodstock	Victoria	$40,000.00
24	C	C	Redoute's Choice / Joie de Vivre	Rogerson Bloodstock	Hamilton	$57,500.00
25	B	C	Montjeu / Joie de Vivre	De Burgh / Farrington	Victoria	$60,000.00
26	BR	C	Cape Cross / Joyfulness	Mr Richard Yuill	Auckland	$130,000.00
27	B	C	Howbaddouwantit / Julie's Sailboat	Mr Bruce Wallace	Auckland	$22,500.00
28	B	C	Montjeu / Kailey Princess	Mr Richard Yuill	Auckland	$210,000.00
29	B	C	Danehill / Kanaka Creek	Mr Paul Perry	New South Wales	$150,000.00
30	B	C	Volksraad / Kape Dancer	New Zealand Bloodstock Ltd	Hong Kong	$100,000.00
31	B	C	Volksraad / Karman Gal	Jillings Yuill Racing Stables	Auckland	$80,000.00
32	B	C	Volksraad / Karsavina	Mr Brian Mayfield-Smith	Victoria	$80,000.00
33	B	F	Cadeaux Genereux / Kassiyaka	Mr Bart Cummings	Sydney	$50,000.00
34	BR	C	Cape Cross / Katlim	Montego Lodge	Matamata	$42,500.00
35	BR	F	Danasinga / Kelly Flinn	Psd $20,000 Res $25,000		$0.00
36	BR	C	Danasinga / Kentucky Lass	New Zealand Bloodstock Ltd	Hong Kong	$100,000.00
37	B	C	Carnegie / Keralia	Darley Australia	New South Wales	$120,000.00
38	C	F	King's Best / Khapkap	Psd $190,000 Res $200,000		$0.00
39	C	C	Elnadim / Kilsheelan Marie	Mr Paul O'Sullivan	Matamata	$60,000.00
40	B	C	Cape Cross / Kindness	Mr David Ellis	Ngaruawahia	$62,500.00
41	C	C	Almutawakel / Kirin Belle	Withdrawn		$0.00
42	RG	C	Stravinsky / Kirov Dancer	Stuart Hale & Co	Cambridge	$75,000.00
43	B	C	Zerpour / Kiss	Paul Moroney Bloodstock	Matamata	$35,000.00
44	C	F	Catbird / Kiss in Vain	Mr David Ellis	Ngaruawahia	$27,500.00
45	B	C	Zabeel / Kiwi Magic	Mr Rob Mcanulty	Auckland	$120,000.00
46	B	C	Zabeel / Kylemore	Mrs Gai Waterhouse	New South Wales	$200,000.00
47	BB	F	Thunder Gulch / La Brillante	Kieran Moore B/Stock P/L	New South Wales	$420,000.00
48	B	C	Volksraad / Lace	Mr Trevor Mckee	Auckland	$50,000.00
49	B	C	Danasinga / La Cent	Mr Tony Pike	Cambridge	$65,000.00

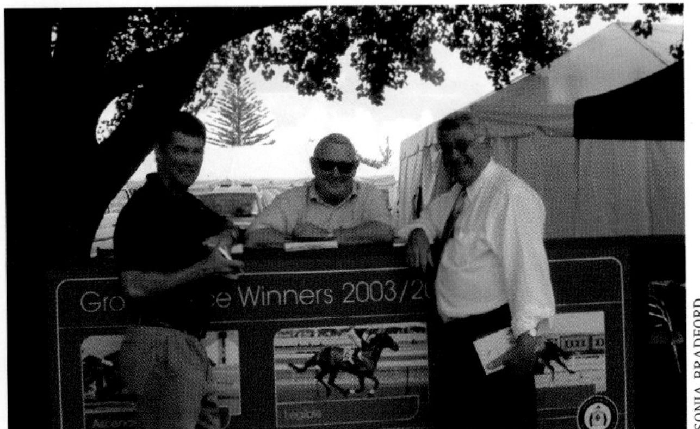

Chief auctioneer Joe Walls (right) with Haunui Farm principal Ron Chitty and son Mark Chitty.

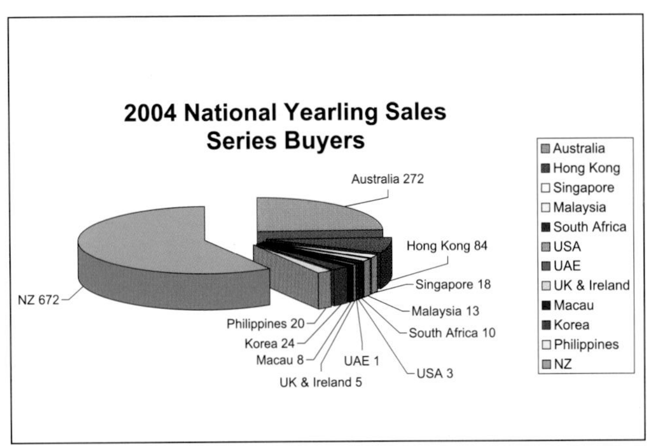

Lot	Col	Sex	Breeding	Purchaser	Location	Price
50	G	C	Zabeel / Lacework	Sanders Racing Stables	Te Awamutu	$95,000.00
51	BR	F	Almutawakel / La Chamane	Psd $37,500 Res $40,000		$0.00
52	B	F	Pentire / Lady Acumen	Paul Moroney Bloodstock	Matamata	$90,000.00
53	B	C	Anabaa / Lady Bay	Mr David Ellis	Ngaruawahia	$72,500.00
54	B	F	Elnadim / Lady Tee	Mr Garry Barlow	Palmerston North	$30,000.00
55	BR	C	Centaine / Laebeel	Mr Paul Willetts	Auckland	$50,000.00
56	B	C	Zabeel / Lake Lucerne	Mr Neville Begg	New South Wales	$160,000.00
57	B	C	Deputy Governor / La Marmalade	Mr Bruce Wallace	Auckland	$82,500.00
58	BR	C	Kaapstad / La Tache	Mr Jerry Sung	Singapore	$130,000.00
59	B	F	Montjeu / La Tebaldi	Psd $30,000 Res $60,000		$0.00
60	B	C	Zabeel / Latte	Dgr Thoroughbred Services	New South Wales	$130,000.00
61	C	C	Kaapstad / Leontyne	Psd $57,500 Res $60,000		$0.00
62	B	F	Danasinga / Light of Night	Mr Paul O'Sullivan	Matamata	$40,000.00
63	B	C	Peintre Celebre / Lihir	Mr Tony Pike	Cambridge	$60,000.00
64	C	C	Danasinga / Lindazam	Psd $22,500 Res $30,000		$0.00
65	B	C	Anabaa / Lisbon	Anzac Lodge	Cambridge	$60,000.00
66	B	F	Montjeu / Little Gem	John Foote Bloodstock Pty Ltd	Queensland	$70,000.00
67	B	C	Volksraad / Llamrei	Psd $22,500 Res $30,000		$0.00
68	BR	C	Danasinga / Lodore Mystic	Kieran Moore B/Stock P/L	New South Wales	$60,000.00
69	C	C	Generous / Love Connection	Mr Bart Cummings	Sydney	$120,000.00
70	B	C	High Yield / Love Dance	Mr John O'Shea	New South Wales	$130,000.00
71	C	C	High Yield / Luna Tudor	Psd $52,500 Res $55,000		$0.00
72	B	C	Danasinga / Macanudo	Jillings Yuill Racing Stables	Auckland	$70,000.00
73	B	C	Volksraad / Madam Valeta	Mr Tim Stakemire	New South Wales	$230,000.00
74	C	F	Thunder Gulch / Madam Zenda	Mr David Ellis	Ngaruawahia	$32,500.00
75	B	C	Montjeu / Madiya	Paul Moroney Bloodstock	Matamata	$110,000.00
76	B	C	Montjeu / Madonna	New Zealand Bloodstock Ltd	Hong Kong	$280,000.00
77	B	F	Carnegie / Madonna Bay	Mr W & Mrs M Milner	Queensland	$25,000.00
78	G	F	Flying Spur / Magpies	Mr David Ellis	Ngaruawahia	$70,000.00
79	B	C	Danasinga / Malberry	Mr Shaun Dwyer	Queensland	$22,500.00
80	B	C	Shinko King / Manchio	Psd $47,500 Res $50,000		$0.00
81	B	C	Carnegie / Mandate	Psd $42,500 Res $50,000		$0.00
82	BR	C	Faltaat / Martina Bel	Mr Paul Willetts	Auckland	$57,500.00
83	B	F	Stravinsky / Mary Josephine	De Burgh / Farrington	Ireland	$65,000.00
84	B	F	Zabeel / Masaiyda	Psd $125,000 Res $150,000		$0.00
85	C	C	Danasinga / Masawa	Mr Gary Hennessy	Matamata	$60,000.00
86	BR	C	Centaine / Match Point	Withdrawn		$0.00
87	BB	F	Danehill / Mattiocco	Mr Tony Bott	Australia	$260,000.00
88	B	F	Montjeu / Maxamore	Mrs Gai Waterhouse	New South Wales	$160,000.00
89	B	F	Almutawakel / Maybe Yes	Paul Harris Bloodstock	Christchurch	$70,000.00
90	B	F	Montjeu / Mazarine	Cambridge Stud	Cambridge	$460,000.00
91	B	C	Montjeu / Meadoway	Dominion Bloodstock	South Africa	$72,500.00
92	B	C	Elnadim / Meryl	Psd $47,500 Res $50,000		$0.00
93	B	C	Volksraad / Methinks	Montego Lodge	Matamata	$35,000.00
94	B	C	Cape Cross / Mimosa	Psd $25,000 Res $40,000		$0.00
95	B	C	Carnegie / Miss Angelina	Rogerson Bloodstock	Hamilton	$65,000.00
96	BR	F	Pins / Miss Daytona			$0.00

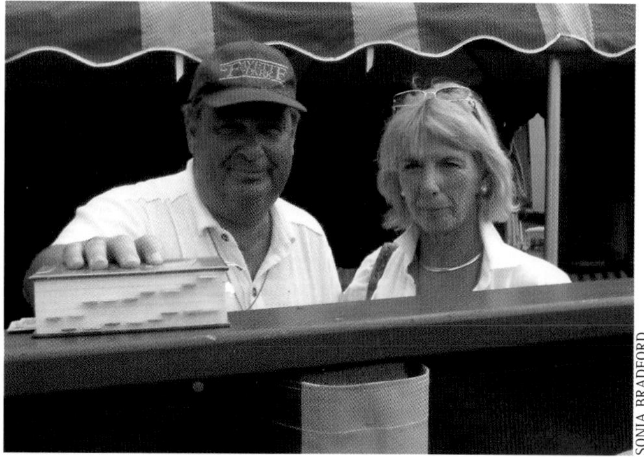

SONIA BRADFORD

David and Masey Benjamin of Fayette Park Stud.

Lot	Col	Sex	Breeding	Purchaser	Location	Price
97	B	F	Montjeu / Miss Fonteyn	Danny Power Bloodstock	Victoria	$50,000.00
98	B	C	Carnegie / Miss Paris	Mr Bruce Wallace	Auckland	$70,000.00
99	B	C	Cape Cross / Miss Rumba	Psd $50,000 Res $60,000		$0.00
100	C	C	Star Way / Miss Sacha	Mr Neville Couchman	Cambridge	$20,000.00
101	B	C	Faltaat / Miss Tree	Robert Roulston Bloodstock	Victoria	$80,000.00
102	BR	C	Centaine / Mistella	Mr Shaun Dwyer	Queensland	$20,000.00
103	B	F	Stravinsky / Misty Angel	Mr David Ellis	Ngaruawahia	$40,000.00
104	B	F	Stravinsky / Misty Gulch	Torryburn Stud	New South Wales	$45,000.00
105	B	C	Stravinsky / Miz Wadleigh	Withdrawn		$0.00
106	B	F	Zabeel / M'Lady's Garter	Mr Shaun Dwyer	Queensland	$80,000.00
107	B	C	Anabaa / Monroe Magic	Paul Moroney Bloodstock	Matamata	$125,000.00
108	B	C	Marauding / Montrose	Mr Chris Waller	Australia	$50,000.00
109	B	C	Stravinsky / Mont Tremblant	Mr Paul Perry	New South Wales	$110,000.00
110	B	C	Danzero / Moon Over Miami	Magus Equine	Hong Kong	$100,000.00
111	B	F	Stravinsky / Moon Vision	The Hon Henry Plumptre	Victoria	$130,000.00
112	B	C	O'Reilly / Morar	Psd $42,500 Res $45,000		$0.00
113	B	C	Carnegie / Morgan Mackie	Rogerson Bloodstock	Hamilton	$65,000.00
114	B	F	Redoute's Choice / Mrs Squillionaire	Bruce Perry Bloodstock Ltd	Masterton	$310,000.00
115	B	C	Zabeel / Musical Note	Dominion Bloodstock	Hong Kong	$300,000.00
116	B	C	Montjeu / My Grace	Waikato Bloodstock 2000 Ltd	Waikato	$95,000.00
117	B	F	Danasinga / Mynzawine	Psd $42,500 Res $60,000		$0.00
118	B	F	Cape Cross / Naadirah	Mr Bevin Laming	Queensland	$65,000.00
119	C	C	Singspiel / Nanaimo	Psd $37,500 Res $50,000		$0.00
120	B	F	Stravinsky / Native Risen Star	De Burgh / Farrington	Ireland	$160,000.00
121	B	F	Pins / Nat the Brat	Psd $27,000 Res $30,000		$0.00
122	B	C	Fusaichi Pegasus / Newgirlintown	Mr Nigel Blackiston	Victoria	$100,000.00
123	B	C	Cape Cross / New Star	Psd $35,000 Res $40,000		$0.00
124	B	F	O'Reilly / Night Star	Mr Robert Burnet	New South Wales	$40,000.00
125	B	F	Montjeu / Nimue	Rogerson Bloodstock	Hamilton	$150,000.00
126	B	C	Montjeu / Niniane	J & I Bloodstock Limited	Auckland	$65,000.00
127	B	F	Stravinsky / No Alimony	Mrs Helen Hart	New South Wales	$60,000.00
128	B	F	Carnegie / Northern Odyssey	Psd $37,500 Res $45,000		$0.00
129	C	C	Langfuhr / North Kiss	Mr Bruce Wallace	Auckland	$35,000.00
130	B	C	Danasinga / Nothing But Net	Psd $32,500 Res $40,000		$0.00
131	B	F	Montjeu / Nothing Less	Mr Craig Ritchie	Auckland	$55,000.00
132	C	C	Hennessy / Obeliah	Mr Robbie Laing	Victoria	$37,500.00
133	B	F	Montjeu / On Air	Mr David Ellis	Ngaruawahia	$82,500.00
134	B	F	Howbaddouwantit / Our Diva	Mr David Ellis	Ngaruawahia	$67,500.00
135	B	F	Zabeel / Our Rosalee	Psd $145,000 Res $150,000		$0.00
136	B	F	Flying Spur / Our Summertime	Rogerson Bloodstock	Hamilton	$125,000.00
137	B	C	Danasinga / Palace Lady	Dominion Bloodstock	South Africa	$55,000.00
138	B	C	Fusaichi Pegasus / Palia	Magus Equine	Hong Kong	$480,000.00
139	C	F	Peintre Celebre / Party Queen	Pendant Equine Syndicate	Victoria	$90,000.00
140	B	F	Carnegie / Phantom's Lady	Psd $22,500 Res $25,000		$0.00
141	B	C	Stravinsky / Philadelphia Fox	James Bester Bloodstock	New South Wales	$80,000.00
142	BR	C	Carnegie / Piccadilly Lily	Mr Gerald Ryan	Sydney	$40,000.00

Lot	Col	Sex	Breeding	Purchaser	Location	Price
143	BR	C	Generous / Pink Melody	Mr Chris Waller	Australia	$40,000.00
144	C	F	Chief Bearhart / Pink Peppercorn	Mr Michael Clout	New South Wales	$37,500.00
145	B	C	Canny Lad / Pireanda	John Foote Bloodstock Pty Ltd	Queensland	$65,000.00
146	B	F	Fusaichi Pegasus / Plaisir d'Amour	Mr John Cornish	New South Wales	$200,000.00
147	B	C	Volksraad / Platinum Blond	Mr Ai & Mrs Sm Fisher	Victoria	$110,000.00
148	B	F	Stravinsky / Pointe	Psd $60,000 Res $80,000		$0.00
149	B	F	Anabaa / Pravda	Mr John Hutchins	Queensland	$275,000.00
150	BR	C	King's Best / Precious Princess	Mr Roger James	Matamata	$37,500.00
151	C	F	More Than Ready / Pretty Wicked	Psd $35,000 Res $70,000		$0.00
152	C	C	Generous / Priada	Psd $10,000 Res $12,000		$0.00
153	C	F	Singspiel / Princess Alea	Mr W & Mrs M Milner	Queensland	$75,000.00
154	C	C	Almutawakel / Princess Gaius	Psd $45,000 Res $50,000		$0.00
155	B	F	Redoute's Choice / Princess Jocinda	Mr Peter Hurdle	Manawatu	$145,000.00
156	B	C	Chief Bearhart / Private Collection	Anzac Lodge	Cambridge	$25,000.00
157	BR	C	El Moxie / Private Gem	Robert Roulston Bloodstock	Victoria	$50,000.00
158	B	F	Pins / Prodigal Lass	Mr Jose Quiros	Auckland	$30,000.00
159	B	C	Danehill / Push a Venture	Bba Ireland	Ireland	$1,000,000.00
160	B	C	Montjeu / Queen Caelia	Mr Nick Moraitis	New South Wales	$260,000.00
161	C	F	Elnadim / Queen Emma	Rafter Co. Ltd	Hong Kong	$30,000.00
162	B	F	Carnegie / Queen of Angels	Landmark Racing Pty Ltd	Victoria	$40,000.00
163	B	F	Generous / Queen of Ballet	Withdrawn		$0.00
164	C	C	Flying Spur / Queen of the Park	Belmont Bloodstock Agency	Victoria	$160,000.00
165	B	F	Cape Cross / Queen's Choice	Olsen Farms Ltd	Pokeno	$52,500.00
166	BR	C	Cape Cross / Quietly Lucky	Psd $45,000 Res $50,000		$0.00
167	BR	C	Danasinga / Rampage Queen	New Zealand Bloodstock Ltd	Hong Kong	$100,000.00
168	C	F	Gilded Time / Rancho Miss	Byron Rogers Bloodstock	Victoria	$60,000.00
169	B	C	Centaine / Ransom Bay	Mr Tony Pike	Cambridge	$47,500.00
170	B	F	Carnegie / Rationable	Tw Archer Trust	Northland	$25,000.00
171	B	C	Zabeel / Real Success	Mr Mark Wyborn	Auckland	$150,000.00
172	B	C	Montjeu / Recant	Mr Jerry Sung	Singapore	$55,000.00
173	B	C	Montjeu / Red l'Engerie	Mrs Donna Logan	Ruakaka	$42,500.00
174	B	C	Commands / Red Slippers	Robert Roulston Bloodstock	Victoria	$380,000.00
175	B	C	Cullen / Red Sugar	Rogerson Bloodstock	Hamilton	$67,500.00
176	B	F	Stravinsky / Refused the Dance	Mr Edmond Moreno	Philippines	$42,500.00
177	B	C	Montjeu / Reining Stars	Gary Alexander Racing Stables	South Africa	$100,000.00
178	B	C	Catbird / Rendezvous	Mr David Ellis	Ngaruawahia	$55,000.00
179	B	F	Danzero / Reno's Best	Psd $35,000 Res $70,000		$0.00
180	B	C	Montjeu / Repetition	Rogerson Bloodstock	Hamilton	$47,500.00
181	BR	C	Kingfisher Mill / Repremand	Psd $30,000 Res $35,000		$0.00
182	BR	F	Montjeu / Rhythm and Black	Mr Robert Laing	Victoria	$80,000.00
183	B	C	Cape Cross / Ricamo	Aquanita Racing Flemington	Victoria	$65,000.00
184	C	C	Strategic / Riesling	Withdrawn		$0.00
185	C	F	Volksraad / Rijeka	Psd $55,000 Res $60,000		$0.00
186	B	F	Zabeel / Rising Eagle			$0.00
187	C	C	Generous / River Flow	Paul Harris Bloodstock	Christchurch	$20,000.00
188	B	F	Danehill / Riverly	Kevin Dagg Bloodstock	Victoria	$220,000.00
189	C	C	Pins / Rivertaine	Withdrawn		$0.00
190	BR	F	Volksraad / Rose World	Paul Moroney Bloodstock	Matamata	$125,000.00

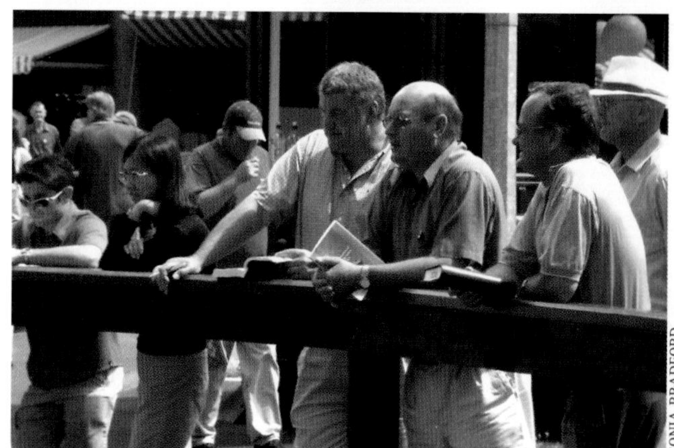

SONIA BRADFORD

Seeking the next champion.

TRISH DUNELL

Sales topping colt spent a lot of time parading with Pencarrow Stud manager Leon Casey.

Lot	Col	Sex	Breeding	Purchaser	Location	Price
191	C	F	Fuji Kiseki / Royal Act	Psd $22,500 Res $35,000		$0.00
192	B	C	Carnegie / Royal Heights	Rogerson Bloodstock	Hamilton	$65,000.00
193	B	C	Zabeel / Royal Magic	Rogerson Bloodstock	Hamilton	$200,000.00
194	BB	F	Cape Cross / Royal Memories	Cambridge Hunt Limited	Wellington	$62,500.00
195	C	C	Stravinsky / Royal Sirt	Withdrawn		$0.00
196	B	C	Redoute's Choice / Royal Zoff	Kieran Moore B/Stock P/L	New South Wales	$145,000.00
197	BB	F	Montjeu / Rune	Mr Robert Priscott	Te Awamutu	$65,000.00
198	C	C	Pins / Sandsend	John Foote Bloodstock Pty Ltd	Queensland	$100,000.00
199	BR	C	Pentire / Sansong	Psd $45,000 Res $50,000		$0.00
200	B	F	O'Reilly / Sarah Fay	Bruce Perry Bloodstock Ltd	Masterton	$47,500.00
201	C	C	Stravinsky / Sarah's Melody	Mr Roger James	Matamata	$75,000.00
202	B	C	Danske / Satin Blush	Belmont Bloodstock Agency	Victoria	$50,000.00
203	B	F	Carnegie / Sauvignon Valley	Mr David Ellis	Ngaruawahia	$60,000.00
204	B	C	Catbird / Savannah	Mr David Ellis	Ngaruawahia	$57,500.00
205	B	F	Montjeu / Scarlet Runner	Kieran Moore B/Stock P/L	New South Wales	$130,000.00
206	B	C	Danehill / Scribbling	Dgr Thoroughbred Services	New South Wales	$210,000.00
207	B	F	Carnegie / Sea of Fashion	Mr David Ellis	Ngaruawahia	$40,000.00
208	BR	F	O'Reilly / Seattle Mint	Psd $37,500 Res $50,000		$0.00
209	B	F	Danehill / Secret Truth	Brian Jenkins	Cambridge	$340,000.00
210	B	F	Stravinsky / Seeking Fortune	Rogerson Bloodstock	Hamilton	$72,500.00
211	B	C	Catbird / Seena Baleena	Truffle Downs Ltd	Auckland	$60,000.00
212	B	F	Stravinsky / Selvorine	Mr Shaun Dwyer	Queensland	$42,500.00
213	B	C	Zabeel / Sequel Sound	Psd $100,000 Res $120,000		$0.00
214	B	C	Danzero / Serotina	Withdrawn		$0.00
215	B	F	O'Reilly / Shear Froth	De Burgh / Farrington	Ireland	$42,500.00
216	B	C	Red Ransom / Sheer Classic	Mr Sd & Mrs Kj Alexander	Matamata	$45,000.00
217	BR	F	Centaine / Shekanwyn	Mr David Ellis	Ngaruawahia	$40,000.00
218	B	F	Zabeel / She's Country	Mr Roger James	Matamata	$150,000.00
219	B	C	Zabeel / She Wishes	Mr Roger James	Matamata	$140,000.00
220	BB	F	Montjeu / Shine on Me	Mr David Ellis	Ngaruawahia	$75,000.00
221	B	F	Last Tycoon / Shirley Sue	Mrs Donna Logan	Ruakaka	$12,500.00
222	B	F	Danasinga / Shorty's Pride	Cook Thoroughbreds	New South Wales	$30,000.00
223	B	C	Octagonal / Silken Fairy	John Foote Bloodstock Pty Ltd	Queensland	$35,000.00
224	B	F	Danasinga / Simple Luxury	Withdrawn		$0.00
225	B	C	Stravinsky / Singalong	Rogerson Bloodstock	Hamilton	$82,500.00
226	B	F	Cape Cross / Sinjani	Rogerson Bloodstock	Hamilton	$52,500.00
227	B	F	Faltaat / Sky Danza	Psd $37,500 Res $60,000		$0.00
228	BL	C	Montjeu / Skylarking	Mr Brian Jenkins	Cambridge	$120,000.00
229	B	C	Danasinga / Slightly Aloof	Mr John Hawkes	Victoria	$60,000.00
230	B	F	Zabeel / Smiling Like	Rogerson Bloodstock	Hamilton	$190,000.00
231	B	C	Stravinsky / Sneetch	New Zealand Bloodstock Ltd	Hong Kong	$300,000.00
232	BR	C	Zabeel / Snow Quill	Rogerson Bloodstock	Hamilton	$320,000.00
233	BLG	C	Align / Snow Reason	Paul Moroney Bloodstock	Matamata	$55,000.00
234	B	C	Carnegie / Society Bay	Mr Matthew Hyland	Victoria	$130,000.00
235	C	C	More Than Ready / So Explicit	Mr Iw Herbert	Palmerston North	$31,000.00
236	BR	C	Almutawakel / Sonchela	Shane Moore Bloodstock	Victoria	$105,000.00
237	B	C	Elnadim / Sophie's Storm	Mr Jerry Sung	Singapore	$70,000.00
238	B	C	Montjeu / Sound of Jazz	Kieran Moore B/Stock P/L	New South Wales	$200,000.00
239	B	C	O'Reilly / Sounds Exciting	Mr Peter Jenkins	South Africa	$50,000.00
240	B	F	Zabeel / Sounds Like Me	Mr Mike Breslin	Palmerston North	$80,000.00
241	C	F	Encosta de Lago / South Pacific	Belmont Bloodstock Agency	Victoria	$45,000.00
242	B	C	Stravinsky / Sparkle 'n Shine	Mr Bruce Lewis	Victoria	$90,000.00
243	BL	C	Danzero / Speedy Topaze	New Zealand Bloodstock Ltd	Hawera	$125,000.00
244	B	C	Danehill / Spell on You	Kieran Moore B/Stock P/L	New South Wales	$100,000.00
245	B	F	O'Reilly / Srikandi	Mr Pn & Mrs K Mckay	Matamata	$45,000.00
246	B	F	Carnegie / Star	Mr David Ellis	Ngaruawahia	$65,000.00
247	B	F	Volksraad / Star of Mercury	Byron Rogers Bloodstock	Victoria	$85,000.00
248	C	F	Pentire / Star Parade	Equine & Livestock Exports	Hamilton	$60,000.00
249	B	C	Faltaat / Star Sixty Seven	Mr David Ellis	Ngaruawahia	$40,000.00
250	C	C	Danasinga / Star Worship	Psd $45,000 Res $60,000		$0.00
251	B	F	Stravinsky / Starzeel	Mrs Helen Hart	New South Wales	$50,000.00
252	B	F	Zabeel / Steluta	De Burgh / Farrington	Ireland	$100,000.00
253	B	C	Cape Cross / Stever House	Hale / Marsh	Cambridge	$135,000.00
254	C	F	Stravinsky / Storm Rail	Bba Ireland	Ireland	$150,000.00
255	B	F	Almutawakel / Stormy Alley	Mr Roger James	Waikato	$60,000.00
256	B	C	Danske / Straussbridge	Mr Gerald Ryan	New South Wales	$35,000.00
257	B	C	King's Best / Street Star	Mr Gary Hennessy	Matamata	$90,000.00
258	BR	F	O'Reilly / Stylish Malt	Mr Bruce Wallace	South Auckland	$20,000.00
259	C	F	Almutawakel / Sulina	Mr Paul O'Sullivan	Hong Kong	$70,000.00
260	C	F	Chief Bearhart / Summary	Psd $30,000 Res $35,000		$0.00
261	B	C	Fusaichi Pegasus / Sunny Lane	New Zealand Bloodstock Ltd	New South Wales	$140,000.00
262	B	F	Fusaichi Pegasus / Superjet	Psd $130,000 Res $150,000		$0.00
263	B	F	Almutawakel / Surfin Bird	Mr Paul Willetts	Auckland	$135,000.00
264	B	C	Elnadim / Sustaad	Kieran Moore B/Stock P/L	New South Wales	$180,000.00
265	B	C	Zabeel / Sweet Vienna	Withdrawn		$0.00
266	B	F	Mujahid / Swift Falcon	Psd $35,000 Res $40,000		$0.00
267	C	F	Howbaddouwantit / Taciturn	Rogerson Bloodstock	Hamilton	$65,000.00
268	B	F	Stravinsky / Tajrebah	The Hon Henry Plumptre	Victoria	$160,000.00
269	B	C	Carnegie / Talaga	Psd $45,000 Res $60,000		$0.00
270	B	C	Howbaddouwantit / Tall Poppy	Mrs Gai Waterhouse	New South Wales	$90,000.00
271	B	F	Montjeu / Tearrunner	New Zealand Bloodstock Ltd	Sydney	$45,000.00
272	B	C	Cape Cross / Temptation	Psd $47,500 Res $50,000		$0.00
273	B	C	Fusaichi Pegasus / The Golden Dane	Mr Peter Moody	Victoria	$150,000.00
274	B	C	Deputy Governor / The Grin	Mr Mark Wyborn	Auckland	$190,000.00
275	B	C	Montjeu / The Lions Roar	Mr B K Ma	Hong Kong	$360,000.00
276	B	C	Danehill / Think Twice	Mr Wing Keung So	Hong Kong	$260,000.00
277	B	F	Cape Cross / Tic Tic Kaboom	Paul Moroney Bloodstock	Matamata	$100,000.00
278	C	C	Spinning World / Tiffany Blue	Mr Neville Atkins	Waiuku	$110,000.00
279	C	C	Faltaat / Tina's Spirit	Mr John Wheeler	New Plymouth	$45,000.00
280	B	F	Danasinga / Tinikadua	Psd $12,500 Res $20,000		$0.00
281	B	C	Orpen / Top Saint	Mr David Ellis	Ngaruawahia	$40,000.00
282	B	C	Cape Cross / Torrance	Psd $15,000 Res $16,000		$0.00
283	B	F	Stravinsky / Tricia Ann	Mark Pilkington Bloodstock	Victoria	$250,000.00
284	B	F	More Than Ready / Trickster	Mr John O'Shea	New South Wales	$45,000.00
285	B	F	Montjeu / Tristachine	Mark Pilkington Bloodstock	Victoria	$380,000.00
286	BR	C	Volksraad / Tristean	Paul Moroney Bloodstock	Matamata	$125,000.00
287	B	C	Montjeu / Trisynd	Mr Tony Olsen	New South Wales	$85,000.00

TRISH DUNELL

The Danehill-Grand Echezeaux colt who topped sale at $1.1 million.

Lot	Col	Sex	Breeding	Purchaser	Location	Price
288	B	C	Zabeel / Trolley Dolly	Sanders Racing Stables	Te Awamutu	$160,000.00
289	BR	C	Marauding / Trotanoy	Mr Laurie Laxon	Singapore	$52,500.00
290	B	F	Kaapstad / True Colours	Mr Roger James	Matamata	$67,500.00
291	B	C	Zabeel / Tudor Era	Paul Moroney Bloodstock	Matamata	$230,000.00
292	B	F	Stravinsky / Tunisia	Withdrawn		$0.00
293	B	F	Montjeu / Tycoon Pet	Mr Danny O'Brien	Victoria	$50,000.00
294	BR	C	Stravinsky / Tycoon's Gold	Mr Graeme Sanders	Te Awamutu	$180,000.00
295	C	C	Stark South / Valley Court	Mr Michael George	Victoria	$65,000.00
296	C	C	Strategic / Vaughan	Mr Apollo Ng	Hong Kong	$45,000.00
297	C	F	Danasinga / Venetian Court	Psd $42,500 Res $50,000		$0.00
298	B	C	Stravinsky / Vicki Buck	Mr Brian Mayfield-Smith	Victoria	$110,000.00
299	B	C	Zabeel / Vie Indienne	Withdrawn		$0.00
300	B	C	High Yield / Vintage Power	Mr David Ellis	Ngaruawahia	$47,500.00
301	B	C	Zabeel / Viva Lyphard	Mr Bevin Laming	Queensland	$200,000.00
302	G	C	Volksraad / Voguessa	Mr Shane Kennedy	Christchurch	$55,000.00
303	BR	F	Kaapstad / Volkschine	Withdrawn		$0.00
304	BR	F	Zabeel / Waihora's Lass	Dgr Thoroughbred Services	New South Wales	$600,000.00
305	B	C	Cape Cross / Wailing	Magic Racing Bloodstock	Australia	$65,000.00
306	C	C	Grand Lodge / Water Sprite	Mr Roger James	Matamata	$70,000.00
307	B	F	O'Reilly / Westmeath	Mr Brian Henderson	Whakatane	$60,000.00
308	B	F	Fusaichi Pegasus / What Can I Say	Vance Racing Stables	Auckland	$105,000.00
309	G	C	Carnegie / Whey to Go	Mr Louis Crimp	Southland	$65,000.00
310	B	F	Quest for Fame / White Queen	Psd $25,000 Res $40,000		$0.00
311	BR	C	Kaapstad / Winds of Conquest	Mr Roger James	Matamata	$57,500.00
312	B	F	Elnadim / Winning Wave	Kevin Dagg Bloodstock	Victoria	$30,000.00
313	B	C	Centaine / Winter Solstice	Mr Trevor Mckee	Auckland	$52,500.00
314	B	F	Carnegie / Wishing Belle	Psd $ Res $60,000		$0.00
315	B	F	Montjeu / Worship	Withdrawn		$0.00

Lot	Col	Sex	Breeding	Purchaser	Location	Price316
	B	F	Carnegie / Wusool	Darley Australia	New South Wales	$50,000.00
317	B	F	Volksraad / Wychwood Lass	Mr Trevor Luke	Christchurch	$125,000.00
318	B	C	Stravinsky / Xwife	Mr David Ellis	Ngaruawahia	$75,000.00
319	B	C	Stravinsky / Yildirine	Mr Rob Mcanulty	Auckland	$80,000.00
320	B	F	Montjeu / Zahra	Robert Roulston Bloodstock	Victoria	$100,000.00
321	B	F	King's Best / Zanetta	Mr Graham Richardson	Matamata	$90,000.00
322	C	F	Align / Zivader	Mr David Ellis	Ngaruawahia	$50,000.00
323	BR	C	Quest for Fame / Zola	New Zealand Bloodstock Ltd	New South Wales	$80,000.00
324	C	F	Peintre Celebre / Acuity	Psd $20,000 Res $30,000		$0.00
325	BR	C	Quest for Fame / Ad Astra	Mr Tony Bott	Australia	$180,000.00
326	B	C	Montjeu / Adrianna	Mr Paul Perry	New South Wales	$120,000.00
327	B	C	Fusaichi Pegasus/A Goodlookin Broad	Mr Tony Bott	Australia	$275,000.00
328	B	C	Stravinsky / Ahorita	Paul Moroney Bloodstock	Matamata	$100,000.00
329	B	C	Elnadim / Alacrity	Dgr Thoroughbred Services	New South Wales	$180,000.00
330	C	C	Danske / Alberton Star	Mr Stephen Chow	Macau	$65,000.00
331	B	F	Centaine / Allez Sel	Mr Shaun Dwyer	Queensland	$75,000.00
332	B	F	Kaapstad / All Night Party	Psd $70,000 Res $80,000		$0.00
333	C	C	Stravinsky / Almaz	New Zealand Bloodstock Ltd	Hong Kong	$80,000.00
334	B	C	Generous / American Express	Miss Chin Ling Chen	Auckland	$45,000.00
335	B	F	Montjeu / Amnesia	Mr Bruce Elkington	Victoria	$135,000.00
336	B	C	Howbaddouwantit / Amore Mia	Waikato Bloodstock 2000 Ltd	Cambridge	$45,000.00
337	B	C	Zabeel / Anakela Bay	Rogerson Bloodstock	Hamilton	$140,000.00
338	B	C	Cape Cross / Anna's Choice	Waikato Bloodstock 2000 Ltd	Cambridge	$115,000.00
339	B	F	O'Reilly / Anne of Tudor	De Burgh / Farrington	Ireland	$37,500.00
340	C	C	Generous / Arctic Heroine	Withdrawn		$0.00
341	B	F	Montjeu / Argante	James Bester Bloodstock	New South Wales	$80,000.00
342	B	C	Zabeel / Argyle	Mr John Hawkes	Victoria	$150,000.00
343	BR	C	Cape Cross / A Shadeed Indeed	Mr Paul Willetts	Auckland	$30,000.00

Lot	Col	Sex	Breeding	Purchaser	Location	Price
344	BR	C	O'Reilly / Aspects of Love	Mr Pn & Mrs K Mckay	Matamata	$40,000.00
345	B	F	Danasinga / Astrology	Mr John Morrissey	Canberra	$90,000.00
346	B	C	Generous / Athykaneyev	Psd $15,000 Res $20,000		$0.00
347	B	F	Zabeel / Attempting	Withdrawn		$0.00
348	B	F	Zabeel / Audencia	Rogerson Bloodstock	Hamilton	$240,000.00
349	B	F	Stravinsky / Augmentation	Psd $37,500 Res $50,000		$0.00
350	B	F	Marju / Aulide	Sanders Racing Stables	Te Awamutu	$52,500.00
351	C	C	King's Best / Aurora Australis	Kieran Moore B/Stock P/L	New South Wales	$100,000.00
352	B	C	Pins / Ausjewel	Rogerson Bloodstock	Hamilton	$120,000.00
353	BR	C	Cape Cross / Avelina	Psd $30,000 Res $50,000		$0.00
354	B	F	Cape Cross / Ayla	Mr David Brideoake	Victoria	$42,500.00
355	B	C	Stravinsky / Azabeel	Mr Jerry Sung	Singapore	$60,000.00
356	G	C	Align / Azarashi	Mr John Hawkes	New South Wales	$75,000.00
357	BR	F	Octagonal / Azurobello	Paul Harris Bloodstock	Christchurch	$55,000.00
358	B	C	Pins / Back to Back	New Zealand Bloodstock Ltd	Hong Kong	$72,500.00
359	B	C	End Sweep / Bala Belle	New Zealand Bloodstock Ltd	Hong Kong	$110,000.00
360	B	F	Stravinsky / Ballycairn	Robert Roulston Bloodstock	Victoria	$180,000.00
361	BB	F	Octagonal / Balmaine	Psd $65,000 Res $100,000		$0.00
362	B	C	Marju / Balm in Gilead	Aquanita Racing Flemington	Victoria	$55,000.00
363	BR	F	Centaine / Barbados	Attunga Stud	New South Wales	$95,000.00
364	B	C	Fusaichi Pegasus / Barents Sea	Psd $80,000 Res $120,000		$0.00
365	B	C	Volksraad / Bashful Lady	Mr Brian Mayfield-Smith	Victoria	$85,000.00
366	C	F	Align / Bass Bidder	Paul Moroney Bloodstock	Matamata	$130,000.00
367	B	F	Montjeu / Be Cool	John Foote Bloodstock Pty Ltd	Queensland	$35,000.00
368	BR	C	Xaar / Bedouin Dancer	Stuart Hale & Co	Cambridge	$67,500.00
369	B	C	Montjeu / Belltello	Mr David Ellis	Ngaruawahia	$57,500.00
370	B	F	Danasinga / Benazir	Psd $25,000 Res $40,000		$0.00
371	B	C	O'Reilly / Better Believe	Mr Gerald Ryan	New South Wales	$75,000.00
372	B	C	Montjeu / Birdles	John Foote Bloodstock Pty Ltd	Queensland	$80,000.00
373	BRB	F	Cape Cross / Black Magic	Withdrawn		$0.00
374	BR	C	Centaine / Blanc de Chine	Mr Stephen Mckee	Auckland	$27,500.00
375	B	F	Chief Bearhart / Blue Tess	Mr Richard Dee	Cambridge	$22,500.00
376	B	F	Carnegie / Bluiski	Psd $17,500 Res $25,000		$0.00
377	B	C	O'Reilly / Blushing Bali	Mr Stephen Mckee	Auckland	$27,000.00
378	B	F	Red Ransom / Bow Street	Mr Alistair Gordon	South Africa	$140,000.00
379	C	C	Danehill Dancer / Bridal	Rogerson Bloodstock	Hamilton	$57,500.00
380	B	C	Chief Bearhart / Brookes Way	J & I Bloodstock Limited	Auckland	$67,500.00
381	C	C	Singspiel / Buncrana	Magus Equine	Hong Kong	$170,000.00
382	C	F	Faltaat / Bushfire Dancer	Cook Thoroughbreds	New South Wales	$115,000.00
383	BR	F	Stravinsky / Bye Bye Affair	Psd $40,000 Res $50,000		$0.00
384	BR	C	Align / Cake	Psd $55,000 Res $60,000		$0.00
385	B	C	Danasinga / Call Minder	W Eagles Plumbing Supplies	New South Wales	$40,000.00
386	B	C	Woodman / Capricious Lass	Mr David Ellis	Ngaruawahia	$60,000.00
387	B	F	Fasliyev / Cause a Scene	Mr Tony Noonan	Victoria	$70,000.00
388	BR	F	Danasinga / Centolde	John Chalmers B/Stock	Australia	$52,500.00
389	B	C	Danehill / Champagne	Mrs Gai Waterhouse	New South Wales	$575,000.00
390	B	F	Stravinsky / Chantenay	Psd $35,000 Res $50,000		$0.00
391	B	F	Desert Prince / Charismatic	Mr John Wheeler	New Plymouth	$45,000.00
392	B	C	Zabeel / Charlott	Belmont Bloodstock Agency	Victoria	$75,000.00
393	B	C	Quest for Fame / Chimeara	Mr Rob Mcanulty	Auckland	$750,000.00
394	BR	C	Cape Cross / Cladagh	New Zealand Bloodstock Ltd	Hong Kong	$180,000.00
395	B	C	Montjeu / Class	Withdrawn		$0.00
396	B	F	Octagonal / Classic Allure	Psd $15,000 Res $16,000		$0.00
397	BRG	C	Elnadim / Classic Moonlight	John Foote Bloodstock Pty Ltd	Queensland	$50,000.00
398	B	C	King's Best / Classic Peerage	Mr Jerry Sung	Singapore	$140,000.00
399	B	C	Carnegie / Clinique	Star Thoroughbreds	New South Wales	$85,000.00
400	B	F	Stravinsky / Close Your Eyes	Mr John O'Shea	New South Wales	$100,000.00
401	B	C	Zabeel / Colors for Life	Rogerson Bloodstock	Hamilton	$80,000.00
402	B	C	Flying Spur / Copa de Oro	Mr John O'Shea	New South Wales	$120,000.00
403	B	C	Howbaddouwantit / Coro Street	Psd $32,500 Res $35,000		$0.00
404	BB	F	Align / Country Road	Rogerson Bloodstock	Hamilton	$57,500.00
405	B	F	Volksraad / Country Rose	Mr John Hutchins	Queensland	$100,000.00
406	B	C	Danehill / Court	Dr Tsoi Wai Wang Gene	Hong Kong	$375,000.00
407	B	C	Chief Bearhart / Courtalista	J & I Bloodstock Limited	Auckland	$37,500.00
408	BL	C	Chief Bearhart / Covered n' Grey	Psd $45,000 Res $70,000		$0.00
409	B	F	Pins / Crash Course	Mrs Gai Waterhouse	New South Wales	$110,000.00
410	B	C	Zabeel / Cravache d'Or	Mr Peter Moody	Victoria	$80,000.00
411	B	F	Montjeu / Cremisi	Mr Peter Mcgregor	New South Wales	$42,500.00
412	B	C	Montjeu / Criceith	Psd $50,000 Res $60,000		$0.00
413	B	C	Stravinsky / Crimson	Withdrawn		$0.00
414	C	C	Chief Bearhart / Cross Country	Mr Shaun Dwyer	Queensland	$30,000.00
415	C	C	Stravinsky / Crystal Hailey	John Foote Bloodstock Pty Ltd	Queensland	$260,000.00
416	C	C	Align / Crystal Jet	Withdrawn		$0.00
417	B	C	Zabeel / Danadevi	Psd $90,000 Res $100,000		$0.00
418	B	F	Generous / Danaselvam	Cook Thoroughbreds	New South Wales	$105,000.00
419	B	F	Howbaddouwantit / Dance for Joy	Stonebridge Farm	Drury	$20,000.00
420	B	F	Generous / Danish Habit	Broadway Partnership	Auckland	$40,000.00
421	B	F	Fusaichi Pegasus / Dantelah	John Foote Bloodstock Pty Ltd	Queensland	$350,000.00
422	B	F	Zabeel / Danzalota	Mr Chris Waller	Australia	$72,500.00
423	B	C	Carnegie / Dare to Win	Paul Moroney Bloodstock	Matamata	$65,000.00
424	B	C	Montjeu / Desert Lily	Withdrawn		$0.00
425	B	F	Carnegie / Desert Wine	Withdrawn		$0.00
426	C	C	City on a Hill / Deysaniya	Psd $32,500 Res $50,000		$0.00
427	BR	C	Fuji Kiseki / Diamond Coast	Withdrawn		$0.00
428	C	F	Align / Diamond Snip	Pendant Equine Syndicate	Victoria	$160,000.00
429	C	C	Generous / Di Luna	New Zealand Bloodstock Ltd	Auckland	$30,000.00
430	B	C	Montjeu / Distant Heights	Belmont Bloodstock Agency	Victoria	$200,000.00
431	B	C	Carnegie / Dominant	Dgr Thoroughbred Services	New South Wales	$60,000.00
432	B	C	Howbaddouwantit / Doodle	Mr David Ellis	Ngaruawahia	$32,500.00
433	B	F	High Yield / Dove Orchid	Mr Edmond Moreno	Philippines	$19,000.00
434	C	F	Volksraad / Down the Avenue	Psd $34,000 Res $50,000		$0.00
435	B	C	Octagonal / Dragoncello	Psd $85,000 Res $120,000		$0.00
436	BR	F	Danske / Dragon Pearl	Psd $42,500 Res $50,000		$0.00
437	C	C	Danasinga / Duchesne	Brandon Farm	Australia	$35,000.00
438	BR	C	End Sweep / Duel at Daybreak	Mr Tony Bott	Australia	$62,500.00
439	B	F	Montjeu / Dunshara	Landmark Racing Pty Ltd	Victoria	$60,000.00
440	BR	C	Pentire / Du Temps	O'Gorman / Sung	Singapore	$140,000.00
441	C	C	Kaapstad / Eartha	Mr Alan Sharrock	Waitara	$30,000.00
442	B	C	Stravinsky / Easter Joy	Mr Paul O'Sullivan	Matamata	$80,000.00
443	B	C	Danasinga / Echostatic	Gary Alexander Racing Stables	South Africa	$60,000.00
444	B	C	Montjeu / Ecole	Psd $50,000 Res $55,000		$0.00
445	B	C	Carnegie / Edina	Mr Bruce Wallace	Auckland	$32,500.00
446	C	C	Almutawakel / Eidercrown	J & I Bloodstock Limited	Auckland	$85,000.00
447	B	F	Almutawakel / Eledance	Psd $27,500 Res $30,000		$0.00
448	C	C	Howbaddouwantit / Elegance	Psd $22,500 Res $25,000		$0.00
449	BR	C	Kaapstad / Eliza	John Chalmers B/Stock	Australia	$75,000.00
450	C	C	Snippets / Eliza Park	Mr Paul Perry	New South Wales	$75,000.00
451	B	C	Montjeu / Elusive Quarry	Hale / Marsh	Cambridge	$235,000.00
452	B	F	Fusaichi Pegasus / Emerald	Mr Demi O'Byrne	New South Wales	$500,000.00

SONIA BRADFORD

Rich Hill Stud team – from left Colin Thompson, Irene Thompson, Colleen Thompson and John Thompson.

Lot	Col	Sex	Breeding	Purchaser	Location	Price
453	B	F	Carnegie / Emerald Cove	Withdrawn		$0.00
454	B	C	Zabeel / Emerald Dream	Bruce Perry Bloodstock Ltd	Masterton	$400,000.00
455	C	C	Chief Bearhart / Eminent Walk	Mr Bruce Wallace	Auckland	$42,500.00
456	B	C	Almutawakel / Emulate	The Hon Henry Plumptre	Victoria	$90,000.00
457	C	C	Testa Rossa / Encantada	New Zealand Bloodstock Ltd	Hong Kong	$160,000.00
458	B	C	Cape Cross / Endless Joy	Withdrawn		$0.00
459	B	F	Montjeu / Enhancer	Wellfield Thoroughbreds Ltd	Palmerston North	$205,000.00
460	BR	C	O'Reilly / Erin Marie	Withdrawn		$0.00
461	BR	C	Pentire / Eulogize	Belmont Bloodstock Agency	Victoria	$150,000.00
462	B	C	Montjeu / Evolution	Mr Dan O'Donnell	Hong Kong	$200,000.00
463	B	F	Danasinga / Exotic Stranger	Bruce Perry Bloodstock Ltd	Masterton	$65,000.00
464	C	F	Pins / Expoeve	Rogerson Bloodstock	Hamilton	$77,500.00
465	B	C	Faltaat / Fairy Lights	Rogerson Bloodstock	Hamilton	$145,000.00
466	B	C	Howbaddouwantit / Fallacy	Halo Bloodstock	Cambridge	$25,000.00
467	B	C	Howbaddouwantit / Fanfare	Psd $24,000 Res $25,000		$0.00
468	B	C	Stravinsky / Farrara	Mr Roger James	Victoria	$65,000.00
469	BR	F	Octagonal / Fayreform	Psd $145,000 Res $150,000		$0.00
470	C	F	Stravinsky / Ferdnand's Flower	Scott Richardson Bloodstock	Auckland	$55,000.00
471	BR	F	Faltaat / Fiasco	Miss Chin Ling Chen	Auckland	$27,500.00
472	B	F	Kaapstad / Fiddle de De	Withdrawn		$0.00
473	B	F	Montjeu / Field Nymph	Withdrawn		$0.00
474	B	C	Canny Lad / Final Show	Mr David Ellis	Ngaruawahia	$72,500.00
475	C	F	Align / Flame of Atlanta	Mr Stuart Munro	Cambridge	$80,000.00
476	B	C	Catbird / Fledged	John Foote Bloodstock Pty Ltd	Queensland	$75,000.00
477	B	C	Montjeu / Fleur de Chine	Mr Tony Bott	Australia	$200,000.00
478	B	C	Zabeel / Fleur des Champs	Aquanita Racing Flemington	Victoria	$67,500.00
479	C	C	Towkay / Flight Queen	Mr John Wheeler	New Plymouth	$50,000.00
480	B	C	King's Best / Flying Bron	Mr David Ellis	Ngaruawahia	$50,000.00
481	B	F	Zabeel / Foreign Copy	Dgr Thoroughbred Services	New South Wales	$300,000.00
482	B	F	Zabeel / Forever Dancing	Rogerson Bloodstock	Hamilton	$230,000.00
483	B	C	Redoute's Choice / Foxtrot	Withdrawn		$0.00
484	B	C	Generous / Fragile Asset	Mark Pilkington Bloodstock	Victoria	$70,000.00
485	B	C	Carnegie / French Flute	Mr Daniel O'Brien	Victoria	$57,500.00
486	C	F	Thunder Gulch / French Frenzy	Paul Moroney Bloodstock	Matamata	$62,500.00
487	C	C	Danasinga / Frisco Ann	Anzac Lodge	Cambridge	$35,000.00

SONIA BRADFORD

Levin trainer Grant Searle at work.

Lot	Col	Sex	Breeding	Purchaser	Location	Price
488	B	C	Singspiel / Fritzy	The Robt Dawe Agency Ltd	Auckland	$90,000.00
489	B	F	Volksraad / Frosting	Withdrawn		$0.00
490	B	F	Fly to the Stars / Full Noise	Psd $30,000 Res $35,000		$0.00
491	B	C	Zabeel / Futile	Mr Tim Martin	Australia	$220,000.00
492	B	F	Stravinsky / Gala Night	Brandon Farm	South Australia	$120,000.00
493	B	C	Fasliyev / Galejade	Mr Tony Bott	Australia	$150,000.00
494	B	F	Zabeel / Gardd	Mr John O'Shea	New South Wales	$180,000.00
495	B	C	Deputy Governor / Georgia	New Zealand Bloodstock Ltd	Hong Kong	$70,000.00
496	B	C	King's Best / Georgiana	New Zealand Bloodstock Ltd	Hong Kong	$360,000.00
497	C	F	Stravinsky / Gesine	Star Thoroughbreds	New South Wales	$75,000.00
498	BR	C	O'Reilly / Gilded Saint	Game Lodge	Hastings	$37,500.00
499	B	F	Pins / Gio	Mr Paul O'Sullivan	Hong Kong	$90,000.00
500	BR	C	Cape Cross / Glenview	Kieran Moore B/Stock P/L	New South Wales	$70,000.00
501	B	F	Montjeu / Glittering Riffles	Mr Roger James	Matamata	$46,000.00
502	B	F	Fusaichi Pegasus / Golden Winds	Psd $180,000 Res $200,000		$0.00
503	B	F	Carnegie / Gold Ingot	Westbury Stud Limited	Auckland	$34,000.00
504	B	F	Zabeel / Good Faith	Withdrawn		$0.00
505	B	F	Cape Cross / Goodness	Mr Alistair Gordon	South Africa	$17,500.00
506	B	C	Zabeel / Goodwood Jazz	Mr Barry Neville-White	Auckland	$55,000.00
507	B	C	Zabeel / Grace and Power	Jillings Yuill Racing Stables	Auckland	$300,000.00
508	BB	C	Elnadim / Grand Archway	Withdrawn		$0.00
509	B	C	Danehill / Grand Echezeaux	Mr David Ellis	Ngaruawahia	$1,100,000.00
510	B	F	Montjeu / Greta Hall	New Zealand Bloodstock Ltd	Auckland	$400,000.00
511	B	C	Montjeu / Grosvenor's Pride	New Zealand Bloodstock Ltd	New South Wales	$100,000.00
512	B	F	Stravinsky / Guardian Angel	Bruce Perry Bloodstock Ltd	Masterton	$50,000.00
513	B	F	Montjeu / Guinevere	Mr Alistair Gordon	South Africa	$110,000.00
514	B	C	Stravinsky / Gypsy Moth	Mr S Chow	Macau	$80,000.00
515	B	C	Danasinga / Gypsy Soul	Psd $75,000 Res $80,000		$0.00

Colts and Fillies Select Session

Lot	Col	Sex	Breeding	Purchaser	Location	Price
516	B	C	Pins / Habalook	Mr Ross Beckett	Invercargill	$17,000.00
517	B	F	Elnadim / H'Ani	Withdrawn		$0.00
518	C	C	Align / Harry's Sister	Aquanita Racing Flemington	Victoria	$47,000.00
519	BR	F	Chief Bearhart / Havitbak	Withdrawn		$0.00
520	B	F	Faltaat / Heale Street	Mr Edmond Moreno	Philippines	$20,000.00
521	B	F	Fly to the Stars / Healy Ridge	Psd $20,000 Res $35,000		$0.00
522	B	C	City on a Hill / Hear's Hoping	Mr Shane Kennedy	Christchurch	$36,000.00
523	BR	C	Cape Cross / Heatherton	Mr G J Mckenzie	Invercargill	$20,000.00
524	BR	C	O'Reilly / Heidi Fleiss	Withdrawn		$0.00
525	C	C	Cullen / Helen's Pride	Psd $8,000 Res $10,000		$0.00
526	C	C	Danasinga / Helen's Song	Withdrawn		$0.00
527	B	C	O'Reilly / Hellriegel	Psd $10,000 Res $15,000		$0.00
528	B	F	Cape Cross / Highland Dancer	Mr John Bromley	Wellington	$30,000.00
529	C	F	Stravinsky / Hilda Hippo	Withdrawn		$0.00
530	BR	C	Cape Cross / Hint	Withdrawn		$0.00
531	B	F	Sakura Seeking / Hollydoll Girl	C & C Company Ltd	Korea	$12,000.00
532	C	C	Stravinsky / Honeymoon Belle	Withdrawn		$0.00
533	B	C	Desert Fox / Honormatic	Mr Bj & Mrs J Lindsay	Auckland	$15,000.00
534	B	C	Generous / Hooker	Psd $16,000 Res $20,000		$0.00
535	C	C	Star Way / Houston	C & C Company Ltd	Korea	$19,000.00
536	B	C	Chief Bearhart / Hula Lei	Mr Graham Richardson	Matamata	$40,000.00
537	B	F	Al Akbar / Hula Rhythm	Weller Racing Stables Ltd	Wellington	$23,000.00
538	BR	C	Volksraad / Hulda	Paul Moroney Bloodstock	Matamata	$45,000.00
539	BRG	C	Chief Bearhart / Humasong	Mr Ross Beckett	Invercargill	$10,000.00
540	BR	C	Centaine / Hussiana	Psd $7,000 Res $10,000		$0.00
541	B	C	Towkay / Hyapatia Lee	Sir James Lodge	Hamilton	$28,000.00
542	B	C	Danasinga / Ice Frantic	Psd $18,000 Res $20,000		$0.00
543	C	C	Towkay / Icicles	Withdrawn		$0.00
544	BR	F	Danasinga / Ilacourt	Psd $37,500 Res $40,000		$0.00
545	C	C	Bahhare / Illusive Icicle	Psd $15,000 Res $20,000		$0.00

Lot	Col	Sex	Breeding	Purchaser	Location	Price
546	B	F	Spectrum / Impassion	Psd $20,000 Res $30,000		$0.00
547	B	C	Danasinga / Impassive Lady	Psd $26,000 Res $30,000		$0.00
548	B	F	Cape Cross / Imperial Ivory	Mr Don Frampton	Wellington	$33,000.00
549	B	C	Cullen / Impress Me	Mr Stephen Mckee	Auckland	$25,000.00
550	B	F	Carnegie / Impulsive	Phillips Thoroughbreds	Auckland	$18,000.00
551	B	F	Cape Cross / Indent	Ainsley Downs	Te Kauwhata	$2,000.00
552	B	C	Faltaat / Infidelity	John Foote Bloodstock Pty Ltd	Queensland	$46,000.00
553	B	C	Sakura Seeking / Innisvale	Mr Kevin T Myers	Wanganui	$21,000.00
554	C	F	Desert King / In the Pink	Mr Ai & Mrs Sm Fisher	Victoria	$30,000.00
555	B	C	Howbaddouwantit / Intricate Style	Mr Stephen W Y Chow	Macau	$20,000.00
556	C	F	Volksraad / Isla Villa	Mr John Bromley	Wellington	$42,000.00
557	BL	F	Centaine / Isn't She Lovely	Withdrawn		$0.00
558	B	C	Deputy Governor / Ivory Kingdom	Psd $17,500 Res $20,000		$0.00
559	C	C	City on a Hill / Ivy Darling	Mr Iw Herbert	Palmerston North	$16,000.00
560	C	C	Deputy Governor / Jackie o'	O'Gorman / Sung	Singapore	$36,000.00
561	B	F	Danasinga / Janus	W E Jeffries Ltd	Hastings	$35,000.00
562	B	C	Cape Cross / Jazzmatazz	The Robt Dawe Agency Ltd	Auckland	$50,000.00
563	C	F	Danasinga / Jewel of Ireland	Psd $15,000 Res $20,000		$0.00
564	B	F	Desert Fox / Joan's Best	Rogerson Bloodstock	Hamilton	$40,000.00
565	B	F	Volksraad / Joie de Chine	Mr Paul Facoory	Queensland	$9,000.00
566	B	F	Volksraad / Jolly Tight	Psd $50,000 Res $60,000		$0.00
567	C	C	Shinko King / Jubilee Princess	Sanders Racing Stables	Te Awamutu	$19,000.00
568	B	C	City on a Hill / Jungle Jill	Psd $20,000 Res $25,000		$0.00
569	BR	F	Cape Cross / Justatik	Psd $12,000 Res $15,000		$0.00
570	B	C	Anziyan / Kaapture the Heart	Psd $8,000 Res $10,000		$0.00
571	B	F	Generous / Karamea Lady	Mr Ai & Mrs Sm Fisher	Victoria	$28,000.00
572	BR	F	O'Reilly / Keating	Psd $20,000 Res $25,000		$0.00
573	C	C	Electronic Zone / Key Issue	Mr Don Frampton	Wellington	$25,000.00
574	BR	F	Favorite Trick / Kharlie Princess	Mr Paul O'Sullivan	Matamata	$25,000.00
575	BR	F	O'Reilly / Kincia	Psd $27,500 Res $30,000		$0.00
576	B	F	Last Tycoon / Kingstonette	Mr Shaun Dwyer	Queensland	$50,000.00
577	B	C	Pins / Kinou	Rogerson Bloodstock	Hamilton	$6,000.00
578	B	F	Pins / Kiri Belle	Mr Trevor Mckee	Auckland	$15,000.00
579	B	C	Volksraad / Kirkberg	The Robt Dawe Agency Ltd	Auckland	$55,000.00
580	BR	C	Perugino / Ko Hula Beach	Mr Richard Collett	Auckland	$65,000.00
581	B	C	O'Reilly / Laa Tansaa	Brandon Farm	Australia	$5,000.00
582	B	F	Deputy Governor / Labasso	Withdrawn		$0.00
583	BRB	C	Bahhare / Lacy Tops	Mr Bruce Wallace	Auckland	$30,000.00
584	G	F	Shinko King / Ladies Bay	Withdrawn		$0.00
585	BR	C	Colombia / Lady Ballina	Mr Brian Jeffries	Bay Of Plenty	$21,000.00
586	B	C	Towkay / Lady Barina	Psd $26,000 Res $30,000		$0.00
587	B	C	Faltaat / Lady Centaine	Psd $40,000 Res $45,000		$0.00
588	B	F	Howbaddouwantit / Lady Cyclops	Psd $7,000 Res $8,000		$0.00
589	BR	C	Centaine / Lady Fergie	Lisa Latta Racing Stables	Palmerston North	$35,000.00
590	B	F	O'Reilly / Lady Fling	Psd $15,000 Res $25,000		$0.00
591	C	C	Spinning World / Lady Guest	Mr Chris Hausman	Palmerston North	$16,000.00
592	B	C	Felix the Cat / Lady in Blue	Psd $7,000 Res $10,000		$0.00
593	B	C	Cape Cross / Lady Nairne	Mr David Brideoake	Victoria	$21,000.00
594	B	C	Zerpour / Lady Nassa	Paul Moroney Bloodstock	Matamata	$25,000.00
595	B	F	Carnegie / Lady Stanhope	Mr Bill Benson	New South Wales	$25,000.00
596	BR	F	City on a Hill / Lady Sunshine	Rivermonte Farm	Cambridge	$18,000.00
597	B	C	Faltaat / La Magnifique	Withdrawn		$0.00
598	B	C	Sakura Seeking / Larrikin Lady	Hale / S Marsh	Cambridge	$14,000.00
599	BR	C	Kilimanjaro / Last Drinks	Mr Rob Mcanulty	Auckland	$100,000.00
600	B	F	O'Reilly / Latour	Withdrawn		$0.00
601	B	F	Chief Bearhart / La Voleur	New Zealand Bloodstock Ltd	Hamilton	$10,000.00
602	B	C	Carnegie / Leander	Mr Paul Willetts	Auckland	$9,000.00
603	B	C	Howbaddouwantit / Leebazane	Psd $22,500 Res $25,000		$0.00
604	B	F	Kashani / Leica Topic	C & C Company Ltd	Korea	$13,000.00
605	B	F	O'Reilly / Lei Lark	Mr Gerald Ryan	New South Wales	$14,000.00
606	B	C	Montjeu / Leto	Papich Racing	Auckland	$72,500.00
607	B	F	Desert King / Libra Belle	John Chalmers B/Stock	Australia	$40,000.00
608	B	C	Danasinga / Libre	Aquanita Racing Flemington	Victoria	$18,000.00
609	C	F	Faltaat / Lidahya	Galaxy Racing	Queensland	$20,000.00
610	B	C	Pins / Liffey	Withdrawn		$0.00

Lot	Col	Sex	Breeding	Purchaser	Location	Price
611	B	F	O'Reilly / Light and Free	Mr Paul O'Sullivan	Matamata	$30,000.00
612	B	C	Kaapstad / Lightning Tree	Mr Kevin T Myers	Wanganui	$33,000.00
613	C	C	City on a Hill / Lillibet	Mr Stephen W Y Chow	Macau	$30,000.00
614	BR	F	Star Way / Limitless	Mr Ross Ancell	United Kingdom	$60,000.00
615	BR	C	Centaine / Logical Miss	Mr Trevor Mckee	Auckland	$27,000.00
616	B	C	Cape Cross / Loreef	Mr Alex Macpherson	Victoria	$20,000.00
617	B	C	Carnegie / Louvain	Tony Pike Bloodstock	Waikato	$30,000.00
618	C	F	Deputy Governor / Lovett's Bay	Psd $2,000 Res $3,000		$0.00
619	B	C	Sandtrap / Lucy Mary	New Zealand Bloodstock Ltd	Waikato	$22,000.00
620	B	C	O'Reilly / Luskin Lady	Mr Richard Collett	Auckland	$26,000.00
621	C	F	Howbaddouwantit / Luskin Lass	Psd $19,000 Res $20,000		$0.00
622	C	C	Danske / Lutece	Psd $14,000 Res $25,000		$0.00
623	B	F	Cape Cross / Lyphard's Reve	Aquanita Racing Flemington	Victoria	$16,000.00
624	B	F	Volksraad / Madamax	Mr John Wheeler	New Plymouth	$50,000.00
625	B	F	Prized / Madame Bardot	Mr Ross Beckett	Invercargill	$8,000.00
626	C	C	Electronic Zone / Madison Avenue	Psd $13,000 Res $15,000		$0.00
627	BL	F	O'Reilly / Magic Strauss	Mr Russell Philp	New Plymouth	$18,000.00
628	B	F	Lion Cavern / Magnetic Belle	Mr Jose Y Quiros	Phillipines	$24,000.00
629	B	C	Tuscany Flyer / Mahala Bay	Aquanita Racing Flemington	Victoria	$8,000.00
630	B	F	Danske / Maiden Over	Landmark Racing Pty Ltd	Victoria	$18,000.00
631	BR	F	Almutawakel / Major Effort	Mr Honorato Nery	Philippines	$14,000.00
632	B	C	Fly to the Stars / Malvina Rose	Mrs Donna Logan	Northland	$50,000.00
633	B	C	Orpen / Manx Symbol	New Zealand Bloodstock Ltd	Hong Kong	$72,500.00
634	B	C	Spectrum / Marasie	Mr Peter Hurdle	Palmerston North	$40,000.00
635	B	C	Daggers Drawn / Marcasite	Withdrawn		$0.00
636	B	C	Spectrum / Marlo Waters	Three Amigos Trust	Christchurch	$22,000.00
637	B	F	Anziyan / Marscade	Withdrawn		$0.00
638	B	C	Carnegie / Mayfair	Psd $22,500 Res $35,000		$0.00
639	BR	F	Faltaat / Mazurka	Mr Paul O'Sullivan	Matamata	$40,000.00
640	C	F	Danasinga / McGinty's Girl	Ultra Recycling New Zealand	Wellington	$20,000.00
641	BR	F	Centaine / McGinty's Lass	Psd $13,000 Res $15,000		$0.00
642	BR	F	Centaine / Military Fun	Psd $15,000 Res $30,000		$0.00
643	B	C	Danske / Mini Heights	Withdrawn		$0.00
644	C	C	Align / Minnie McGinnis	Papich Racing	Auckland	$42,000.00
645	BR	F	Align / Mirakesh	Withdrawn		$0.00
646	B	F	Danasinga / Mirima	Aquanita Racing Flemington	Victoria	$34,000.00
647	C	F	Volksraad / Miss Bailey	Psd $30,000 Res $40,000		$0.00
648	B	C	Towkay / Miss Beam	Mr Pn & Mrs K Mckay	Matamata	$37,500.00
649	B	C	Desert King / Miss Grosvenor	Mr Joe Barnes	Auckland	$30,000.00
650	C	C	City on a Hill / Miss Jimeale	Mr Paul Willetts	Auckland	$21,000.00
651	B	F	Volksraad / Misskap	Psd $22,000 Res $30,000		$0.00
652	B	F	Kaapstad / Miss Max	Mr Mike Breslin	Palmerston North	$52,000.00

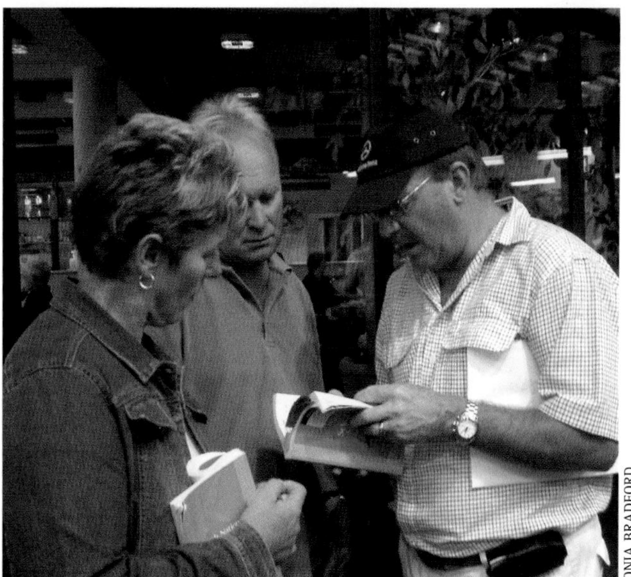

SONIA BRADFORD

Colleen and Chris Wood with bloodstock agent Stuart Hale.

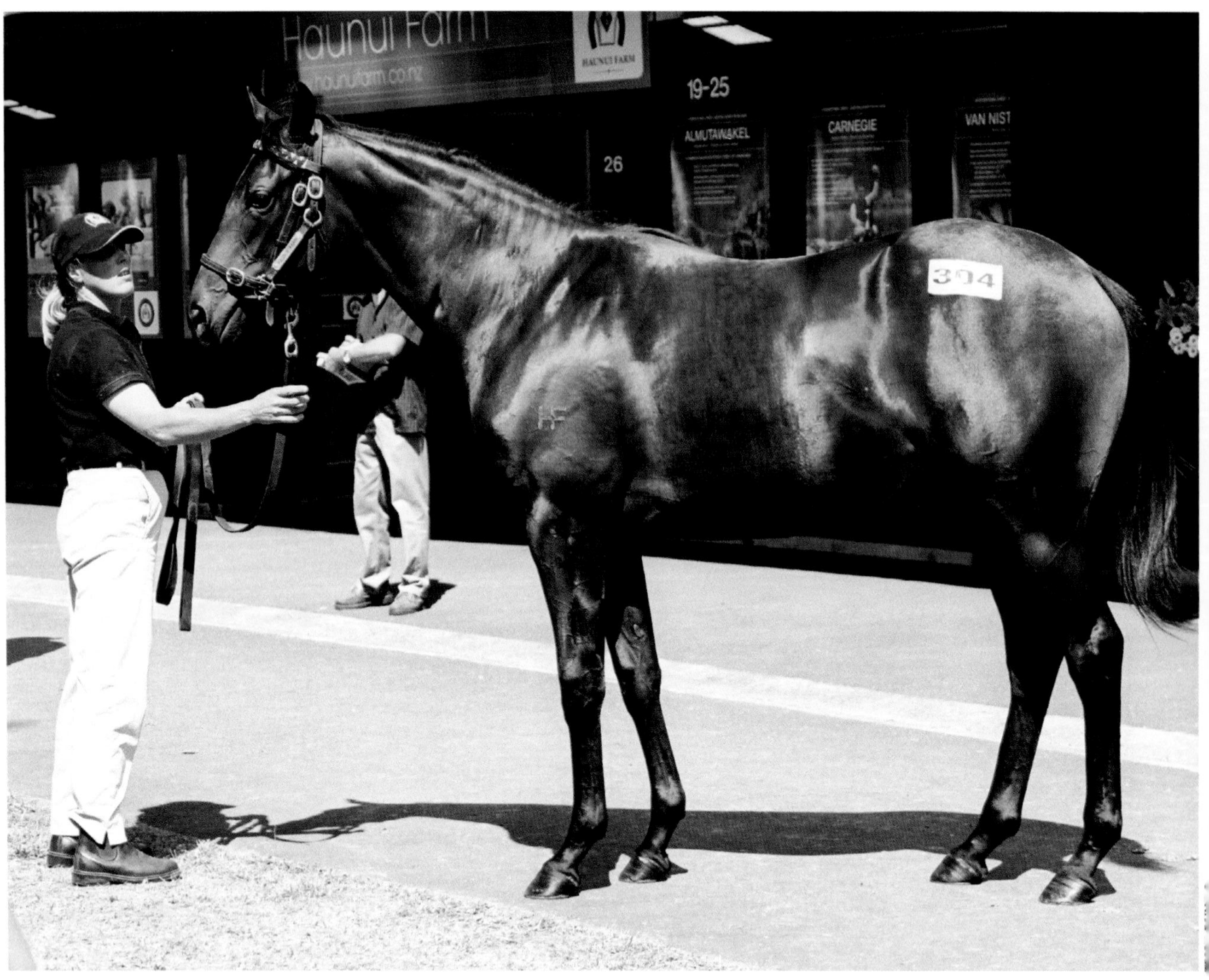

The top-priced filly by Zabeel from Waihora's Lass.

Lot	Col	Sex	Breeding	Purchaser	Location	Price
653	C	F	Chief Bearhart / Miss Moonshine	Stoney Creek Lodge	Wellington	$3,000.00
654	B	C	Volksraad / Miss Opera	Mr Richard Dee	Cambridge	$65,000.00
655	B	F	Stravinsky / Miss Rory	Paul Moroney Bloodstock	Matamata	$55,000.00
656	B	F	Stravinsky / Miss Saigon	Mr Bj & Mrs J Lindsay	Auckland	$95,000.00
657	B	F	Danasinga / Mixed Up	Psd $10,000 Res $12,000		$0.00
658	C	C	City on a Hill / Mohaves Lass	Mr Doug Harrison	Victoria	$25,000.00
659	B	F	O'Reilly / Mon Cheri	Mr Paul O'Sullivan	Matamata	$30,000.00
660	C	C	Star Way / Morangie	Withdrawn		$0.00
661	BR	C	Faltaat / Morgan Glory	New Zealand Bloodstock Ltd	Bay Of Plenty	$23,000.00
662	B	C	Kaapstad / Mrs Bond	Laurel Oak Bloodstock Pty Ltd	New South Wales	$75,000.00
663	B	C	Danasinga / Mrs Poole	Mr Peter Williams	Christchurch	$18,000.00
664	B	F	Cullen / Muchacha	Rogerson Bloodstock	Hamilton	$27,000.00
665	B	F	Almutawakel / Musical Charm	Paul Moroney Bloodstock	Matamata	$30,000.00
666	C	F	Howbaddouwantit/My Amazing Grace	Psd $12,000 Res $14,000		$0.00
667	B	C	Danske / My Chameleon	Mr Ron Cook	Victoria	$37,500.00
668	B	C	Centaine / My Girl Elise	Mr Brian Mayfield-Smith	Victoria	$16,000.00
669	B	F	Shinko King / My Good Omen	Withdrawn		$0.00
670	B	C	Elnadim / My Marilyn	Mr Peter Walker	Auckland	$30,000.00
671	B	F	Montjeu / Mystic Flight	Mr John Bromley	Wellington	$34,000.00
672	B	C	Centaine / Nasajuanita	Mr Ad & Mrs Ka Yorke	Manawatu	$15,000.00
673	B	F	Faltaat / Native Hawk	Psd $28,000 Res $30,000		$0.00
674	B	C	Danasinga / Neela	Mr Doug Harrison	Victoria	$22,000.00
675	C	C	Almutawakel / Neutron Dancer	Mr Kevin T Myers	Wanganui	$26,000.00

Lot	Col	Sex	Breeding	Purchaser	Location	Price
676	B	F	Centaine / Never Blue	Mr Alan Sharrock	Waitara	$21,000.00
677	B	C	Volksraad / Never Bluffs	Mr Jeremy Gask	South Australia	$45,000.00
678	BR	F	Align / Niece's Gift	John Chalmers B/Stock	Australia	$30,000.00
679	BR	C	Danasinga / Night and Day	Withdrawn		$0.00
680	B	C	Desert Fox / Night Dancer	Aquanita Racing Flemington	Victoria	$18,000.00
681	B	F	Danasinga / Night Dancer	Psd $14,000 Res $15,000		$0.00
682	C	F	Deputy Governor / Nijsha	C & C Company Ltd	Korea	$13,000.00
683	BR	C	Desert Fox / Nite Jewel	Withdrawn		$0.00
684	B	F	Danasinga / Nivea	C & C Company Ltd	Korea	$14,000.00
685	B	C	Bahhare / Noubeel	Mr Murray Baker	Cambridge	$40,000.00
686	B	C	Volksraad / Nuccina	Mr Brian Jenkins	Cambridge	$60,000.00
687	B	C	High Yield / Nymph Errant	Mr Kevin T Myers	Wanganui	$38,000.00
688	B	F	Faltaat / Of Value	Psd $24,000 Res $30,000		$0.00
689	B	C	Kashani / Oh Heavens	Withdrawn		$0.00
690	BR	F	Cape Cross / Okahu	Withdrawn		$0.00
691	B	C	Cape Cross / Olga's Pal	New Zealand Bloodstock Ltd	Hong Kong	$26,000.00
692	C	C	Bahhare / Olivain	Mr David Enright	Manawatu	$13,000.00
693	C	F	Bahhare / Omoto Lass	C & C Company Ltd	Korea	$19,000.00
694	BR	C	Cullen / One Good Reason	Mr Chris Wood	Auckland	$28,000.00
695	BR	C	Pentire / On My Tour	Anzac Lodge	Victoria	$30,000.00
696	B	C	Daggers Drawn / Opals	Aquanita Racing Flemington	Victoria	$23,000.00
697	B	F	Prized / Opera Singer	Psd $14,000 Res $15,000		$0.00
698	B	F	Cape Cross / Operatic	John Chalmers B/Stock	Australia	$31,000.00

Lot	Col	Sex	Breeding	Purchaser	Location	Price
699	B	C	Last Tycoon / Orland	Mr B & Mrs M Jenkins	Cambridge	$9,000.00
700	B	C	Volksraad / O'sequita	Mr David Howarth	Christchurch	$35,000.00
701	BR	F	Kaapstad / Our Sportsgirl	Messrs Bj & A Bennett	Victoria	$30,000.00
702	B	C	Jade Robbery / Our Star Tate	Mr David Ellis	Ngaruawahia	$30,000.00
703	B	F	Secret Savings / Outstanding Affair	Mr Jose Y Quiros	Phillipines	$37,500.00
704	B	C	Zerpour / Overview	New Zealand Bloodstock Ltd	Auckland	$20,000.00
705	BR	F	O'Reilly / Oxford Echo	Sanders Racing Stables	Te Awamutu	$18,000.00
706	B	F	Howbaddouwantit / Pageant	Mr Murray Baker	Cambridge	$40,000.00
707	C	C	Star Way / Pakatoa Princess	C & C Company Ltd	Korea	$16,000.00
708	C	F	Almutawakel / Palace Bound	Mr Graham Richardson	Matamata	$30,000.00
709	B	C	Elnadim / Pan for Glitter	Mr John Carran	Invercargill	$30,000.00
710	C	F	Generous / Parfore	Psd $2,000 Res $4,000		$0.00
711	B	F	Danasinga / Party Belle	Danny Power Bloodstock	Victoria	$22,000.00
712	B	C	Faltaat / Peace of Mind	John Foote Bloodstock Pty Ltd	Queensland	$77,500.00
713	BR	F	Faltaat / Peppers	Psd $28,000 Res $30,000		$0.00
714	B	F	I Conquer / Perfect	Tim Roberts Syndicate	Australia	$31,000.00
715	BR	F	Volksraad / Persistance	Brandon Farm	Australia	$23,000.00
716	B	C	Bahhare / Perspicacious	Halo Bloodstock	Hamilton	$16,000.00
717	BB	C	Danske / Petite	Mr Brian Jeffries	Te Puke	$20,000.00
718	B	C	Sandpit / Piece of Cake	Mrs Donna Logan	Northland	$35,000.00
719	B	C	Danasinga / Pina Colada	John Chalmers B/Stock	Australia	$12,000.00
720	C	C	Generous / Pinwheel	Mr Alan Sharrock	Waitara	$18,000.00
721	BR	F	O'Reilly / Plentiful	Psd $10,000 Res $12,000		$0.00
722	B	F	Spectrum / Polly's Pocket	Mr Paul Jelicich	Kumeu	$27,000.00
723	B	C	Elnadim / Price to Pay	Rogerson Bloodstock	Hamilton	$26,000.00
724	BR	F	O'Reilly / Proms	The Robt Dawe Agency Ltd	Auckland	$50,000.00
725	B	C	Danske / Purple Tone	C & C Company Ltd	Korea	$13,000.00
726	C	F	Align / Quack	Rogerson Bloodstock	Hamilton	$65,000.00
727	B	C	Al Akbar / Quasin	Stuart Hale & Co	Cambridge	$10,000.00
728	B	F	Pins / Quiet One	Mr Edmond Moreno	Philippines	$16,000.00
729	C	C	Springsteen / Quiet Queen	Psd $9,000 Res $10,000		$0.00
730	B	F	Towkay / Racing Waters	Psd $19,000 Res $20,000		$0.00
731	B	C	Carnegie / Racy Belle	Mr John Morrisey	Canberra	$24,000.00
732	B	C	Volksraad / Radigund	Mr Paul Perry	New South Wales	$70,000.00
733	BR	F	Danasinga / Ranch	Withdrawn		$0.00
734	C	F	Volksraad / Rapunzel	Psd $27,500 Res $30,000		$0.00
735	C	C	Stravinsky / Rare Bits	Mr Paul Perry	New South Wales	$150,000.00
736	BR	F	Towkay / Reasonable	Stuart Hale & Co	Cambridge	$47,500.00
737	BRB	C	Centaine / Reasonably	Mr Aaron Purcell	Victoria	$13,000.00
738	B	F	Danske / Rebecca Sharp	Psd $48,000 Res $50,000		$0.00
739	B	C	Bahhare / Rebus	Mr Paul O'Sullivan	Matamata	$47,500.00
740	B	F	Danske / Red Baroness	Mr Stephen Mckee	Auckland	$32,000.00
741	BR	C	Kaapstad / Red Letter Day	Withdrawn		$0.00
742	B	C	Woodborough / Regal Kate	Posa'S Lodge Waikato	Waikato	$14,000.00
743	B	C	Pins / Reputedly	Mr Brian Mayfield-Smith	Victoria	$90,000.00
744	BR	F	Cape Cross / Restrain	Rivermonte Farm	Cambridge	$6,000.00
745	B	F	Cape Cross / Rhinestone	John Chalmers B/Stock	Australia	$15,000.00
746	B	F	Volksraad / Ribbons	Withdrawn		$0.00
747	BR	C	Cape Cross / Righteous Lady	Rogerson Bloodstock	Hamilton	$85,000.00
748	C	F	Daggers Drawn / Right Tune	Psd $10,000 Res $12,000		$0.00
749	BR	C	O'Reilly / Robbers Aunty	Hale / S Marsh	Cambridge	$45,000.00
750	BR	C	Centaine / Rock the Kasbar	John Foote Bloodstock Pty Ltd	Queensland	$45,000.00
751	C	F	Chief Bearhart / Romance and Roses	Mr Bill Benson	New South Wales	$9,000.00
752	BR	F	Sandtrap / Rondstat	Mr Paul O'Sullivan	Matamata	$14,000.00
753	C	C	Almutawakel / Rory's Helen	Mr Alan Sharrock	Waitara	$50,000.00
754	B	C	O'Reilly / Roscrea	Withdrawn		$0.00
755	B	F	King of Kings / Rose of Ockie	Mr Bruce Wallace	Auckland	$27,000.00
756	B	C	Deputy Governor / Rosetena	Mr John Carran	Invercargill	$25,000.00
757	B	C	Cullen / Rouge Etoile	Mr Bruce Wallace	Auckland	$31,000.00
758	C	C	Spectrum / Royal Empire	Psd $24,000 Res $30,000		$0.00
759	C	F	City on a Hill / Royal Pay	Psd $18,000 Res $20,000		$0.00
760	BL	C	The Commander / Royal Proposal	Mr Jeremy Gask	Australia	$27,000.00
761	B	C	Haayil / Ruakiwi Sunshine	Mr Brian Jeffries	Te Puke	$20,000.00
762	B	F	Cullen / Ruby's River	Withdrawn		$0.00
763	C	C	City on a Hill / Russian Slice	Mr Roger James	Matamata	$20,000.00

Lot	Col	Sex	Breeding	Purchaser	Location	Price
764	R	C	Volksraad / Saffie	Mr Brian Mayfield-Smith	Victoria	$70,000.00
765	C	C	Chief Bearhart / Sailor's Lift	Withdrawn		$0.00
766	BR	C	Lord Ballina / Salaam	Aquanita Racing Flemington	Victoria	$14,000.00
767	C	C	Faltaat / Sandy's Angel	Taylors Bloodstock	Wellington	$40,000.00
768	B	C	Cape Cross / San Ysabeel	Michael Stedman Bloodstock	New South Wales	$42,000.00
769	B	F	Volksraad / Saree's Grove	K J Hickman	Christchurch	$17,000.00
770	G	F	O'Reilly / Satonda	Galaxy Racing	Queensland	$18,000.00
771	B	F	Thunder Gulch / Saveur	William H Masters	New South Wales	$36,000.00
772	BG	C	Diamond Express / Saving Grace	Mr V & Mrs S Lianto	New South Wales	$14,000.00
773	B	C	Danske / Scarlet	Withdrawn		$0.00
774	B	F	Montjeu / Scenic Bay	Withdrawn		$0.00
775	B	C	Howbaddouwantit / Scenic Victoria	Withdrawn		$0.00
776	B	C	Stark South / Seadreamer	Mr Kingsley Peach	Victoria	$22,500.00
777	C	F	Chief Bearhart / Sea Encounter	Mr Robbie Laing	Victoria	$30,000.00
778	C	C	Volksraad / Search	Mr Mike Breslin	Palmerston North	$40,000.00
779	BR	F	Anabaa / Seersha	Psd $20,000 Res $40,000		$0.00
780	C	F	Danske / Selene Star	Psd $10,000 Res $15,000		$0.00
781	BR	F	Carnegie / Sensuality	Psd $7,500 Res $10,000		$0.00
782	B	C	Fly to the Stars / Sent to War	Psd $30,000 Res $35,000		$0.00
783	B	F	O'Reilly / Serenova	Psd $17,500 Res $25,000		$0.00
784	B	C	Cape Cross / Set Up	Mr Kevin T Myers	Wanganui	$40,000.00
785	B	F	Kilimanjaro / Shafty Lady	Kumeroa Station	Hawkes Bay	$16,000.00
786	B	F	Danasinga / Shannon Marie	Gundaroo Stud Pty Ltd	New South Wales	$22,500.00
787	B	C	Bahhare / Sharazad	Mr Iw Herbert	Palmerston North	$17,000.00
788	B	C	Stravinsky / Shariat	Paul Moroney Bloodstock	Matamata	$150,000.00
789	C	F	Danasinga / She's First Class	Psd $24,000 Res $25,000		$0.00
790	B	C	Cape Cross / She's Possessed	New Zealand Bloodstock Ltd	Hong Kong	$20,000.00
791	B	F	Almutawakel / Show No Fear	Paul Moroney Bloodstock	Matamata	$52,000.00
792	B	C	My Halo / Showtimecanterbury	Withdrawn		$0.00
793	B	F	Howbaddouwantit / Showzeel	Stuart Hale & Co	Cambridge	$37,500.00
794	B	C	Zerpour / Silk's Lady	Mr Shaun Ritchie	Cambridge	$6,000.00
795	B	C	Danasinga / Silver's Sister	Michael Stedman Bloodstock	New South Wales	$85,000.00
796	C	F	Deputy Governor / Simonette Dee	Withdrawn		$0.00
797	C	C	Stark South / Simply Sally	The Robt Dawe Agency Ltd	Auckland	$50,000.00
798	B	F	Chief Bearhart / Sitting Pat	Mr Honorato Nery	Philippines	$20,000.00
799	C	F	Kaapstad / Skimmer	Psd $22,000 Res $30,000		$0.00
800	B	C	Woodman / Sky Haven	Sir James Lodge	Hamilton	$20,000.00
801	B	F	Howbaddouwantit / Sky Mist	Hale / S Marsh	Cambridge	$21,000.00
802	B	F	Haayil / Slewzanner	Anton Koolman Bloodstock	New South Wales	$18,000.00
803	B	F	Carnegie / Smytzer's Krstina	Psd $13,000 Res $15,000		$0.00
804	B	C	Carnegie / Snadame	New Zealand Bloodstock Ltd	Hong Kong	$40,000.00
805	C	F	Align / Snippets' Miss	Mr Rd & Mrs Ja Collett	Auckland	$42,500.00
806	BR	C	O'Reilly / Snow Cloud	Mr Bevin Laming	Queensland	$40,000.00
807	B	F	Danske / So Happy	Galaxy Racing	Queensland	$15,000.00
808	B	C	O'Reilly / Soleil Vite	Michael Stedman Bloodstock	New South Wales	$20,000.00
809	B	F	Beautiful Crown / So Like Lae	Psd $25,000 Res $30,000		$0.00
810	B	C	Volksraad / Somehow	Psd $35,000 Res $40,000		$0.00
811	B	C	O'Reilly / Somethingregal	Mr R J Williams	Christchurch	$16,000.00
812	C	F	Align / So Soon	Kumeroa Station	Hawkes Bay	$20,000.00
813	B	C	Howbaddouwantit / Spandex	Stuart Hale & Co	Cambridge	$36,000.00
814	C	C	Deputy Governor / Spectaculac	Tony Pike Bloodstock	Cambridge	$15,000.00
815	B	C	Lujain / Spice Girl	Mr Jeremy Gask	Australia	$45,000.00
816	B	F	Danske / Spider	Psd $17,500 Res $25,000		$0.00
817	B	F	Almutawakel / Spindrift	Mr Paul O'Sullivan	Matamata	$75,000.00
818	B	F	Pins / Spring Reason	W Freestone Pty Ltd	Queensland	$11,000.00
819	C	F	Danasinga / Sriwijaya	Dr & Ec Mackintosh	Ashburton	$5,000.00
820	B	C	Commands / Starmix	Mr Mike Breslin	Palmerston North	$60,000.00
821	B	F	Peintre Celebre / Star of Namibia	Mr Peter Walker	Clevedon	$30,000.00
822	B	C	Generous / Star on Ice	Palace Lodge	Levin	$10,000.00
823	BR	C	Cape Cross / Startling Lady	Mr Bevin Laming	Queensland	$38,000.00
824	B	F	Danasinga / Steady as a Cat	Withdrawn		$0.00
825	C	C	Align / Steingrubler	Rogerson Bloodstock	Hamilton	$45,000.00
826	B	C	Kaapstad / Stella Stargazer	Tony Pike Bloodstock	Cambridge	$52,500.00
827	B	C	Howbaddouwantit / Step in Time	Mr Trevor Mckee	Auckland	$7,000.00
828	B	C	Pins / Stirling Jo	Mr Doug Rawnsley	Auckland	$16,000.00

Lot	Col	Sex	Breeding	Purchaser	Location	Price
829	B	C	Catbird / Stitches	Withdrawn		$0.00
830	B	C	Generous / St Lucia	Paul Moroney Bloodstock	Waikato	$18,000.00
831	B	C	Carnegie / Straight Cut Jeans	Beamish Bloodstock Ltd	Bay Of Plenty	$42,000.00
832	B	C	O'Reilly / Straight Lip	Psd $35,000 Res $40,000		$0.00
833	BR	C	Ebony Grosve / Stretto	Mr V & Mrs S Lianto	New South Wales	$22,500.00
834	B	F	Cape Cross / Strike Twice	Magic Racing Bloodstock	Australia	$30,000.00
835	B	C	Pins / Stuck Up	New Zealand Bloodstock Ltd	Hong Kong	$50,000.00
836	C	C	General Nediym / Stunning Crystal	Psd $57,500 Res $60,000		$0.00
837	B	C	Align / Super Reason	Sanders Racing Stables	Te Awamutu	$40,000.00
838	B	C	Volksraad / Surprize Offer	New Zealand Bloodstock Ltd	Cambridge	$41,000.00
839	B	C	Shinko Forest / Susie Speaking	Karapiro Bloodstock	Waikato	$40,000.00
840	C	C	Danasinga / Sweetliner	Mr Robert Priscott	Te Awamutu	$32,500.00
841	B	C	Real Quiet / Sweet Talinga	Stuart Hale & Co	Cambridge	$12,000.00
842	C	C	Deputy Governor / Sylph	Tony Pike Bloodstock	Cambridge	$40,000.00
843	B	F	O'Reilly / Symphius	Mr Stephen Mckee	Auckland	$12,000.00
844	C	F	Daggers Drawn / Take the Chance	Cunnlang Partnership	New Plymouth	$16,000.00
845	B	C	Howbaddouwantit / Talk Talk	C & C Company Ltd	Korea	$17,000.00
846	BR	C	Prized / Tango	Gundaroo Stud Pty Ltd	New South Wales	$32,000.00
847	C	C	Daggers Drawn / Tbaareeh	Paul Moroney Bloodstock	Matamata	$22,500.00
848	B	C	Volksraad / Tedzerror	Mr Jim Gibbs	Matamata	$44,000.00
849	B	C	Deputy Governor / Theydon Bois	Mr John Wheeler	New Plymouth	$59,000.00
850	C	C	Danasinga / Timamou	Kevin Dagg Bloodstock	Victoria	$30,000.00
851	C	F	Chief Bearhart / Timely Flight	Withdrawn		$0.00
852	C	C	Sakura Seeking / Time of My Life	Mr Daniel Flavell	Auckland	$12,000.00
853	C	F	Volksraad / Timpani	Mr Ray Cleaver	Victoria	$16,000.00
854	BR	F	Cape Cross / Tina's Dream	Mr Honorato Nery	Philippines	$5,000.00
855	B	C	Al Akbar / Tinsel	Withdrawn		$0.00
856	B	F	Danasinga / Tio Lotus	Psd $18,000 Res $25,000		$0.00
857	B	F	Volksraad / Tio Violet	Psd $22,000 Res $30,000		$0.00
858	BR	F	Kaapstad / Tivoli Hero	Withdrawn		$0.00
859	BB	F	Cape Cross / Totoka	Mr Greg Shirley	Auckland	$15,000.00
860	C	F	Deputy Governor / Touch Wood	Psd $22,000 Res $30,000		$0.00
861	B	F	Danasinga / Tralae	Psd $15,000 Res $25,000		$0.00
862	C	C	Pins / Tramaurea	Celebrity Thoroughbreds	Invercargill	$40,000.00
863	B	C	Carnegie / Tramontane	Withdrawn		$0.00
864	BL	C	Cape Cross / Transluscent	Mr Brian Jenkins	Cambridge	$52,500.00
865	B	C	Howbaddouwantit / Trapeze	Mr Bruce Wallace	Auckland	$15,000.00
866	B	F	Howbaddouwantit / Treasure Chest	Psd $9,500 Res $10,000		$0.00
867	B	F	Centaine / Tresor	Psd $16,000 Res $20,000		$0.00
868	B	C	Almutawakel / Trice Time	Withdrawn		$0.00
869	B	C	Volksraad / Trickery	Psd $30,000 Res $40,000		$0.00
870	B	C	Carnegie / Tricon	C & C Company Ltd	Korea	$26,000.00
871	B	F	Pins / Tri Halo	Psd $11,000 Res $15,000		$0.00
872	BR	F	Kaapstad / Trimmings	Mr Bill Benson	New South Wales	$15,000.00
873	B	F	Danasinga / Trisha's Belle	Rogerson Bloodstock	Hamilton	$31,000.00
874	B	C	Hula Town / Truly Mystic	Withdrawn		$0.00
875	B	C	Dangerous / Turtle Beach	Sanders Racing Stables	Te Awamutu	$46,000.00
876	C	F	Thunder Gulch / Twinklebelle	Mr John Couch	Auckland	$14,000.00
877	B	C	Catbird / Ugandan Gold			$0.00
878	C	F	Generous / Urgent Move	C & C Company Ltd	Korea	$13,000.00
879	BR	C	Danasinga / Vaguely Sneeky	Sir James Lodge	Hamilton	$30,000.00
880	B	F	Pins / Vain Kiwi	Paul Moroney Bloodstock	Matamata	$70,000.00
881	B	F	Howbaddouwantit / Valentine Girl	Mr Paul O'Sullivan	Matamata	$10,000.00
882	B	F	Volksraad / Vanderbilt	K J Hickman	Christchurch	$40,000.00
883	B	C	Align / Vanity Fair	Mr Peter Hurdle	Palmerston North	$37,500.00
884	B	F	Carnegie / Vasadanya	Mr Aaron Purcell	Victoria	$15,000.00
885	B	C	Fly to the Stars / Village Dancer	Triassic Park	Cambridge	$25,000.00
886	B	F	Spectrum / Vital Curves	Mr Gb & Mrs Re Chamberlain	Christchurch	$15,000.00
887	B	F	Almutawakel / Vive la France	Mr David Ellis	Matamata	$32,500.00
888	B	C	Pins / Vizelle	Mr Warren Bolton	Taranaki	$25,000.00
889	B	C	Danske / Volstrata	Galaxy Racing	Queensland	$20,000.00
890	B	C	Carnegie / Vorst	C & C Company Ltd	Korea	$19,000.00
891	B	F	Pins / Vote	Mr Alan Sharrock	Waitara	$20,000.00
892	B	C	O'Reilly / Vreeland	Withdrawn		$0.00
893	B	F	King of Kings / Waikiki Princess	Mr David Ellis	Ngaruawahia	$37,500.00

Lot	Col	Sex	Breeding	Purchaser	Location	Price
894	C	C	Generous / Wait	Mr Dean Wiles	Malaysia	$21,000.00
895	BR	C	Prized / Waitohi Gold	Mr Doug Harrison	Victoria	$20,000.00
896	B	F	Towkay / Wake Up Suzie	Psd $2,000 Res $3,000		$0.00
897	B	C	Almutawakel / Wauwinet	Rivermonte Farm	Cambridge	$38,000.00
898	B	F	Carnegie / Way Leggo	Psd $25,000 Res $35,000		$0.00
899	B	C	Felix the Cat / Wayward	Mr Shane Kennedy	Christchurch	$20,000.00
900	B	F	Danasinga / Whakanui Heights	Psd $10,000 Res $20,000		$0.00
901	C	C	Electronic Zone / Whata Beauty	Mr John Wheeler	New Plymouth	$11,000.00
902	C	C	Volksraad / Whence	Mr Marcus Corban	Cambridge	$27,000.00
903	B	F	Howbaddouwantit / Whyte Haze	Mr Trevor Mckee	Auckland	$8,000.00
904	BR	F	Faltaat / Wicked	Psd $25,000 Res $40,000		$0.00
905	B	C	Cape Cross / Wild Blue	Taylors Bloodstock	Wellington	$50,000.00
906	C	F	Kaapstad / Wild Wood	Mr Paul O'Sullivan	Matamata	$55,000.00
907	B	C	Volksraad / Windfield Dancer	Mr Richard Collett	Auckland	$57,500.00
908	BR	C	Cape Cross / Winds of War	Withdrawn		$0.00
909	B	F	Almutawakel / Windsor Walk	Mr Sd & Mrs Kj Alexander	Waikato	$22,500.00
910	C	C	Faltaat / Witch Partner	Psd $30,000 Res $35,000		$0.00
911	BR	F	Danasinga / Wobinda Lass	Aquanita Racing Flemington	Victoria	$44,000.00
912	B	C	Al Akbar / Work of Art	Mr Tom Jamison	Wellington	$20,000.00
913	BR	C	City on a Hill / Xativa	Mr Wj Thurlow	Taranaki	$3,000.00
914	C	F	Pins / Xmas Eve	Dominion Bloodstock Agency	Waikato	$22,000.00
915	B	C	Bahhare / Xzanadu Lady	Mr Stephen Montgomery	Christchurch	$32,500.00
916	B	C	Shinko King / Yama Dansu	Mr Richard Yuill	Auckland	$15,000.00
917	B	F	Align / Zabrina	Withdrawn		$0.00
918	B	C	Danske / Zam's Girl	Tony Pike Bloodstock	Cambridge	$15,000.00
919	C	C	Howbaddouwantit / Zippo	C & C Company Ltd	Korea	$23,000.00
920	B	C	Align / Abenezra	Lisa Latta Racing Stables	Palmerston North	$45,000.00
921	C	F	Faltaat / Adeliza	Stoney Creek Lodge	Wellington	$3,000.00
922	C	F	Howbaddouwantit / Affidavit	Psd $7,000 Res $8,000		$0.00
923	C	F	Bahhare / Agena	C & C Company Ltd	Korea	$12,000.00
924	C	C	Chief Bearhart / Alchemy	Mr Roger James	Matamata	$40,000.00
925	C	F	Danske / Alfred's Jewel	Lisa Latta Racing Stables	Palmerston North	$25,000.00
926	B	F	Faltaat / Al Katcha	John Chalmers Bloodstock	Australia	$44,000.00
927	B	F	Howbaddouwantit / Also	Psd $6,000 Res $8,000		$0.00
928	B	C	Stravinsky / Amaroo	Landmark Racing Pty Ltd	Victoria	$52,000.00
929	B	C	O'Reilly / Amber Ace	Psd $16,000 Res $18,000		$0.00
930	B	C	Volksraad / Amythest	Psd $67,500 Res $70,000		$0.00
931	BR	C	Ebony Grosve / Andra	Withdrawn		$0.00
932	B	C	Kingdom Bay / Annifrid	Mr Richard Collett	Auckland	$25,000.00
933	B	C	Stravinsky / Arena Pride	New Zealand Bloodstock Ltd	Cambridge	$85,000.00
934	B	C	Shinko King / Argyll Dazzler	Mr John Wheeler	New Plymouth	$12,000.00

Sydney's Neville Begg looking for another winner from Fairdale Stud.

Lot	Col	Sex	Breeding	Purchaser	Location	Price
935	B	C	Casual Lies / Astec Gold	Mr Rj Bergerson	Palmerston North	$22,000.00
936	B	F	O'Reilly / Auchtric	Mr Paul O'Sullivan	Matamata	$30,000.00
937	B	C	Desert Fox / Audrey Rose	Mr Joe Barnes	Auckland	$20,000.00
938	C	F	Danske / Avondawin	Mr Doug Rawnsley	Auckland	$6,000.00
939	B	C	O'Reilly / Avonrose	Psd $15,000 Res $20,000		$0.00
940	B	C	Cullen / Awave	Tony Pike Bloodstock	Cambridge	$30,000.00
941	C	C	Zerpour / Babillard	Mr Iw Herbert	Palmerston North	$42,500.00
942	B	F	Desert Prince / Bacharach	Psd $2,000 Res $4,000		$0.00
943	C	F	Generous / Baez	Psd $14,000 Res $15,000		$0.00
944	B	C	Thunder Gulch / Baie des Chaleurs	Mr Chris Hausman	Palmerston North	$16,000.00
945	C	C	Sakura Seeking / Balfasching	Psd $9,000 Res $10,000		$0.00
946	B	F	Fly to the Stars / Balinchy	Mr Sd & Mrs Kj Alexander	Matamata	$14,000.00
947	C	F	Danske / Ballamanda	Mr Murray Baker	Cambridge	$12,000.00
948	B	C	Generous / Balleroo	Withdrawn		$0.00
949	B	C	Almutawakel / Balletia	United Bloodstock	Korea	$30,000.00
950	B	C	O'Reilly / Ballina Magic	Mr Roger Williams	Christchurch	$3,000.00
951	B	F	Danske / Bank Burst	Psd $16,000 Res $20,000		$0.00
952	B	C	Daggers Drawn / Banshee	Mr Dean Wiles	Malaysia	$32,500.00
953	B	F	O'Reilly / Barcombe Mills	Rogerson Bloodstock	Hamilton	$30,000.00
954	C	F	Danasinga / Barlisa	Psd $15,000 Res $20,000		$0.00
955	BR	C	Danske / Bay Doll	Mr Bruce Wallace	Auckland	$13,000.00
956	BR	C	Kaapstad / Bay Folly	Mr Gary Hennessy	Matamata	$24,000.00
957	B	F	Centaine / Beautiful Sea	New Zealand Bloodstock Ltd	Melbourne	$90,000.00
958	B	C	Prized / Beau Zena	Psd $24,000 Res $25,000		$0.00
959	B	C	Casual Lies / Belle Star	Beamish Bloodstock	Taupo	$47,500.00
960	C	F	Volksraad / Best of Times	K J Hickman	Christchurch	$45,000.00
961	B	C	Sandtrap / Better View	Withdrawn		$0.00
962	B	F	Desert King / Bibi Maizoon	Dr Gene Tsoi	Waikato	$25,000.00
963	B	C	Pins / Bicheno Gold	Mr Shane Kennedy	Christchurch	$12,500.00
964	B	C	Bahhare / Bis Cat	Sir James Lodge	Hamilton	$35,000.00
965	C	C	Sandtrap / Black Mist	Mr Dean Howard	Hastings	$20,000.00
966	G	F	Stark South / Blue Heaven	R T A Bloodstock	Victoria	$10,000.00
967	B	C	Cullen / Blue Paris	Psd $28,000 Res $30,000		$0.00
968	C	F	Prized / Blue Satin	C & C Company Ltd	Korea	$21,000.00
969	B	C	Danasinga / Blue Symbol	John Foote Bloodstock Pty Ltd	Queensland	$70,000.00
970	B	C	Danske / Blue Water Lady	Mr Ross Beckett	Invercargill	$12,000.00
971	C	C	Chief Bearhart / Bold Vision	Six Sigma Racing Ltd	Christchurch	$32,000.00
972	C	F	Align / Brancoli	Mr Dean Howard	Hastings	$18,000.00
973	C	C	Prized / Breath of Life	Mr Sd & Mrs Kj Alexander	Hamilton	$25,000.00
974	C	C	Kaapstad / Brief Courtship	Mr Bill Benson	New South Wales	$17,000.00
975	C	F	Deputy Governor / Brilliant Victory	Mrs Donna Logan	Northland	$30,000.00
976	B	F	Align / Brindillemousse	Mr Warren Bolton	New Plymouth	$50,000.00
977	C	C	Align / Brooke's Express	Rogerson Bloodstock	Hamilton	$28,000.00
978	B	F	Mujahid / Brulant	Mr Bruce Wallace	Auckland	$14,000.00
979	BR	F	Pins / Burwood Road	Rogerson Bloodstock	Hamilton	$90,000.00
980	B	F	Pins / Cajun Affair	Mrs Ml Murdoch	Auckland	$26,000.00
981	B	F	Volksraad / Calceolaria	Psd $25,000 Res $40,000		$0.00
982	B	C	Sandtrap / Calm As	Mr Kevin T Myers	Wanganui	$27,000.00
983	B	C	Bahhare / Calm Courage	Celebrity Thoroughbreds	Invercargill	$32,000.00
984	C	F	Bahhare / Calm Lover	Anzac Lodge	Cambridge	$33,000.00
985	B	C	Faltaat / Cantango	Mr Paul O'Sullivan	Matamata	$40,000.00
986	C	C	Bahhare / Captivating	New Zealand Bloodstock Ltd	Auckland	$16,000.00
987	BR	C	Cullen / Caranti	Mr Brian Jeffries	Bay Of Plenty	$28,000.00
988	B	C	Pins / Carla Rossi	New Zealand Bloodstock Ltd	Hong Kong	$55,000.00
989	B	F	Howbaddouwantit / Cascade	Mr Murray Baker	Cambridge	$18,000.00
990	B	C	Volksraad / Caserio	Mr Bob Emery	Auckland	$65,000.00
991	C	C	City on a Hill / Cayna	Mr Stephen Mckee	Auckland	$21,000.00
992	B	F	Carnegie / Cenphic	C & C Company Ltd	Korea	$10,000.00
993	B	F	Pins / Centakin	Mr Robert Burnet	New South Wales	$36,000.00
994	B	C	Carnegie / Centri Belle	Kevin Dagg Bloodstock	Victoria	$30,000.00
995	B	C	O'Reilly / Centro Star	Mr Dean Howard	Hastings	$35,000.00
996	G	C	Iglesia / Ceptor Smile	J & I Bloodstock Limited	Auckland	$35,000.00
997	BR	C	Daggers Drawn / Chameleon	Withdrawn		$0.00
998	B	C	Faltaat / Change Partners	Psd $17,000 Res $20,000		$0.00
999	G	C	Dracula / Chapel Light	Lisa Latta Racing Stables	Palmerston North	$20,000.00

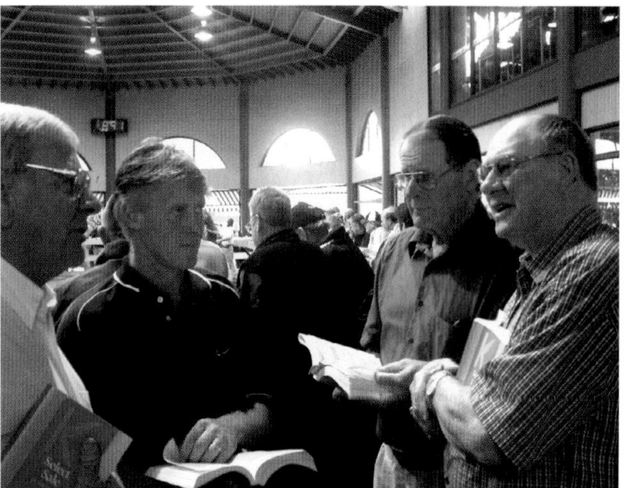
SONIA BRADFORD

In earnest discussion, well-known kiwi racing identities from left, John Davey, Richard Yuill, Peter Grieve and Colin Jillings.

Lot	Col	Sex	Breeding	Purchaser	Location	Price
1000	B	C	Success Express / Charybdis	Mr Bruce Wallace	Auckland	$26,000.00
1001	B	C	Carnegie / Chaste	Kevin Dagg Bloodstock	Victoria	$46,000.00
1002	C	C	Danasinga / Chataigne	Chipmunk Lodge Ltd	Invercargill	$11,000.00
1003	B	F	Mujadil / Chestnut Ridge	Withdrawn		$0.00
1004	BR	C	O'Reilly / Chezasinga	Chipmunk Lodge Ltd	Invercargill	$8,000.00
1005	B	C	Monolith / Chianina	Psd $36,000 Res $50,000		$0.00
1006	B	F	O'Reilly / Chicallina	Lisa Latta Racing Stables	Palmerston North	$15,000.00
1007	B	F	Green Perfume / China Girl	Mr Brian Jenkins	Cambridge	$34,000.00
1008	C	F	Chief Bearhart / Chosen Ploy	Mr Brian Jenkins	Cambridge	$33,000.00
1009	B	C	Mellifont / Clara Duthie	C & C Company Ltd	Korea	$24,000.00
1010	C	C	Bahhare / Clare Valley	John Foote Bloodstock Pty Ltd	Queensland	$20,000.00
1011	B	F	Cape Cross / Classic Call	Prudential Bloodstock	Cambridge	$20,000.00
1012	BR	C	Towkay / Classic Realm	Hale / S Marsh	Cambridge	$28,000.00
1013	BR	C	Almutawakel / Classy Liz	Mr Alan Jones	Cambridge	$18,000.00
1014	B	C	O'Reilly / Clockwork	Mr Paul Willetts	Auckland	$24,000.00
1015	B	F	Carnegie / Comely's Pride	Mr Ross Beckett	Invercargill	$14,000.00
1016	B	F	Mellifont / Conifer Bay	Psd $16,000 Res $17,000		$0.00
1017	B	C	Almutawakel / Cool Babe	Mr Dean Wiles	Malaysia	$30,000.00
1018	B	F	Chief Bearhart / Cool Rock'a	C & C Company Ltd	Korea	$20,000.00
1019	C	F	Volksraad / Coraletta	Galaxy Racing	Queensland	$20,000.00
1020	B	C	Deputy Governor / Country Classic	Mr Neville T Couchman	Cambridge	$27,500.00
1021	B	C	Centaine / Courtly Queen	Mr Lance Noble	Matamata	$25,000.00
1022	B	C	Desert Fox / Cousin Ann	Psd $6,000 Res $9,000		$0.00
1023	B	F	Align / Crest View	C & C Company Ltd	Korea	$17,000.00
1024	B	C	Danasinga / Crystal Brook	Mr John Sargent	Matamata	$28,000.00
1025	B	C	Carnegie / Crystal Rose	Psd $36,000 Res $40,000		$0.00
1026	C	C	Almutawakel / Culburra Beach	Mrs Ml Murdoch	Auckland	$35,000.00
1027	B	C	Deputy Governor / Culture Shock	Withdrawn		$0.00
1028	B	C	Volksraad / Curt	Psd $34,000 Res $35,000		$0.00
1029	BB	F	Generous / Dahlom	Paul Moroney Bloodstock	Matamata	$32,000.00
1030	C	C	Generous / Dainty Diva	The Robt Dawe Agency Ltd	Auckland	$43,000.00
1031	B	C	Towkay / Dancing Reason	Psd $28,000 Res $30,000		$0.00
1032	C	C	Stark South / Dans'ore	Hale / S Marsh	Cambridge	$30,000.00
1033	B	C	Faltaat / Danzapak	Mr Richard Collett	Auckland	$22,000.00
1034	BR	F	Prized / Daring Daphne	Psd $8,000 Res $10,000		$0.00
1035	BR	C	Cape Cross / Daulomani	Mr Mark Brooks	Cambridge	$10,000.00
1036	B	C	Chief Bearhart / Daylight Dawning	Mr Chen Zhichai	Indonesia	$13,000.00
1037	C	C	Stark South / Dazzle Me	Paul Moroney Bloodstock	Matamata	$54,000.00
1038	B	C	Sandtrap / Deceo	Mr Robert Priscott	Te Awamutu	$25,000.00
1039	C	C	City on a Hill / Deune	Galaxy Racing	Queensland	$20,000.00
1040	B	F	Prized / Diaga	Withdrawn		$0.00
1041	BR	F	Cape Cross / Diamond Fire	Mrs Donna Logan	Northland	$24,000.00
1042	B	F	O'Reilly / Disciple	Psd $9,000 Res $10,000		$0.00

Lot	Col	Sex	Breeding	Purchaser	Location	Price
1043	B	C	Stark South / Divvy	Mr Kevin T Myers	Wanganui	$15,000.00
1044	B	F	Stark South / Dolcezza	Mrs Johanna Bruniges	Queensland	$10,000.00
1045	C	F	Danasinga / Donna's Gold	Withdrawn		$0.00
1046	B	C	Desert Fox / Dot the I	New Zealand Bloodstock Ltd	Melbourne	$30,000.00
1047	BR	C	Lord Ballina / Double Babu	Withdrawn		$0.00
1048	BR	C	Haayil / Drambuie	Psd $19,000 Res $20,000		$0.00
1049	B	F	Fly to the Stars / Dream Bay	Argonaut Racing & Breeding Ltd	Te Kauwhata	$31,000.00
1050	B	F	Bahhare / Dresden Gold	Psd $10,000 Res $15,000		$0.00
1051	B	C	Iglesia / Dubai Century	Psd $22,000 Res $25,000		$0.00
1052	BR	F	Cape Cross / Durga Mai	Psd $20,000 Res $30,000		$0.00
1053	BLG	C	Centaine / Earina Lass	Withdrawn		$0.00
1054	BR	F	Kaapstad / Eastend	Withdrawn		$0.00
1055	C	C	Kaapstad / Easy Way	Psd $16,000 Res $25,000		$0.00
1056	BR	F	Danasinga / Ebony Heights	Mr Alan Jones	Cambridge	$21,000.00
1057	B	F	Brief Truce / Ebony Tudor	Fennessy & Associates Ltd	Dunedin	$50,000.00
1058	C	F	Made of Gold / Echo Beach	Jillings Yuill Racing Stables	Auckland	$35,000.00
1059	B	F	Desert Sun / Edradour	Stoney Creek Lodge	Wellington	$40,000.00
1060	BR	C	Danske / Elabama Star	Sanders Racing Stables	Te Awamutu	$28,000.00
1061	B	C	Faltaat / Electric Dream	Withdrawn		$0.00
1062	B	C	Colombia / Ellena Dawn	Mr Roger James	Matamata	$26,000.00
1063	B	C	Centaine / Epi Tahi	Sir James Lodge	Hamilton	$16,000.00
1064	C	C	Align / Equalizer	Posa'S Lodge Waikato	Cambridge	$26,000.00
1065	G	F	Last Tycoon / Ethel	Mr David Ellis	Ngaruawahia	$14,000.00
1066	C	F	Generous / Etoile d'Amore	Psd $44,000 Res $45,000		$0.00
1067	BB	C	Danske / Fabrication	C & C Company Ltd	Korea	$23,000.00
1068	B	F	Howbaddouwantit / Fairdale Lass	New Zealand Bloodstock Ltd	Matamata	$26,000.00
1069	B	C	Woodman / Fairy Princess	Psd $18,000 Res $20,000		$0.00
1070	B	F	Anziyan / Faithful Thought	C & C Company Ltd	Korea	$11,000.00
1071	C	F	City on a Hill / Falcons Fire	Psd $11,000 Res $15,000		$0.00
1072	BR	C	Ebony Grosve / Fanny Black	Mr Mark Sweeney	Te Awamutu	$27,000.00
1073	B	F	O'Reilly / Far South	Paul Moroney Bloodstock	Matamata	$17,000.00
1074	B	C	Volksraad / Fashionista	Mr John Wheeler	New Plymouth	$15,000.00
1075	B	C	Align / Fayette	Mr Kingsley Peach	Victoria	$90,000.00
1076	B	F	Elnadim / Fib's	Withdrawn		$0.00
1077	B	C	Almutawakel / Filament	Hale / S Marsh	Cambridge	$55,000.00
1078	B	C	Hennessy / Flaming Nature	Mr Shane Kennedy	Christchurch	$27,500.00
1079	B	C	Cullen / Flight Amal	Mr R N Elliot	Macau	$22,000.00

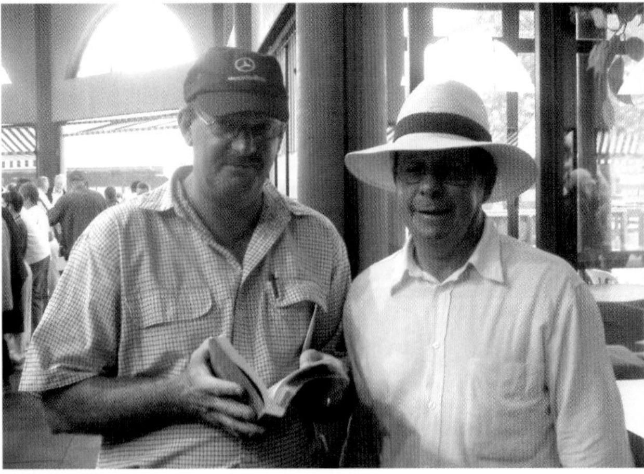

Bloodstock agent Stuart Hale and high profile trainer Bruce Marsh.

Lot	Col	Sex	Breeding	Purchaser	Location	Price
1080	B	C	Stark South / Flint Seal	Mr Russell Philp	New Plymouth	$10,000.00
1081	B	C	Align / Flying Features	Paul Moroney Bloodstock	Matamata	$55,000.00
1082	C	F	Stark South / Fly So Free	Mr Shaun Ritchie	Cambridge	$13,000.00
1083	BB	C	Desert Fox / Forbidden Poison	Danica Guy	Auckland	$3,000.00
1084	B	C	Centaine / Frau Zam	New Zealand Bloodstock Ltd	Cambridge	$24,000.00
1085	B	F	Sandtrap / Full Detail	Psd $24,000 Res $25,000		$0.00
1086	B	C	Pins / Funny Features	Dominion Bloodstock Agency	Waikato	$40,000.00
1087	BR	F	Fly to the Stars / Galore	Psd $16,000 Res $30,000		$0.00
1088	B	C	Cape Cross / Gardenia	Sanders Racing Stables	Te Awamutu	$190,000.00
1089	BR	F	Snippets / Garden Walk	Rogerson Bloodstock	Hamilton	$75,000.00
1090	B	C	Volksraad / Gillygate	New Zealand Bloodstock Ltd	Wanganui	$40,000.00
1091	BB	F	Zerpour / Golden Sound	Mr Iw Herbert	Palmerston North	$30,000.00
1092	B	C	Cullen / Goldilocks	Mr Sd & Mrs Kj Alexander	Matamata	$16,000.00
1093	G	C	City on a Hill / Gold Raider	Mr Greg Shirley	Auckland	$14,000.00
1094	C	C	Align / Got a Woodie	Hale / Wheeler	Cambridge	$30,000.00
1095	B	F	Volksraad / Grand Princess	Mrs Ann Gibbs	Matamata	$55,000.00
1096	BR	F	Deputy Governor / Grosvenors Pearl	Mr Sd & Mrs Kj Alexander	Matamata	$33,000.00
1097	B	F	Carnegie / Guiding Angel	Mr Mark Mullane	Auckland	$15,000.00

Waikato Stud grooms take a respite between parades.

THE HANGING OF MRS MOSS

A Rare Coincidence

Sometimes stories improve with the second telling. Sometimes they don't. That is why "The Hanging Of Mrs Moss", first published in David Bradford's weekly Sunday News feature "Inside Running", finds its way into this publication in its original form. Fairytales should never be tampered with and the outcome of the Bloomsbury Stud 1400 at Matamata on February 14 was in every sense of the word a fairytale come true.

The length of cord pulled tight. Thankfully there was little movement as the strong fibres took the full weight. Mrs Moss had been hung. Her feet were a full metre and a half from the floor. With life having now passed her by, her legacy would be a permanent niche in racing folklore.

The other Mrs Moss stood back, studied her handiwork and gave thanks to her two accomplices – husband Danny and friend Henrietta, dowager Duchess of Bedford.

No. This is not an extract from the latest Dick Francis novel. This is for real. Dick Francis stories are good. But never as good as the outcome of last week's Bloomsbury Stud 1400 at Matamata. For it was a photo decision to that race which saw the stud's owner, the Duchess of Bedford, present Mrs Moss with a painting of the duchess's beloved and world-famous mare – Mrs Moss. The trophy was a special gesture putting an extra focus on the upmarket breeding property just a kilometre from the racetrack.

Racing-mad Mrs Judy Moss, wife of local farmer and Matamata Racing Club president Danny Moss, had long had

Mrs Judy Moss with Mrs Moss.

her heart set on getting her hands on the other Mrs Moss. Family had been well and truly briefed that a portrait of the namesake would be hanging in the new home currently in the planning stages. Yet to be decided was just how Judy would procure it. Then providence intervened with a 24-carat golden opportunity.

Hot early favourite Amazing One, shortly bound for Hong Kong, was a shock scratching from the Bloomsbury Stud 1400 and Judy and Danny suddenly had new favourite Campari Belle running for them. After a tooth and nail battle with Star Of Rio, Campari Belle got Judy Moss into the hanging busi-

Campari Belle (No. 9) closing in for win over Star of Rio.

ness by a long head. No day at the races had been quite like it. Few trophies are likely to be more treasured.

So what's special about the equine Mrs Moss? Heaps. To begin with she had 15 foals – 12 got to the races and 11 won. Among them was Jupiter Island, whose 14 wins included the Japan Cup and other group wins in England, America and France. Precocious, Krayyan and Pushy were also group performers. It is a dynasty of which the Duchess of Bedford and her late husband Robin became immensely proud as it gave a new lustre to the Tavistock family's racing colours. The purple livery, with white stripes and black cap with a tassel, was first registered in 1791.

The duke, who died last year [2003], thought of Matamata as his second home to Woburn Abbey after becoming enraptured with its rural informality during a visit to New Zealand in the 1990s. Ten years ago, with the assistance of Matamata's famous O'Sullivan family, the couple set up Bloomsbury Stud, now comprising 116 hectares and home to 40 of the duchess's own broodmares. The latest addition to the broodmare band is a grand-daughter of Mrs Moss named Herself, who has been booked for two successive matings with Zabeel. Herself won the group three Nell Gwynne Stakes, while dam Pushy included among her wins the group two Queen Mary Stakes.

The Duke of Bedford's love affair with Matamata and its closely knit racing fraternity has been recognised by the duchess, who has taken over the sponsorship of the group two Matamata Breeders Stakes. This year the $70,000 juvenile fillies feature had its first airing as the Robin, Duke of Bedford, Matamata Breeders Stakes. It was the 35th running of what has become one of the jewels of New Zealand two-year-old racing.

WORLD'S RICHEST OF

Hong Kong Cup Day Extravaganza

By David Bradford

There is no racing jurisdiction in the world which comes close to matching the unique and fulfilling status of the Hong Kong Jockey Club. To begin with it's a dedicated charity fund-raiser from which nearly 200 charities get to share the equivalent of $NZ250 million a year – a mind boggling amount made possible by strict adherence to a business mission tied into the objective of being a world leader in horse racing and betting entertainment.

Already hosting the world's greatest day of turf racing every December, the HKJC has to a large degree achieved its objective. But its administrators see it only as a beginning. They want nothing less than total customer satisfaction for all stakeholders in the industry and the whole community. The essential stepping stone to making this happen has been identified as putting on a racing show which embraces the best horses, the best trainers and the best jockeys operating under the umbrella of an efficient and dedicated administration structure of the highest integrity.

New Zealand has long standing links with Hong Kong racing as a major provider of racing stock. Currently Shane Dye is one of the star jockeys and Greg Childs and Lance O'Sullivan are other riders to have made their mark there in recent years. Now the final link in the New Zealand connection has been forged with Paul O'Sullivan becoming the first Kiwi to be granted a trainer's permit.

O'Sullivan won ten New Zealand training premierships in partnership with his father Dave and in 2002/03 won his first solo title. Had it not been for his move to Hong Kong in June of 2004 he would have most likely picked up his second. Now the challenge is to re-craft his skills to achieve matching results in a totally new environment. Perhaps his greatest comfort rests with hugely successful transitions made by former Australian trainers David Hayes and John Size – Kiwis don't relish playing second fiddle to Aussies.

But he will have to make his own way. No one knows that better than his former champion jockey brother Lance who in three separate stints there rode more than fifty winners. Speaking of his own initiation to Hong Kong racing, Lance recalls: "From the time you step off the plane you've got to make your own luck. The competition is fierce and you get no favours."

So what awaited Paul – a 44-year-old champion at home – when he stepped off the plane to start a new career in what many consider to be the mecca of world racing?

First of all he had to go there in the full realisation he was the new boy on the block. It was like he had climbed down from the top of Mt Cook and was standing at the foot of Mt Everest – facing a completely new challenge in a completely new and unique environment.

Even the bookkeeping is unique in Hong Kong. The club provides all the staff and free stabling and the trainers live in an apartment complex on Sha Tin racetrack. Trainers receive a retainer for each horse in their stable and nine percent commission on stake earnings.

In the 2003/04 season, John Size's horses won $18 million which earned him the New Zealand equivalent of almost $1.5 million in percentages. At no time did he have more than 60 horses in his stable – the maximum allowed by the HKJC. Size was the leader in the money race but not the absolute standout. The top five on the trainers' table were all in the million dollar bracket. Hong Kong has flat tax rate of 15 percent.

Training in Hong Kong is labour intensive. One groom – known locally as a mafoo – is allocated to every three horses. They are among the best paid stable staff in the world. When housing, commissions and superannuation is factored in they

DAY
TURF RACING

HONG KONG JOCKEY CLUB

Jockey Frankie Dettori does his traditional flying dismount after winning the Hong Kong Cup.

factored in they earn around $NZ4550 a month. Each trainer has an allocated local Cantonese-speaking assistant trainer who copes with the problem of a large number of non-English speaking staff. Paul O'Sullivan was given the choice of three and after interviews said he would have been more than happy with any one of them.

But he was particularly impressed with the credentials of Raymond Tsui who landed the job. Tsui formerly worked for Alex Wong whose stable always had a sprinkling of New Zealand horses he had either bought here or had bred from a

HONG KONG JOCKEY CLUB

group of mares based at Highview Stud. Locals told O'Sullivan Tsui was one of the best assistant trainers in the business.

The other bit of early good news for O'Sullivan came when a new client told him he would eventually be getting the Stravinsky-Horlicks colt which had fetched $240,000 at the 2004 Karaka yearling sales. Horlicks, trained by O'Sullivan in partnership with his father and ridden by Lance O'Sullivan, had given the family one of its most cherished moments in racing when she won the Japan Cup.

The overall direction of the Hong Kong training setup is

under the control of expatriate Australian John Ridley, who took up the position ten years ago after becoming well-known to New Zealanders as the Auckland Racing Club's property manager.

Ownership also comes under rigid control in Hong Kong. Owners have to meet strict financial and integrity criteria and pay their bills directly to the HKJC. It is essential for them to be members of the HKJC and hold permits to import racing stock. All imports undergo strict veterinary inspection.

It is the carefully structured nature of Hong Kong racing which makes it so successful and such an important cog in the enchanting mix of eastern and western culture of the local society. Hong Kong Cup Day in December is more than just a celebration of the world's greatest day of racing on turf. It's a statement of pride, the exciting culmination of an invitation to the world to come not only to enjoy the racing but also the sights and sounds of one of the most vibrant cities in the world.

The invitation to visitors is an all-year, around-the-clock affair. Since Hong Kong ceased to be a British colony in 1997 and reverted to Chinese control, there has been a huge influx of mainland tourists. In October 2003 they accounted for 878,000 of the 1.67 million record total for the month.

October 2003 came as a great relief to the tourism industry after the disastrous downturn earlier that year brought about by the SARS epidemic. The attitudes of the Hong Kong Tourist Bureau run parallel with those of the Hong Kong Jockey Club.

At the time of the Hong Kong Cup the Tourist Bureau chief executive director Clara Chong said that while mainland visitors represented the biggest market and highest spenders, marketing had to be open ended.

"Maintaining a balanced portfolio of visitors from different markets is important both from a business perspective, to minimise risk, and as a way of ensuring Hong Kong retains its cosmopolitan, multi-cultural atmosphere in keeping with its status as Asia's world city," she said.

Those sentiments were clearly on display when visitors of western origin flew into Hong Kong in December for the Hong Kong Cup extravaganza. On November 27 the Hong Kong Winterfest had been launched to run through to January 4. Santa Claus and jingle bells were everywhere – a warm and friendly reminder of traditions developed during British colonial days.

Centrepiece of the festive decorations was the Christmas wishing tree standing 12 storeys – 33.5 metres tall – and lit in different colours by 28,000 light bulbs. As with so many Hong Kong activities the HKJC was enthusiastically involved. It was represented by the reindeer express – a miniature reindeer sleigh in motion and four full-size horse sculptures.

The street decorations flowed into hotels, bars, restaurants and shopping malls, creating an atmosphere making it almost compulsory for visitors to reach for their wallets and invest in the orient. On December 14, Rudolph the reindeer stepped aside and it was the day of the horse at Sha Tin.

Racing began in Hong Kong in the early 1840s and the HKJC was formed in 1884. Until 1971 it was conducted as an amateur sport at Happy Valley. Sha Tin, reclaimed from the sea, was opened in 1978. Constant upgrading has kept it as one of the most modern racecourses in the world, with a capacity for 80,000 fans; Happy Valley accommodates 55,000.

Delving into the betting activities of Hong Kong residents turns up some bewildering statistics. Between them Sha Tin and Happy Valley produce the highest betting per capita in the world to achieve an annual turnover of $NZ14.3 billion from 78 racedays and 710 races. Ten percent of that money is bet on-track; the rest through 100 off-track outlets or by electronic means. Four thousand telebet operators handle about a million calls a day.

Standing trackside and taking in the view of the massive Sha Tin grandstands is an awesome experience and never diminishes. The Hong Kong Jockey Club has 4200 permanent employees and another 15,000 casuals. They include 1000 chefs and assistants who on raceday provide for 23,000 members, visitors and the public.

In the course of a year 146,000 whole chickens are consumed, along with 18,000 lobsters, 350,000 pieces of sushi and sashimi, 90,000 bottles of vintage wine and 5000 kegs of beer. But the most popular dish among the always predominantly Chinese racegoers is a simple bowl of noodles.

New Zealand racing had one of its glorious moments in 2000 when Sunline gained a heart-stopping win over local idol Fairy King Prawn in the Hong Kong Mile. As a small band of Kiwis cheered on their own idol their voices were drowned by the chant of Prawn, Prawn, Prawn as Fairy King Prawn bravely but unsuccessfully cut into Sunline's precious lead. The Australian flag was raised when Falvelon won the Hong Kong Sprint. It was Australasia's day.

The following year the western world was rocked when Japanese horses dominated. But in 2002 Hong Kong racing imprinted itself on the world when local horses won three of the four features. It was a poignant moment at the media debrief at the end of the day when HKJC chief executive

Runners in the Hong Kong Vase turning into the home straight.

Another one! Tony Cruz (right) and jockey Felix Coetzee celebrate the win by Lucky Owners in the Hong Kong Mile following Silent Witness' sprint success.

HONG KONG JOCKEY CLUB

Jockey Dominique Boeuf (Vallee Enchantee) on his return to the scale after winning the Hong Kong Vase.

A magnificent fireworks display rounded off a magnificent day of international racing.

SONIA BRADFORD

世界馬壇盛會 香港國際賽事

WORLD CITY - WORLD SPORT

HONG KONG JOCKEY CLUB

Some of the international photographers covering the 2003 Hong Kong international races at Sha Tin.

HONG KONG JOCKEY CLUB

Falbrav's owners and jockey Frankie Dettori celebrate their great Hong Kong Cup win.

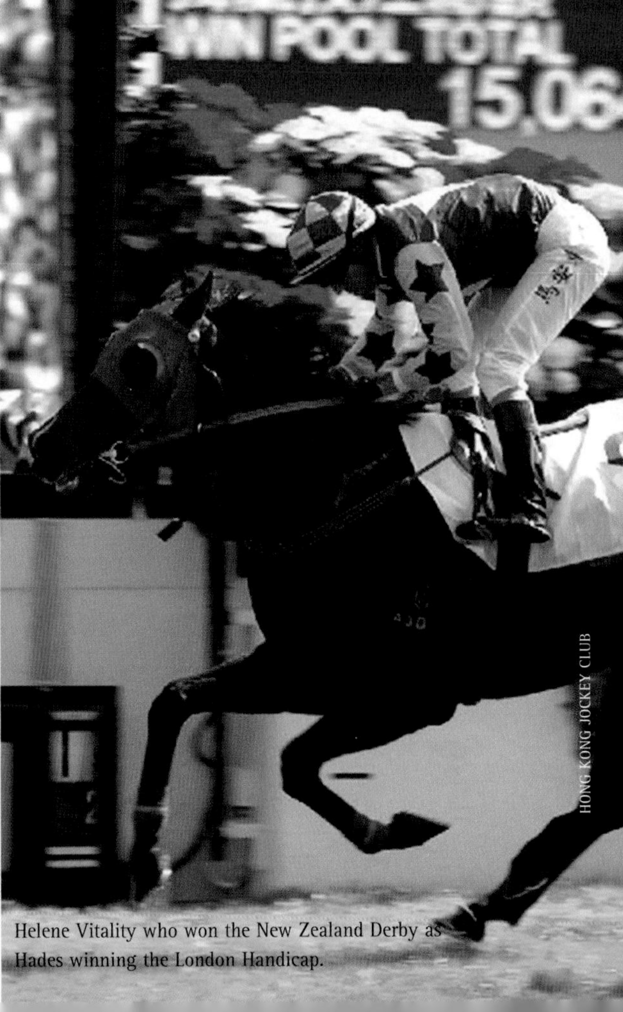

HONG KONG JOCKEY CLUB

Helene Vitality who won the New Zealand Derby as Hades winning the London Handicap.

Lawrence Wong and racing director Winfried Engelbrecht-Bresges opened the session with enthusiastic high-fives. Payday had at last come as reward for years of planning and investment.

It was to that background that Hong Kong Cup Day of 2003 unfolded into more stunning results for the locals. Afterwards an invited international media corps of 250 was reaching for more superlatives as it crafted reports about great horses and an even greater occasion.

Falbrav's easy win in the Hong Kong Cup, which cemented his claims to being the best horse in the world, should have been the lasting reminder of the day. But quite incredibly he was upstaged by a team of locals who captured two of the support group one races on the mouth-watering programme. The horses concerned were Silent Witness and Lucky Owners – their partners trainer Tony Cruz and jockey Felix Coetzee.

Australian-bred Silent Witness maintained an unbeaten 11-race winning sequence when he beat South African champion National Currency. New Zealand-bred Lucky Owners won the Hong Kong Mile, digging deep in his reserves of stamina to beat fellow local Bowman's Crossing and top class Japanese contender Lohengrin.

Lucky Owners is by Danehill from Miss Priority, a daughter of Kaapstad and herself a three-quarter sister to the champion Might and Power. He was bought at the Sydney Easter Sales from the Cambridge Stud draft by Tony Vasil on behalf of Leung Kai-fai. After the win Leung said he had decided on the name as he had personally selected the horse at sale time and because he was a lucky owner.

But there was more than luck attached to Tony Cruz becoming the first trainer to win two group one races on a Hong Kong Cup Day programme. It was a fitting tribute to the skills of a great horseman. Cruz, 46, is Hong Kong's favourite racing son. As a jockey he won six Hong Kong premierships while during the 1980s he was first jockey to the Aga Khan and rode the great Triptych in seven of her 13 European group one wins. What the locals love about him most is that he grew up in Hong Kong.

A star performer among Hong Kong jockeys since the 1990s, Coetzee had been absolutely confident about Silent Witness winning, describing him as the best horse he's ever likely to ride and arguably the best sprinter in the world.

In the minds of those present Falbrav's win in the Hong Kong Cup stamped him as at least equal if not better than world series winner High Chaparral. He was having his tenth group one start of the season and recording his fifth win of the campaign. On a glorious winning note he came into the full ownership of

BELOW: Local favourite Silent Witness (Felix Coetzee) captures the Hong Kong Sprint from South African runner National Currency.

BOTTOM: Jockey Tosten Mundry partners the New Zealand bred Figures to success in the Champions Mile.

Shadai Farms to stand at stud in Japan.

The remaining feature, the 2400 metre Hong Kong Vase, fell to the diminutive French filly Valee Enchantee, giving the French their fifth victory in ten runnings of the race.

New Zealand-breds were prominent in supporting races. New Zealand Derby winner Hades – racing as Helene Vitality – won for the David Hayes stable in the second race, Gem of India won race six and Figures race nine. Helene Vitality is a son of Zabeel, Gem of India is by Defensive Play and Figures, who raced so well out of the Colin Jillings and Richard Yuill stable as Marcurous, is by Maroof.

Paul O'Sullivan was not in Hong Kong for the 2003 international meeting, but famous jockey brother Lance was there as part of the media invasion. The pair have good reason – apart from friendship – for remembering now Singapore-based Australian trainer John Meagher. Back in 1985 Koiro Corrie May, trained in partnership by Paul with father Dave and ridden by Lance, lost the Melbourne Cup in the last stride to the Meagher-trained What A Nuisance.

Meagher was on hand for 2003 Hong Kong Cup Day and his comments about the best single day of racing on turf would have added fuel to Paul O'Sullivan's desire to become an active part of the scene.

HONG KONG JOCKEY CLUB

HONG KONG JOCKEY CLUB

TOP: French filly Vallee Enchantee (Dominque Boeuf) prevails in the international group one Hong Kong Vase with a 3/4 length margin over Polish Summer.

ABOVE: Jockey Frankie Dettori captures the Hong Kong Cup aboard Falbrav.

"It rivals the Melbourne Cup," Meagher said, while showing some surprise an Aussie could say such a thing. "It's the greatest single day of racing in the world – the world turf championship.

"I go to Royal Ascot every year and it's the greatest racing week, but this is the greatest racing day. You have to put it into categories like that," he told the South China Morning Post.

"It's without doubt the best single day's racing in the world."

Equally ecstatic about the Hong Kong Jockey Club's show was Taso Christoforou, multi-millionaire co-owner of National Currency, following his horse's defeat at the hands of Silent Witness.

"The whole show they put on, they way they treat their guests like royalty – it is the world's best," he said.

Despite the bigger money at Dubai – venue for the world's richest race – Christoforou was adamant Hong Kong was better. "Better atmosphere, better vibes."

The Hong Kong Jockey Club set some lofty goals in 1998 when setting a path toward international recognition. The hard yards have been travelled, the accolades now coming its way are richly deserved.

NAIL-BITING FINISH TO BIG FILLIES RACE

Matamata Breeders Stakes

By David Bradford

When you're running hot you're running hot. And nothing keeps the temperature up better than a slice of luck. The first piece of luck for the Tankard family of Cambridge came when Judy Tankard won the lucky draw for a $46,000 Class A Mercedes on the final day of the Ellerslie summer carnival. Only weeks later son Bryce trained the winner of the Robin, Duke of Norfolk, Matamata Breeders Stakes.

In a nail-biting finish, the Tankard trained Velasco won the group two race for two-year-old fillies by a whisker. Behind her success was a fine training feat performed by a member of a family steeped in racing. But Lady Luck again played a major part. With the filly still a maiden when race entries closed, Bryce Tankard didn't bother to nominate the Australian-bred but got the chance to reconsider when the Matamata Racing Club, faced with small numbers, extended the closing time. An eleventh-hour change of heart saw Melbourne owners and breeders Julian Sullivan and Julie Andrews collect the $43,750 winner's stake.

Unfortunately, the couple were not on hand to witness the win. On January 26, while attending the national yearling sales at Karaka, Velasco's owners had seen her finish third at Avondale. It was not the sort of effort suggesting a step up to group two company at her next start and certainly not the sort to indicate she could go to Matamata and give her rivals a beating after first giving them a start.

A chance ride for Andrew Calder when Gary Grylls opted to ride Can't Hackit in preference, Velasco missed the jump when rearing at the start and early on looked a 100 to 1

Velasco snatches victory in The Robin, Duke of Bedford, Matamata Breeders Stakes.

Keeninsky romping away with The Fairview Ford Slipper.

chance. But Calder kept a cool head, found all the right gaps when making his last-to-first run and hit the winning post locked with the Michael Walker-ridden Acupuncture. It was not until the photo gave Velasco the verdict by a nose that Walker was prepared to concede defeat. Can't Hackit was three-quarters of a length astern and following were Volk Dancer and the favourite Prickles. Steffi, who had made the long haul from Winton, apparently was feeling the stress of the trip and beat only one home in the 11-horse field.

Tankard was quick to declare Velasco's win the high point of his eight-year training career. But the 30-year-old wasn't exactly short on fond memories. He was able to recall the seven wins of Shatin Heights, including the 3200 metre Duke of Norfolk Stakes at Flemington. Then, of course, there was Dollars 'N Gold who notched 11 wins, 24 seconds and 10 thirds. Winning jockey Andrew Calder had some more recent fond memories, like winning the Avondale Cup on Regal Krona in December and the Wellington Cup on Cluden Creek in January.

The winner's co-owner Julian Sullivan manages the VOBIS stakes incentive scheme for Victoria Racing and is an active breeder, selling his colts and racing his fillies. Velasco was the result of the mating of his McGinty mare Vital Curves with Flying Spur.

Two-year-old colts and geldings are catered for on the Matamata programme with the $30,000 Fairview Ford Slipper, won in comprehensive fashion by emerging star Keeninsky from Shastri and the Southland runner Lotzatow.

The wayward Keeninsky had made an inauspicious start to his career with bolshie behaviour at his first two trials outings. The first at Taupo led to him being put aside for two months. Then on January 8 at Paeroa the stroppy colt bucked Allan Peard off and co-trainer Stephen Autridge responded by sending the pair around again in another heat, in which they finished third. Peard's part in getting Keeninsky under control was rewarded by him becoming the colt's regular jockey, winning with him at Trentham at his only start prior to Matamata.

Keeninsky was in total command in the closing stages of the Fairview Ford Slipper, winning by two and a quarter lengths. Later he was to emphasise his class further by winning the group three Two-Year-Old Classic at New Plymouth and the group one Manawatu Sires Produce Stakes.

BELOW LEFT TO RIGHT: Rick Wiley, manager of Bloomsbury Stud, Ginger Tankard, Andrew Calder, Danny Moss, The Duchess of Bedford and Bryce Tankard.
BOTTOM: Velasco returns to scale.

BROWNE STABLE DOMINATES

Great Northern Carnival

By David Bradford

As on so many previous occasions the Auckland Racing Club's Great Northern jumping carnival became the Ken and Ann Browne show. Apart from winning their ninth Mercedes Great Northern Steeplechase, they also snared the featured McGregor Grant Steeples, a supporting steeplechase and two hurdle races. The winning jockey on each occasion was Michelle Hopkins.

Two important hurdle races did elude the stable. The Friday Flash Great Northern Hurdles was won in dashing style by the versatile Cuchulainn and the Racing Minister's Hurdles went the way of Willie Montague at the expense of the Browne runner Drizzle.

The Browne camp takes a pretty phlegmatic approach to its big scale racing activities, but hearts were being worn on sleeves after Wanderlust's Great Northern Steeples triumph.

To begin with the winner was lucky to be alive, let alone taking out the southern hemisphere's most gruelling race, giving this ninth win in the great race more meaning to the Brownes than so many of the previous eight. After being down for the count not once but twice, Wanderlust's indomitable spirit had won over all adversity. He also vindicated a prediction made by Ken Browne four years earlier when he branded the horse a potential Great Northern winner after an 18-length win in a minor steeplechase at Ellerslie.

In 2000 Ken Browne was still riding and when he made his

Wanderlust takes the water jump during the Great Northern Steeples.

prediction for Wanderlust he had just ridden his 100th steeplechase winner. Now permanently on life-support following a horrendous training fall, he watched Wanderlust win from the fifth floor of Ellerslie's members stand and then, assisted by his caregivers, participated in the birdcage presentation ceremony. He may have been there in his capacity of co-trainer and co-owner but his smile had more than a little "I told you so" edge to it.

The Great Northern Steeplechase Ken Browne originally had in mind for Wanderlust was the 2001 event. But injuries were to put an end to those plans when, within a couple of months, Wanderlust bowed a tendon which required an implant. Being the resilient character he is, he bounced back within 12 months to win the Pakuranga Hunt Cup by 10 lengths. But the comeback was short-lived. He then broke a forearm and two vets believed he would have to be destroyed.

Ken and Ann Browne offered Wanderlust a lifeline. He was confined to his stable box and it was over to the horse to show the patience to allow the break to mend. After months of confinement he emerged structurally fit, but physically facing a long haul back to racing trim. Twenty months from injury time he was back racing. Though not forward enough for a tilt at the Great Northern, he won twice at Ellerslie in August. The most important of these wins was his second Pakuranga Hunt Cup and he followed up with a September win at Paeroa on national jumps day at the expense of Grand National winner Cuchulainn.

That show of form and his obvious liking for Ellerslie meant the Great Northern was more than a dream. Through the summer and autumn he did his muscle-toning hillwork on the Browne farm on the outskirts of Cambridge and in May had two leadup races at Te Rapa, including a third in the Waikato Steeplechase and, after a somewhat rocky run, another third in the Northern Trial at Ellerslie.

He was ready, but he was still faced with the task of beating sentimental favourite Golden Flare, who was seeking a third win to match the feat of Hunterville. In Wanderlust's favour was that in six encounters with Golden Flare he had finished in front five times. But Golden Flare was still very much on Ann Browne's mind when she gave Michelle Hopkins her riding instructions.

Ann Browne figured Golden Flare, if following his usual pattern of racing, would be at the rear with 1400 metres to run. He was also noted for his ability to make ground rapidly descending the famous Ellerslie hill. So, departing from convention, she instructed Hopkins to push the button going up the hill – usually regarded as suicidal tactics.

Said Hopkins afterwards: "Mrs Browne said if I could get far enough ahead, I would be down the hill when Golden Flare was still going up it." The instructions worked to perfection, with Wanderlust waltzing home by 14 lengths from the maiden Aquaria Dancer, with Golden Flare just half a head back third. Fifteen lengths further away, Cool Conductor headed the others.

Hopkins said the win had sparked more emotion within her than her historic deadheat in the race on Smart Hunter with Sir Avion in 2001. "He's just a brave, brave horse," she said. "To come back from the sort of injuries he's had is just remarkable. I'm so proud of him."

Appropriately the second-to-last jump in the Great Northern is the Ken Browne brush at the foot of the hill. When Hopkins was asked if she felt confident when so far clear at that point she said, "I wasn't sure where the others were and I daren't look back. I said, 'sorry buddy, we've got to keep going, I'll take a look after we get over the last' and that's just how it has to be. I didn't want to push him more than I had to – he'd given his all – but I couldn't take chances, either."

In the course of getting that all sorted with the media she dropped a bombshell, announcing her pending retirement and that she and fiance Jason Strawbridge had set a December wedding date. At the time with 106 jumps wins to her credit, she said she could ride for another 10 years and be no better off financially. "But I could end up with a lot of twisted and broken bones."

Listening in the wings with an approving smile was Strawbridge, who was probably thinking the Smart Hunter – Sir Avion deadheat hadn't been half bad either. Sir Avion had been trained by his grandfather Kevin O'Connor and it was during the after-race celebrations he had met his wife-to-be.

The first of the Brownes' Great Northern Steeplechase winners was Ascona, who won in 1977 and again in 1979. The next was Ardri in 1990, who in successive years was followed by Brother Bart and Lord Tennyson. Sydney Jones stepped up to the plate in 1995 and '97 and Smart Hunter deadheated in 2001.

Celebrating the win. Foreground: Ken Browne, Ann Browne and Michelle Hopkins. Rear: Lyn Stevens (ARC chairman), Ernie Ward (Mercedes/Benz), Graham Morgan (Morgan Furniture) and Auckland Mayor John Banks.

YOUNG ENOUGH FAST ENOUGH

Cuchulainn's Great Northern Hurdles Win

By David Bradford

Feelings ran deep when Cuchulainn missed out on an invitation to contest the Nakayama Grand Jump, the world's richest steeplechase. The primary reason given was an opinion he lacked the pace to be successful in Japan. Wrong, said trainer Bob Autridge, and instead of leaving it at that he hatched a plan to prove his point.

That plan was to win New Zealand's richest hurdle race, the Friday Flash Great Northern Hurdles. A couple of days before the event the plan looked to be going so well Autridge and some friends backed the horse at the $20 fixed-odds being offered by the TAB. Autridge's judgment was spot on. On raceday the fixed-odds price had tumbled to $9 while the totalisator dividend was $8.

The Cuchulainn camp is all smiles after dashing win in the Friday Flash Great Northern Hurdles.

In the previous winter Cuchulainn's wins had included the Wellington Steeplechase and the Grand National Steeplechase, a huge turn-around in form for a horse who had gone to Autridge as a rogue. Looking back two years, Autridge said it was really a case of Cuchulainn getting some of the aggro out of his system or going to the pet food factory. The pair now obviously have a huge respect for one another but genuine affection could be stretching the relationship to its limits. What is certain is that Autridge is a true horseman in the old sense of the word and Cuchulainn is a talented and game character to be respected in any company.

An intimate association has also been forged between Cuchulainn and regular jockey Finbarr Leahy. As Leahy is quick to remind people, the horse is named after a rugged and somewhat bloodthirsty Irish warrior. And those who listen are never in doubt from whence Leahy migrated to New Zealand four years ago. In the Great Northern Hurdles both horse and rider were at their best.

Leahy later admitted to going into the race with plenty of confidence and things went pretty well to script during the running. Patronage set up a suitably strong pace and Leahy delayed his run until the point of the home turn. Cuchulainn took the last hurdle in front and carried on to win by four and a half lengths from Al Burkan, who was making ground at the finish. Challenge, who had looked a real chance at one stage, wilted slightly to be third, ahead of Patronage.

For Autridge, a farrier before he became a horse trainer, it was his second training success in the Great Northern Hurdles. The other came in 1969 with Foxonewa, who remains his special favourite. Following that Northern win he took the horse to Trentham and, riding as an amateur against the professionals, added the Wellington Hurdles.

The big let-down was topweight My Willie Montague, who dropped out of the contest on the home turn. Trainer-jockey

Craig Thornton said the horse was making a noise and got the wobbles. It looked the end of the road for the injury-plagued jumper, but he gained one more day in the sun a fortnight later when winning the Racing Minister's Hurdles at the expense of Drizzle. After that a recurrence of his leg problems saw him retired with a record of five wins from eight starts over hurdles.

Drizzle, the mount of Michelle Hopkins, was the favourite for the Prime Minister's Hurdles by stint of two easy wins earlier at the Auckland Racing Club's spectacular winter carnival. But she didn't have to wait long to be in winning mode again when partnering the much improved Kia King in the Dilmah McGregor Grant Steeples. Like so many of the horses from the Ken and Ann Browne stable, Kia King was bought cheaply, this time for just $600.

Part of his appeal was that he belonged to the same family as the Auckland Cup winner Kia Maia. He didn't show a great deal of promise early on and his career was put on hold when he had to undergo tendon implants. Much of his preparation for the winter campaign was restricted to swimming and hour-long stints on a walking machine. Yet he was fit enough to win a minor steeplechase on the opening day of the Northern carnival and followed up with a 13-length win in the McGregor Grant. It was an effort which immediately pointed to him being a serious contender for the 2005 Great Northern Steeples.

The shock failure of the McGregor Grant was Golden Flare, chasing his third win in the event. He botched the water jump, which comes early in the race, and according to rider Clayton Chipperfield was never going well afterwards. He was retired without racing again. The other shock for punters was the early exit of Aquaria Dancer, who had run so bravely for second in the Great Northern. He, too, botched the water jump, causing his saddle to slip and rider Lance Macfarlane had no option but to pull the horse up.

Cuchulainn takes the last jump in the Friday Flash Great Northern Hurdles.

HASTINGS PROVIDI

Gold Jet and Fontera

By David Bradford

Wingatui steeplechaser Gold Jet and Wanganui hurdler Fontera had their supporters seeing double in July after they respectively won the Ashwell Farm Hawke's Bay Steeples and the Placemakers Hawke's Bay Hurdles. Back in May the same pair had won the Ecolab Waikato Steeplechase and the Dunstan Feeds Waikato Hurdles. Neither competed at Ellerslie's Great Northern jumps carnival.

Gold Jet didn't go into the Waikato Steeplechase favourite, but he was certainly the hottest talking point. At his previous start at Gore his rider Stewart Moir believed there was another lap to run and passed the winning post in second place with his mount full of running. At Te Rapa, trainers Brian and Shane Anderton replaced the suspended Moir with the vastly more experienced Tom Hazlett. After a ding-dong battle over the closing stages Gold Jet out-finished Doctor Heights by a long head, with a gap to subsequent Great Northern Steeples winner Wanderlust.

It was the first time Hazlett had ridden Gold Jet, but he's had a long-standing association with the Anderton family after being apprenticed to Brian. These days he's based in Methven after being one of Australia's foremost jumps jockeys. After the race Cool Conductor's rider Jonathan Riddell claimed Hazlett had interfered with his mount three fences from home and caused him to fall. Stewards studied films of the incident and said there was no case for Hazlett to answer.

In the Waikato Hurdles Fontera outpaced his rivals and outjumped them until the final obstacle when he gave rider Isaac Lupton a bit of a fright. The win was a little old hat for trainer Kevin Myers, who had won the 2001 contest with Stacey Jones and in 1986 with Doctor Sam. His father Bill won it with Even Terms in 1973 and Phrase in 1980, while brother Peter claimed the 1984 contest with Outright.

Fontera's own family ties are with the O'Leary brothers – Dan, Humphrey, Michael and Shaun – who farm at Whangaehu, just south of Wanganui. They are all dairy farmers and during recent flooding in the district one of their properties had suffered a million dollars' worth of damage so Fontera's win brought

RACE IMAGES, PALMERSTON NORTH

The dashing Fontera in full flight.

S DOUBLE DOUBLE

LEFT: South Island visitor Gold Jet on the way to victory in the Hawke's Bay Steeples.
BELOW: A jubilant Tom Hazlett after Gold Jet's big steeples win at Hastings.

about a most welcome change of fortune. A five-year-old by Kingsttenham – sire also of McGregor Grant Steeples winner Kia King – Fontera cost $7000 as a two-year-old and owes his name to a variation of the giant dairy company Fonterra.

When Gold Jet went to Hastings he was in familiar territory, having been bred there by Isabel Roddick, who retains an interest in the horse and who earned her niche in racing history by breeding Rough Habit. Tom Hazlett again rode Gold Jet quietly in the Hawke's Bay Steeples until the second to last fence where a huge leap signalled victory was in sight. Going strongly to the finish, he comfortably accounted for Great Northern Hurdles winner Cuchulainn, who was back to his normal role of steeplechasing. Third placed Doctor Heights was more than 12 lengths from the winner after leading through the middle stages.

Fontera was again too slick and too good for his rivals when scoring an easy end-to-end win in the Hawke's Bay Hurdles. He beat the hardy Al Burkan by five and a quarter lengths, while Narousa battled into third almost ten lengths further back.

GOOD SAMARITANS SAV

Paeroa

By David Bradford

Last winter cash-strapped Paeroa Racing Club looked to be at the end of the trail, down and out. One hundred and twenty years of history was about to go down the gurgler. Then three good samaritans emerged from the woodwork. The first was transtasman trainer Graeme Rogerson, who stepped up to the plate with a $200,000 interest-free loan. This quite magnificent gesture provided breathing space and the chance to explore a more permanent solution. Bearers of the solution were local identities Tony and Barbara Richards, who purchased the racecourse property for $900,000 and then leased it back to the club. The deal was struck in the name of the Barbara L. Anderson Family Trust, of which Tony and Barbara Richards are the trustees. The Richards name is firmly entrenched in the district with Tony Richards vehicle dealerships in Paeroa, Thames and Whitianga.

The lease is for a 15-year term worth $68,000 annually and includes a sponsorship of $15,000 each year. The trust owns other properties within the Waikato and Thames Valley region but has no plans for further racecourse investments. Though the 37 hectare Paeroa Racing Club property has a prime location, it was bought out of a desire to see it continue as a racing venue and community asset.

Graeme Rogerson had a matching desire to see racing continue at Paeroa, declaring racing had been good to him and he welcomed the opportunity to put something back. Throughout his colourful training career in New Zealand, Australia and briefly in Dubai, Rogerson has always sung the virtues of the New Zealand thoroughbred industry – backing his words by investing millions in New Zealand bloodstock. His contribution to racing was recognised in June when he was awarded the New Zealand Order of Merit.

The intervention of Graeme Rogerson and Tony and

TRISH DUNELL

TRISH DUNELL

TOP: Tony and Barbara Richards.
ABOVE: Graeme Rogerson.

Barbara Richards made safe National Jumps Day at Paeroa on September 7. A clash with Father's Day and wet weather was unfortunate but keenly contested racing further cemented a permanent spot on the racing calendar. The open steeplechase was won by Wanderlust, who went on to win the Mercedes Great Northern Steeplechase, while the open hurdles victor Oliverdance went on to contest the Nakayama Grand Jump in Japan.

PAEROA RACING CLUB

Oliverdance after winning the big hurdles in the colours of raceday sponsor Sunday News.

KIWIS TAKE THEIR PLACE IN AMERICAN OAKS

Hollywood Park Classic

By Mike Dillon
Photos: Hollywood Park

There were a lot of reasons why James Cassidy was thrilled with Ticker Tape's dashing win in the US$750,000 American Oaks. One of them was to wash away the memory of his beloved New York Yankees being beaten for the second consecutive day by the Mets.

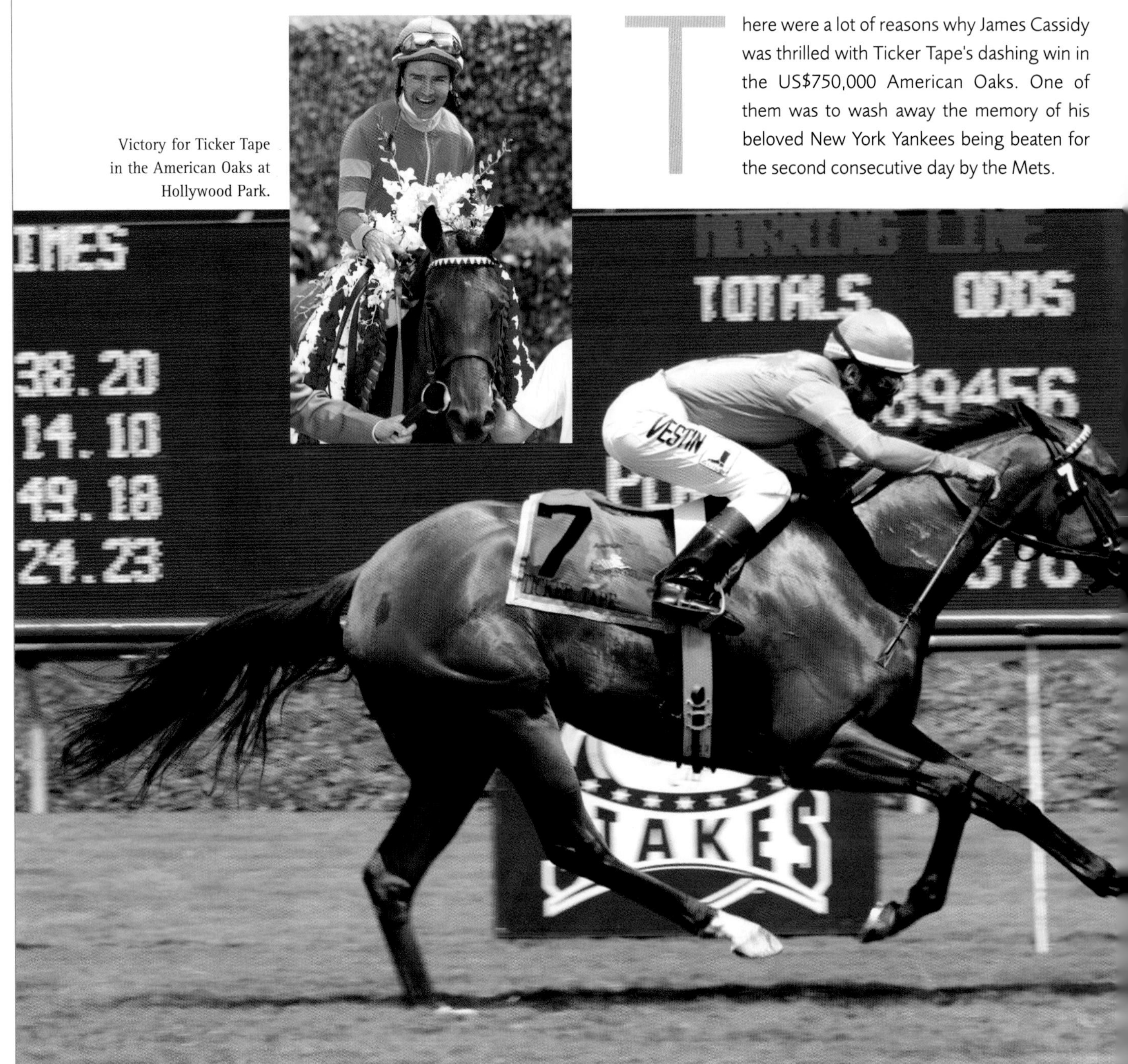

Victory for Ticker Tape in the American Oaks at Hollywood Park.

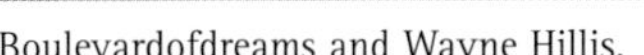

Boulevardofdreams and Wayne Hillis.

Racing to the wire in The American Oaks.

Nothing can erase bad thoughts quicker than your first Group One victory as a trainer.

Cassidy is 58, but the first win at racing's highest level did not take as long coming as you might think – he was an assistant trainer for many years then left that side of the industry to work in the veterinary field for 10 years. He has been training less than 10 years.

The New Zealand thoroughbred industry was also looking over its shoulder in the American Oaks.

July saw just the third running of the race and Boulevardofdreams was New Zealand's first runner.

She was invited into the race via her third placing in the AJC Oaks at Randwick at Easter, along with French Lady, who was second in the Sydney event. After that race French Lady was bought by a client of Californian trainer Neil Drysdale.

Remarkably, New Zealand had a third runner, Eternal Melody, who has been sold to leading trainer Bobby Frankel from Kevin Hughes' Riccarton stable.

It's just as well horsemen are fatalistic, or Boulevardofdreams' trainer Wayne Hillis would have had an inferiority complex in California.

Stabled alongside Boulevardofdreams was the American Oaks entry Dance In The Mood, who some make a case for as the best filly in the world.

Boulevardofdreams was a $6000 paddock purchase and Dance In The Mood earned US$1.7 million in just four unbeaten performances leading up to her fourth in the Japan Oaks before leaving for the United States.

Dance In The Mood is owned and raced by Shadai Race Horse Syndicate and obviously will never be on the market, but the Japanese put a value of US$10 million-plus on her.

That may have increased significantly had she won the American Oaks, as many expected her to do.

On Hollywood Park's tight inside track it was always going to come down to tactics – everyone agreed the horse with the best run was pretty much going to get the job done.

Like a lot of Hollywood scripts, this one ran true to form.

The horse with the best run won, but it was not Dance In The Mood.

Local rider Kent Desormeaux saw to that. It was obvious that to win this race, a filly had to produce a lightning 200m sprint somewhere close to the home turn. Desormeaux cut loose on Ticker Tape approaching the bend and appeared to catch Yutaka Take on Dance In The Mood by surprise.

That was the end of the race right there, but Take was adamant afterwards that Ticker Tape had boxed him in before she cut loose and that if you reversed the runs, Dance In The Mood would have won.

Desormeaux had his own hard luck Hollywood Oaks stories to tell – he was first over the line in the inaugural running in 2002, but lost the race on protest after some dramatic interference to the runner-up.

"Yeah, I've got my history in this race, most of which I'd like to forget," said Desormeaux.

Boulevardofdreams held her end up well for New Zealand.

When Wayne Hillis and New Zealand jockey Gary Grylls walked the track two days before the race, they agreed that to maximise any chance the Kiwi filly would need to be in the best part of the track at the 400m – which was three widths out from the rail – and pushing forward before straightening. Also, that to come from the tailend was going to be next to impossible.

Turning for home in the American Oaks.

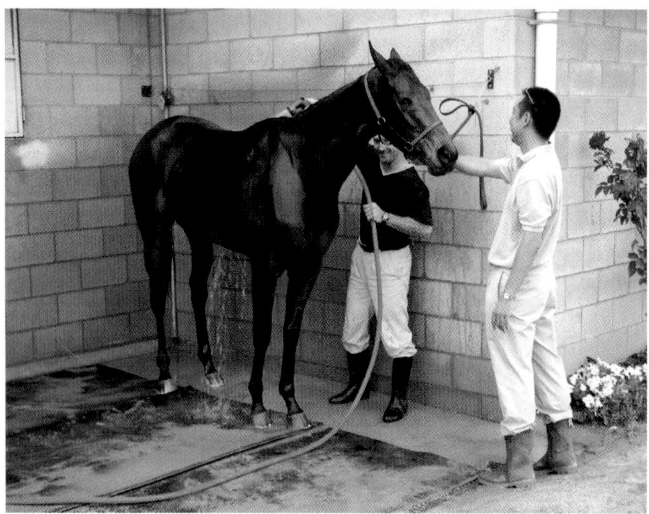

Boulevardofdreams gets a hose down before the big race.

Unfortunately, Boulevardofdreams clipped the side of the barrier stalls when the start was made, had her momentum checked sufficiently to see her settle in the back four.

From that point it was self-defeating for Gary Grylls to look for a run wide out and down the back straight committed himself to staying in close.

To finish seventh under those circumstances was a very sound effort for a filly who lacked that fraction of zip-sprint required to win on the grass tracks of California.

It showed that New Zealand will be extremely competitive in the race in coming years.

A NEW FACE FOR NORTHERN RACING?

Clubs to pool resources

By David Bradford

In the last few days of the 2003/04 season sweeping administration changes were looming, including the 19 clubs from Taupo north being welded into a defined northern region. Within that region there would be three cluster groupings, modelled largely on the highly successful TRAC consortium.

The clubs comprising TRAC are Bay of Plenty, Rotorua, Matamata, Te Aroha and Taupo. Thames and Paeroa come within the new cluster grouping although they are separate from TRAC. The Waikato cluster covers the Waikato, Cambridge, Waipa and Taumarunui clubs, while the northern one comprises Auckland, Avondale, Counties, Whangarei, Dargaville and the Pakuranga Hunt.

TRAC has been the trendsetter in showing how individual clubs can benefit from joining with others to maximise assets and commercial opportunities. A key factor in TRAC's success has been the fact that all the clubs involved have retained their own identities and committees. That philosophy will continue within the clusters and over the extended regional concept.

Guy Sargent, chairman of New Zealand Thoroughbred Racing and the proponent of the cluster concept, had always perceived it should grow over a period of three or four years

Surprize Surprize garlanded after Te Aroha group one win.

Sunray, winner of The Centra Rotorua Challenge.

TRISH DUNELL

to a broader regional model. Naturally he was immediately supportive when clubs north of Taupo expressed a willingness to begin with the ultimate model.

At the change of season the clubs concerned were working through the nuts and bolts issues. A major among those issues was whether the one cheque book would be in the hands of the three clusters or the regional administration. Then there was the management structure. The early preference was for a regional board plus three cluster boards to deal with day-to-day issues confronting particular clusters and the individual member clubs. What wasn't wanted was the creation of an unwieldy bureaucracy.

The desirability of putting a regional spin on the presentation of New Zealand racing has been strongly mooted for more than fifty years but proponents of the concept have generally fought a losing battle against parochialism. Declining attendances and a constant battle for meaningful sponsorship have at last given the old maxim "united we stand, divided we fall" a place in racing. Hopefully it is made clear in the new season it is a philosophy here to stay.

Obviously that spirit was already alive and well with TRAC in 2003/04. Accounting for 25 percent of the race meetings held north of Taupo, it paid $3,198,000 in stakes and staged seven group races. The most important of these prestige events was the group one $120,000 New Zealand Bloodstock Breeders Stakes (won by Surprize Surprize) at

Surprize Surprize (rails) powers home to win The NZ Bloodstock Breeders Stakes.

Te Aroha. Matamata chimed in with the Robin, Duke of Bedford Matamata Breeders Stakes (Velasco), New Zealand's most important race for two-year-old fillies and holding group two status.

Group two races were also run at Tauranga and Rotorua – the $100,000 Westernbay Finance Japan/NZ Trophy (Silky Red Boxer) and the First Sovereign $80,000 Rotorua Cup (No Fibs). Also at Rotorua, Pay My Bail won the group three Lion Red Plate and Sunray the group three Centra Rotorua Challenge, while at Tauranga Just Aqua claimed the group three Tauranga Stakes.

With member clubs all claiming financial benefits, TRAC certainly proved to be on track. Now the highway beckons.

TOP: Pay My Bail (Lee Rutherford) scored in the Lion Red Stakes at Rotorua.
ABOVE: Japan/New Zealand trophy winner Silky Red Boxer poses with Heather Weller.

HIGH EMOTION AND A BIG SHOUT

International Day Te Rapa

By Aidan Rodley

TRISH DUNELL

When the best horses in the land front on the same day on the same track race-goers go along breathing expectation. That was the case at Te Rapa in February – with all expectations exceeded. In a day of spectacular racing Lashed, Sedecrem and Taatletail all turned in breathtaking performances.

The photo decision which gave Lashed victory over Penny Gem in the $100,000 Whakanui Stud International plunged owner and Cambrige Stud principal Sir Patrick Hogan into a state of euphoria. He'd been dreaming of plucking some money from friend and rival breeder Tim Bodle, whose breeding operation had sponsored the race.

"I've really been waiting for this – getting some of the Bodle money, " he chuckled as he set off to lead Lashed back to scale in the company of grandsons Liam and James Hunt. Of course, besides the friendly banter with his mate, Hogan was also quick to appreciate the significance of having another group one win behind the name of the Encosta De Lago mare who one day would be joining the Cambridge Stud band of broodmares. That sort of result also tends to get studmasters hyped up.

While Sir Patrick continued to jibe Bodle for hours after the trophy presentation, the other group one feature created mayhem among a different section of the vocal Te Rapa crowd.

Euphoric after Sedecrem's tenacious Waikato Draught Sprint victory, part-owners Ernie Ward and Peter Walker, in their acceptance speech, announced they would shout $3000 of the sponsor's product over the public bar. The pair, who race Sedecrem with Winston McDonald and Colin Giltrap, received the loudest cheer of the day for their gesture, especially from a large group of young men in uniform t-shirts as they made haste for the bar.

"It's been so much fun – you've got no idea. One thing's for sure, I won't be driving back to Auckland," said Ward, chief executive of Daimler Chrysler, and like his co-owners a driver of a Mercedes – which backwards spells Sedecrem.

And it was no less of a party atmosphere for connections of Taatletail, winner of the International day's third feature race, the Cambridge Stud Sir Tristram Fillies Classic.

Painter-decorator Dean McLuckie, a one-sixth part-owner in the filly, reckoned he had half of Huntly on course to celebrate Taatletail's win and there was certainly a large crowd gathered around the barbeque and convoy of chilly-bins his mates had assembled.

"Brilliant, that's unbelievable," said McLuckie after the group two 2000m win. "This is our day. We've brought our beers and our barbeque. There's half of Huntly here and that's just great for the races . The 2000 metres was no worries and she's the best filly in New Zealand bar no-one today.

"I was just shaking after the race – I thought I was going to have a heart attack. We'll be partying all night now, I can tell you."

But the carnival atmosphere around the racecourse was not without reason – the action on the track was straight from the top draw.

It took a withering late sprint from the Graeme Rogerson and Stephen Autridge-trained Lashed to just haul in Penny Gem in the final stride. Already a group one winner of the Captain Cook Stakes earlier in the season, Penny Gem and rider Michael Coleman established what looked like a winning break only for Lashed and Opie Bosson to grab them with a perfectly timed finish.

The mare's will to win even caught Bosson by surprise.

"I had the rest of the bunch covered but I couldn't get to

TOP: Sir Patrick and Lady Hogan accompanied by grandsons Lian and James Hunt share the moment with Lashed.
TOP LEFT: Taatletail proves superior in Sir Tristram Fillies Classic.
BOTTOM: Part owner Ernie Ward leads Sedecrem and jockey Grant Cooksley back to scale.

Penny Gem until the very last stride. That was a huge effort," he said afterwards.

In the stand, Sir Patrick had all but given up hope. "Fifty metres out I took my eye off her and looked at the post and hoped it would move further forward," he said. "It's a fairytale because we bought her for $80,000 and she's now won us almost $1 million."

Coupled with Lashed's success, Taatletail's remarkable Sir Tristram Fillies Classic win made for one of the most satisfying days of Autridge's training career.

"It was a fantastic day," Autridge said later in the week. "My head was on the chopping block with Taatletail in more ways than one. There were people saying she wouldn't go 2000 metres, especially since she hadn't raced for six weeks and when she was beaten at Ellerslie there were a lot of people quick to knock her.

"That's how you always picture it but it never seems to work out that way. That's her – as good and as game as you'd ever find. I didn't gallop her on Thursday, which Rogey said I should have. His words were, 'Well, she wouldn't want to stop.'

"It's very satisfying. And for her to win on the same day as Lashed was just enormous. The Hogans have been pretty good clients for me; even before I came here they supported me. They owned Singalong, who won the Sir Tristram Classic for me three years ago."

Regular rider Michael Walker was again astounded at Taatletail's resilience.

"It's like having a V8 motor under you with her," he said. "When I want her to kick she doesn't just kick, she just won't let the others past. She's just so tough. She's such a pleasure to ride. She was up against it but she's proven she's the best filly in the land. She's done that on her ear."

Taatletail's win secured her the title of New Zealand Bloodstock Filly of the Year but it was to be her final race. She was humanely destroyed after a tragic stable accident less than three weeks later.

Sedecrem's sprint win was no less meritorious. Against arguably the best domestic field assembled in the 2003/04 season, the Colin Jillings and Richard Yuill-trained gelding turned in something special.

Ridden by globe-trotting Auckland jockey Grant Cooksley, Sedecrem as usual got back and was still at the rear of the field with 300 metres to run. Angled into the clear, he unleashed his characteristic sizzling finish to overtake a host of group one-performed sprinters on the outside and score by one and a quarter lengths.

It was Sedecrem's 11th win from 24 starts and his second group one success, following his Easter Handicap victory at Ellerslie the previous season. His winning stake of $62,500 took his career earnings past $420,000.

Afterwards Jillings revealed Sedecrem's farrier Kevin Crampton had made alterations to the way he shod the gelding, whose notorious hooves needed a filling of fibreglass to enable him to race. In the past Crampton had shod Sedecrem then added the fibreglass filling but in the month leading up to the race he had filled the hoof with fibreglass then nailed the shoe into the filling.

Jillings paid credit to Crampton's work but also made no secret of his own admiration for the horse.

"What a great performance. He's a marvellous horse," Jillings said. "He's not a hard horse to train, except for his feet."

But it was Ward who summed the galloper up best. "He looks like the Six Million Dollar Man at his front feet but he's got the motor of a $5 million Mercedes."

NEW BLOOD

"A LONG TERM COMMITTMENT TO BREED AND RACE SUCCESSFUL WORLD CLASS BLOODLINES"

A new owner, the purchase of a 150-acre neighbouring property, and the start of an on-going expansion programme is set to establish The Oaks Stud as one of Australasia's top stud farm properties. Already The Oaks has increased the original broodmare band of 42 young mares to more than 80 mares heading into the 2004 breeding season.

With world-class facilities and land holdings of more than 350 acres, The Oaks Stud has set out to achieve sustained growth in the business. As well as the acquisition of young mares the Stud stands foundation stallion Traditionally and has more recently purchased the dual Gr. 1 winning 2YO Spartacus, who stands his first season at The Oaks Stud in 2004. Always looking to the future the brilliant Gr. 1 winning two year old Keeninsky has also been purchased for stud duties at the conclusion of his racing career.

AT THE OAKS

THE OAKS STUD **STALLIONS**

The only Group One winning son of Champion sire Mr Prospector standing at stud in New Zealand. Sire of outstanding first crop foals in 2003. Stands his third season at The Oaks in 2004.

Dual Group One winning son of champion sire Danehill. The only son of Danehill to win two Group One races in Europe in 2002. Stands his first season at The Oaks in 2004.

BROODMARES

The Oaks Stud has built up a collection of over 80 of the finest Northern Hemisphere-bred mares purchased from the United Kingdom, Ireland, France and the United States coupled with a carefully selected line-up of Australasian mares to form a truly international broodmare band.

RACING TEAM

The brilliant Gr. I winner **Keeninsky** will race for The Oaks this season together with a number of well bred fillies including such quality families as:
Zaria (Zabeel - Snow Quill) Full sister to Queensland Oaks winner Zagalia
Blooming (Stravinsky - Down The Avenue) Full sister to Shaftesbury Avenue
Evana (Entrepreneur - Miss Trump) Out of a 1/2 sister to Lohnro and Niello.

GROUP ONE WINNERS ARE IN OUR BLOOD

For all enquiries contact Rick Williams (General Manager, The Oaks Stud) 021 733 962

THE OAKS STUD

RD3 Cambridge New Zealand. Phone 64 7 823 3026 Fax 64 7 823 3019
Email oaks.stud@xtra.co.nz Website www.theoaksstud.co.nz

POMP AND GLORY'S EASTER PARADE

Big metric mile win

By David Bradford

Pomp And Glory collects the coveted Easter Handicap.

Ellerslie's Easter Handicap remains New Zealand's most important metric mile – even if overshadowed by Sydney's corresponding race, the Doncaster Handicap. One horse, Sleepy Fox, achieved the incredible feat of winning it four times from 1944 after the incomparable Kindergarten had ushered in that decade by wining in 1941 and '42. And although there were no Kindergartens or Sleepy Foxes in the 2004 edition, it was still a reasonably slick field.

On the day, Pomp And Glory proved the slickest of them all. But the race began and ended in drama. To begin with, Pomp And Glory's owners replaced regular rider Lynsey Hofmann with Opie Bosson, who had become available when he failed to make Rodrigo Rose's weight. The training partnership of Allan Jones and Brett McDonald were not overly impressed by the switch. Hofmann was openly brassed off but her feelings were partly soothed when she bet $100 each-way on the winner and collected $565. However, it was not quite like riding a group one winner.

Pomp And Glory is raced by retired Perth businessman Terry Crommelin and Aucklander John Clydesdale. Unfortunately, Crommelin had to put celebrations on hold to rush back to Perth to be at the side of his wife, who had suffered a heart attack only hours earlier. Happily, the news on arrival was good.

It had been an eventful time for Crommelin, who had originally expected to see Pomp And Glory contesting the Doncaster Handicap. Instead, when it became apparent on the preceding Tuesday the horse was not going to make the Sydney field, he was switched to the Easter Handicap.

Digesting the fact that Pomp And Glory had covered the 1600 metres in 1:32.9, Jones was quick to declare Pomp And Glory would have been highly competitive in the Doncaster. Though he conceded Opie Bosson had ridden a good race, he remained staunchly in support of Hofmann and said the horse would have still won had she been the rider.

One positive Jones took from Pomp And Glory's win was the breaking of a jinx. The Easter Handicap had been something of a hoodoo race for him after Bay Sovereign and Mr Sovereign had both run seconds and Cool Deal notched a third. At last Jones had an Easter Handicap to go with his two Auckland Cups, a Railway Handicap and a New Zealand Derby.

The Paul O'Sullivan-trained Diamond Like set a fast pace for the Easter Handicap and Pomp And Glory swept past her with 250 metres to run. Just short of the line he started to gawk and Rodrigo Rose, ridden by the Australian Reece Wheeler, got to within half a length. Almost in line next was Jetski, recording his third successive third in the race. There was a break of a length and three-quarters to Travellin' Man, who ran on, and the weakening Diamond Like.

The New Zealand breeding fraternity knows Terry Crommelin best as the man who introduced the Mr Prospector blood to New Zealand through the sires Straight Strike and Cache Of Gold. But he perhaps deserves equal praise for the level of perseverance he showed to breed a group one winner from the stakes performer Aptitude, whom he bought off Aucklander Henry Norcross for $10,000.

Between 1986 and 1999, Aptitude slipped or missed eight times. Her first two foals were born dead. It was not until her tenth year at stud that she produced a live foal. There were only two more and Pomp And Glory (from the second-to-last crop sired by Pompeii Court) was the last of them. Then more patience was called for when Pomp And Glory had to have bone chips removed from both front fetlock joints.

The Easter Handicap was Pomp And Glory's eighth win from just 17 starts, with his best beforehand the group two Jerry Clayton Classic during the Ellerslie summer carnival. His big winter assignment was the Stradbroke Handicap in Brisbane but he dropped out over the closing stages after being one of the early leaders.

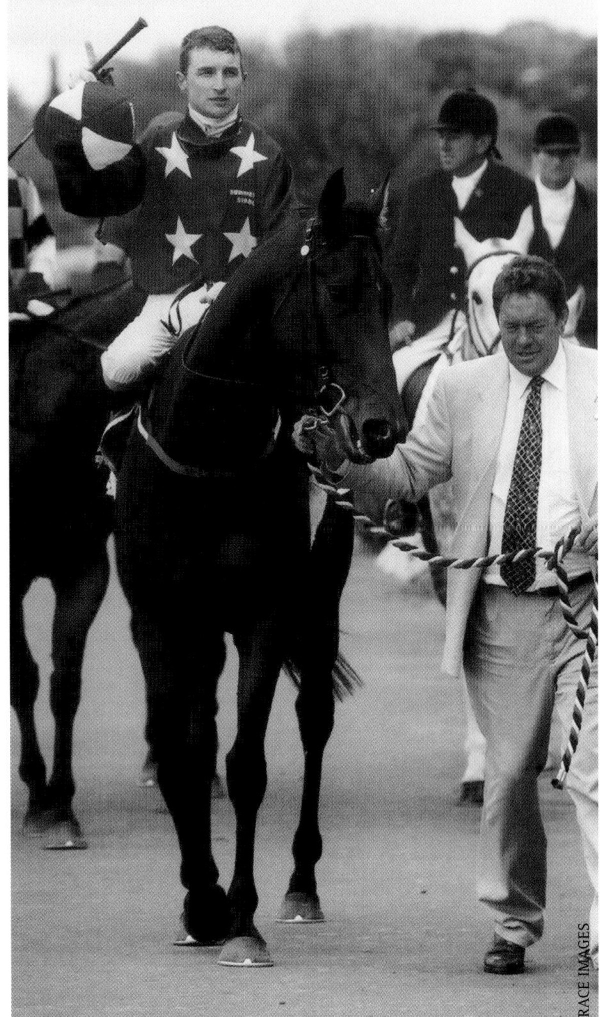
RACE IMAGES

AUCKLAND RACING CLUB

TOP: Part-Owner John Clydesdale leads Pomp And Glory in after Easter Triumph.

ABOVE: Terry Crommelin.

NEWSMAKERS AND EVENTS

Summary of comings and goings

By David Bradford

August

LANCE O'SULLIVAN RETIRES

Twelve times New Zealand champion jockey Lance O'Sullivan announced his retirement, quitting while still at the top with a record 2479 wins and holding every record on offer. No other jockey had won so many premierships, he had collared every group one race in New Zealand, won most prizemoney, had won most races at Ellerslie, scored the fastest 100 winners in a season and on six occasions rode six winners on a programme.

For all that, perhaps his greatest achievement was coming back from life-threatening injuries suffered in an horrific race smash at Moonee Valley in 1997. Two years later, against all odds, he returned to the saddle to win three more premierships. He made a winning debut as an apprentice at Te Awamutu and ended his career with a winning treble at Tauranga. The highlight of his remarkable career was winning the Japan Cup on Horlicks when it was the world's richest race. In a short semi-retirement he worked as a Trackside comments man and then before season's end branched out as a trainer when brother Paul vacated Wexford Stables to move to Hong Kong.

TRISH DUNELL

Lance O'Sullivan.

BRAVE BATTLE LOST

Former jockey Neil Hain lost his life, aged 46, to crippling injuries sustained in a training accident. Big flat wins for the versatile horseman were the Auckland and Wellington Cups on Secured Deposit and the Avondale Cup on Eva Grace. The best jumper he rode was Airmond on whom he won the Grand National Hurdles at Riccarton and the Hiskens Steeples in Melbourne. Neil is survived by wife Jill, daughter Cherie and jockey son Daniel.

BIG JACK SAYS FAREWELL

In Australia, especially around the traps in Sydney, Jack Ingham was known as Big Jack – simply because he was a larger-than-life figure in racing and commerce. He died 50 years after he and brother Bob took over the family poultry business which as Ingham Enterprises grew to be one of the most successful family-owned ventures in Australia. The brothers – known as the chicken kings – approached racing with the same zeal. Their Crown Lodge and Woodlands Stud spearhead a thoroughbred operation second in size to only that of Dubai's ruling Maktoum family, which operates under the Godolphin banner.

The combined annual turnover of the Ingham chicken and thoroughbred activities is $1.2 billion and not long before Jack Ingham's death he and his brother were estimated to have a joint personal wealth of $800 million. Two of Jack Ingham's most treasured thoroughbreds were the New Zealand bred Octagonal and his son Lonhro. New Zealanders figured strongly in his wide circle of friends, who enjoyed the warmth of his companionship and appreciated the significance of the Ingham company slogan of "Doing the right things and doing things right" which was so manifested in Jack himself. Jack Ingham, man of commerce, man of racing and philanthropist died aged 75.

September

WEATHER MAN RULES

The weather couldn't keep out of the headlines in September as it dealt two cruel blows to the Hastings spring carnival. In the original script the best horses were headed for Hastings on August 23 for the very good reason that at that time of the year there's a better chance of good spring footing than anywhere else. Wrong. Rain washed out the meeting and the group one Mudgway Partsworld Stakes (won by Miss Potential) had to be included in the Wanganui programme. That meant a whole heap of horses had to have their racing programmes rescheduled. But worse was to come. The Hastings meeting on September 13, featuring the group two Glenmorgan Generous Stakes (Irish Rover) and Highview Stakes (Taatletail) was also hit by bad weather and had to be transferred to Otaki. By September 27 the sun had finally broken through in Hawke's Bay and it was the racing fraternity and not the farmers who were smiling when Distinctly Secret romped away with the Kelt Capital Stakes.

AUCKLAND RACING CLUB

Paul Moroney.

SOLD TO AMERICA

Matamata bloodstock consultant Paul Moroney negotiated the sale of three-year-old filly Katana to America for $1 million. The Matamata Breeders Stakes winner, who had also pushed Maroofity so close in the Manawatu Sires' Produce Stakes the previous season, had originally been bought by Moroney as a yearling for Tauranga owners Alan and Christine Abel. The new American owners are John and Jerry Amerman, who bought Happyanunoit from Moroney to win three grade one races for them. Katana is by Volksraad from the Sir Tristram mare Tristean.

BARRED FROM BETTING

The TAB initiated some surprise headlines about the previous season's champion two-year-old Maroofity when he was barred from fixed-odds betting for the Wanganui Guineas. This meant the second placed horse would be regarded as the winner if Maroofity performed as expected. He didn't, running sixth, with Stardane being the winner from Wee Winkle and Green Machine.

October

NEW BONUS SCHEME

In an industry joint venture, the New Zealand Thoroughbred Bonus Scheme was introduced to replace the former New Zealand Bloodstock Mercedes Super Bonus Series and the FAMIS Series. Behind the innovation were the New Zealand Racing Board, New Zealand Thoroughbred Racing, the New Zealand Thoroughbred Breeders' Association and New Zealand Bloodstock Ltd. The scheme has been designed for every foal crop being able to compete for 180 bonuses. Level A bonuses are worth $15,000 and level B $7500. Much of the funding comes from the New Zealand Racing Board and the remainder from an $1125 entry fee. When enrolments closed in July there were some 700 entries.

SUNLINE IN FOAL

Champion mare Sunline was reported safely in foal to seven-time group one winning stallion Rock Of Gibraltar. It was her second covering after failing to conceive first-up to the Coolmore shuttle stallion, who stands his southern hemisphere season in New South Wales.

ROSINA LAD WINS

Rosina Lad gave Levin trainer David Haworth his biggest thrill in racing when winning the group two Waterford Crystal Mile at Moonee Valley. Successful jockey Greg Childs said the addition of blinkers was a crucial factor in Rosina Lad's win – his first in Australia after eight from 13 starts in New Zealand.

WANDERING DAYS OVER

International jumps jockey Craig Thornton returned from a three-month stint in Japan to announce his wandering days were over. "It was an experience riding in Japan and very rewarding financially, but it's great to be back home," he said. "It was just too tough emotionally being away from my family that long." Thornton secured his financial security as America's

TRISH DUNELL

Craig Thornton.

champion jumps rider and later in the season he and jockey wife Trudy bought Jim Gibbs' Parkvale Farm to set up their own training and agistment operation.

November

HALL OF FAME

Australian trainer David Hall hit the world's racing headlines when Makybe Diva won the Melbourne Cup for South Australian owner Tony Santic. That day he would probably would have been happy to accept that as the crowning glory of his career. But it got better. In May the Hong Kong Jockey Club granted him the final available permit to train there – giving him a toehold on some of the most lucrative racing in the world.

JACK BENNETT

One of New Zealand's most influential racing administrators between 1980 and '92, Jack Bennett died in Palmerston North on November 15. A local barrister and solicitor, he was a one-time president of the Manawatu Racing Club and joined the TAB board in 1972 then later became chairman of both the TAB and the New Zealand Racing Authority. Initiatives introduced during his days in administration included the TAB taking a shareholding in Radio Pacific, establishing Action TV (now Trackside) and the restoration of racecourse amenities. The family association with racing administration continues with his eldest son David being vice-president of the Manawatu Racing Club and his nephew Guy Sargent the chairman of NZ Thoroughbred Racing.

ZIRNA SUPREME IN SINGAPORE

Westbury Stud's Zirna bathed herself in more Singapore glory when winning the $1.5 million Singapore Gold Cup, just three weeks after she had taken out the Raffles International Cup. The winning mount went to Mark Du Plessis, the former Zimbabwean who was then stable rider for the mare's Singapore trainer Malcolm Thwaites. Since then Thwaites has relocated to Macau, Du Plessis has returned to New Zealand and Zirna (to become Singapore's horse of the year) has retired after failing to acclimatise early into a Dubai campaign.

TRISH DUNELL

Zirna.

December

HAPPY BIRTHDAY KAREN

AUCKLAND RACING CLUB

Karen Fursdon.

Matamata trainer Karen Fursdon was handed the best possible birthday present when Upsetthym won the Hamilton Stayers' Plate at Te Rapa on December 13. "That settles that," she said. "She can go for the Auckland Cup now. She'll have no weight and the way she rolls along they could have a job picking her up." Prophetic words indeed. Next time out she won the Queen Elizabeth Handicap and then, of course, the Auckland Cup.

ANOTHER WIN FOR BUSTLING BILL

There was a special twist to Him A Gotta Go clearing maiden ranks at Awapuni on Boxing Day. One of his owners was jockey legend Bill Skelton, these days immobilised by a stroke suffered in 1994. Bill Skelton's bustling style saw him win more races in New Zealand than any other jockey apart from Lance O'Sullivan. Numerous big races also fell to him in Australia. On retirement from riding he set up as a trainer at Levin, where one of his good winners was Carpark Flyer, dam of Him A Gotta Go. Carpark Flyer was raced by Cliff and Betty Condren of Wellington who gifted Skelton a share in her foal by Al Akbar.

RACING REVAMP

New Zealand Thoroughbred Racing boss Guy Sargent announced plans for an administration revamp for 70 individual clubs. His proposal was that New Zealand be divided into five largely self-governing clusters. The regions would be bulk funded and share one chequebook. The fine-tuning process was still underway at season's end.

January

DAVID LLOYD STEPS DOWN

Thirty-three years of racing club administration came to an end on January 17 when David Lloyd stepped down as chief executive of the Auckland Racing Club. He left big shoes to fill. Few administrators have had such a sound industry knowledge from grassroots up. His grounding came with 14 years as secretary of the Te Aroha Jockey Club, then eight years as chief executive of the Canterbury Jockey Club, followed by 15 months as director racing with the Macau Jockey Club.

He was head-hunted by the Auckland Racing Club at a time when it was facing massive financial problems – a $23 million debt and a mountain of deferred maintenance. He left with the debt cleared, money in the bank and an effective maintenance programme in place – plus a huge amount of industry respect. That respect spread to other racing jurisdictions. At various global conferences he delivered papers in Bangkok, Macau, South Africa, Australia and Japan.

TRISH DUNELL

David Lloyd

Lloyd's successor, who took up his duties in June, was Chris Weaver, formerly an executive with Lion Breweries and until his appointment a director of the Auckland Racing Club.

SIMON COOPER ARRIVES

If New Zealand racing lost an old hand when David Lloyd quit, the industry was immediately to welcome a new one when Simon Cooper was appointed assistant chief executive of New Zealand Thoroughbred Racing. The brief of the been-there-done-that Englishman was to enhance communications, public relations, industry profile, ownership initiatives and encourage the NZTR board's "The Way Forward" programme. Everything was on the list except how to enjoy the trout streams, snow capped mountains and the toheroa beds. But Cooper has been pretty successful at answering challenges.

He's worked in the racing media, with the International Racing Bureau – promoting races such as the Japan Cup, Hong Kong Cup and English Derby – and then for eight years was at the coal face of lifting Hong Kong racing to its present international status. England had lost its appeal when he went back there to live and he believes New Zealand will be a better place for himself, wife Alex and children Adam (11) and Joel (7). For the sake of New Zealand racing, hopefully Alex, Adam and Joel will get to ski Ruapehu, catch a trout in Lake Taupo and munch a toheroa fritter in the carpark at the Dargaville races.

February

NEW APPOINTMENT

A global search for a CEO for the new Racing Board (the merger of the TAB and Racing Industry Board) ended with the appointment of Graeme Hansen. A New Zealander who had been living in Canada, Hansen went to the job with extensive top-level experience in banking. He had headed Barclays Bank in Canada, Australia and New Zealand and most recently had been CEO of Barclays private banking in London. Other baggage taken into his new position is a broodmare and a couple of horses in training.

In announcing the appointment, Racing Minister Damien O'Connor said it was great to see a talented New Zealander returning home to face the challenge of reinvigorating racing.

HAPPY EVER AFTER

The Sunday papers of February 1 carried one of those happy-ever-after stories which crop up from time to time in racing. It centred around Matamata trainer John Sargent who had watched his $20,000 yearling purchase Successor plough through the mud and rain the previous day to win the $500,000 Mercedes Super Bonus Classique. Originally he had bought the horse as a spec, but when there were no takers he was left to race Successor himself.

Even so he was lucky to be still the owner after Hong Kong buyers, only four days before the race, had turned the gelding down as being too small. It was Sargent's biggest win since landing the Magic Millions Classic with Vedodara in the late 1980s. In between times he had been based in Malaysia, where he won two training premierships, but these days he's firmly established at Matamata.

AUCKLAND RACING CLUB

Bridgette O'Sullivan

ELLERSLIE AMBASSADOR

There were plaudits all round for the Auckland Racing Club when it appointed Bridgette O'Sullivan as the club's special ambassador to promote the thrills of racing to the younger generation and encourage ownership. The wife of famous jockey turned TV comments man (and now trainer) Lance O'Sullivan, Bridgette O'Sullivan not only possesses great people skills but is actively engaged in ownership.

March

MICHAEL PREPARES FOR WALKABOUT

In an interview with leading Auckland racing writer Mike Dillon, published in Thoroughbred Racing Monthly, superstar apprentice Michael Walker, a newsmaker from day one of his career, offered a glimpse into his personal life and his hopes for the future as his apprenticeship wound down. As well as speaking of investments such as a 21-acre pre-training operation just outside New Plymouth and an apartment block in Auckland, he spoke also of the maturity which developed during his riding stint in Hong Kong, which provided only two winners. "It brought me back to earth; made me realise there's a world out there bigger than New Zealand."

He spoke warmly of the Sharrock family – Allan, to whom he was apprenticed, and Bruce, who was his manager. He rated ill-fated filly Taatletail as the best he had ridden and how upset he was when he learned of her death. "She was a very special horse to me. When we went across the finish line in her last win at Te Rapa this enormous emotion overcame me. I turned around and Mark Sweeney was right behind and I yelled 'I love this filly' and Mark said, 'I know'. The photo of me kissing her when we were coming back made the newspapers and I really meant it."

Another meaningful quote from the article was, "When I finish riding I want people from everywhere to say, 'remember that good rider from New Zealand' – but I don't want to be big-headed." By the time Walker's apprenticeship ended in May he was already set to ride in Melbourne under the management of Bruce Clark – also manager of Damien Oliver. Immediately successful and following his motto of "Have saddle, will travel" he journeyed forth on a raid to Queensland and won the Brisbane Cup on Danestorm.

BRUNO CANNATELLI

Michael Walker

BET OF THE MONTH

An unnamed expat Australian living in Hong Kong had a $1 million bet on Lonhro to win the Australian Cup. It was placed with Sportingbet and when Lonhro won he collected $1.55 million. For Lonhro, a son of New Zealand-bred champion Octagonal, it was his 25th win from 33 starts. But it came the hard way, as he was pocketed at a crucial stage of the race and Darren Beadman only got him up in the last stride.

April

ONE THOUSAND WINNERS

April 17, 2004, is a date Palmerston North-based jockey Darryl Bradley will never forget as the winning mount on Sun Hawke provided him with his 1000th winner in New Zealand. This significant milestone had come from 8191 mounts and had amassed $9.15 million in stakes. Among the thousand wins were group one successes on Avedon in the New Zealand Two Thousand Guineas and the Bayer Classic and another 41 at group two, group three or listed status. Bradley's extended career tally also includes the group one Doomben Cup, on Sapio in 1997. In the 1998/99 season he won the New Zealand jockeys' premiership with 133 wins, 28 ahead of Opie Bosson.

RACE IMAGES, PALMERSTON NORTH

Darryl Bradley

NEW RATINGS SYSTEM

The April meeting of New Zealand Thoroughbred Racing approved a critical change to the handicapping system – the introduction of a ratings-based handicapping system for implementation on August 1, 2004. From that point handicappers will give each horse a domestic rating figure to which interested parties can compare ratings given to horses of a similar class. The main significance of the move is that owners and trainers will be able to assess the quality of their own horses and the opposition before nomination time.

The system will make it easier for trainers to place their horses to best advantage and have access to vital information. It should also prove an important guide to clubs in framing programmes. There will be computer capacity to update ratings every two days.

DEATH OF ROBERT SANGSTER

The overriding theme of obituaries for Robert Sangster were that his life revolved around wine, women and winning. Certainly a website www alwaysmypleasure@anytime.com would not have gone astray. But, as bountiful as his love life and socialising might have been, it will be his racing activities for which he will be longest remembered. At the height of his success he had about a thousand horses at stud or in training in England, Ireland, America, Venezuela, Australia and New Zealand.

Leading British owner five times between 1977 and '84, his northern hemisphere wins included two English Derbys, four Irish Derbys and three Prix de l'Arc de Triomphes. Among his many Australian wins were the 1999 Victoria Derby with Blackfriars.

In the 1970s he went into a partnership with John Magnier and Vincent O'Brien in Coolmore Stud, Tipperary. The trio tried to corner the Northern Dancer line, buying yearlings at the Kentucky sales. Their breathtakingly bold plan was to secure all the best colts with the potential to become classic winners and ultimately high profile stallions. There were some significant failures, but two who filled expectations were Caerleon and Sadler's Wells.

Sangster saw breeding simply as a commercial venture. "Horseflesh," he once said, "is a very commercial currency, an asset, unlike property, that can always be shifted." He was the son of Vernon Sangster, founder of Vernon's Pools, the family company he sold in 1988 for $270 million.

His romantic adventures meant he was seldom out of the gossip columns. In 1978 he ended his 18-year marriage to former model Christine Street to take up with Susan Peacock, wife of Australian politician Andrew Peacock. This second marriage was a fizzer.

In 1982 he became involved with Mick Jagger's consort, Texan model Jerry Hall and in 1985 Susan Lilley, daughter of Peter Lilley, head of the Lilley and Skinner shoe empire, became the third Mrs Sangster. He was generous with his money, loved champagne, helicopters and private planes and women. But most of all he loved thoroughbreds.

May

FAYETTE PARK PUT ON MARKET

The superbly appointed and picturesque Fayette Park stud was placed on the market by David and Maisey Benjamin. The world-class 132 hectare property is the result 16 years of hard work and forward thinking by the Benjamins. Their reward came when Fayette Park became breeder of the year in 2003 after earlier nominations in 2000 and '01. Since the sale of the property the Benjamins have relocated to Cambridge, where they are standing Postponed and Don Eduardo but generally operating on a much smaller scale.

HALL OF FAME

The late Jack Ingham, his brother Bob and their trainer John Hawkes were all inducted into the Australian Racing Hall of Fame on May 20. The success of the trio is spelled out in a few simple statistics. Hawkes, at the time of his induction, had trained 70 group one winners, for Woodlands Stud 35. In the 1998/99 season, Hawkes-trained horses won $11.2 million and in the 1999/2000 season he set an Australian record of 315 wins.

LURE OF HONG KONG

Paul O'Sullivan had been keeping tight-lipped but at last the rumours were confirmed that he was answering the call to train in Hong Kong. At the same time the question of what was to become of Wexford Stables was answered. Paul's successor was to be his famous jockey brother Lance, who would start his training career under the fatherly eye of, mentor of both, retired icon trainer Dave O'Sullivan.

TRISH DUNELL

Paul (left) and Lance O'Sullivan.

June

LEGEND LOSES CANCER BATTLE

When Awapuni trainer Noel Eales died, aged 73, racing lost one of its finest trainers on record. But more than his ability to train winners, Noel Eales will be remembered for his personal qualities. He was loyal to those he trained for and to those who worked with him. He was respected for his integrity, dedication, uncompromising work ethic, attention to detail, the warmth of his company and willingness to pass his great knowledge on to others.

His career in racing began in 1943 as an apprentice and came to a halt in 1949 because of increasing weight with a modest 13 winners on the board. He began training in 1954

Noel Eales

and quickly met with success. When ill health forced him to take a break in 1971, he went to Sydney with the intention of holidaying with Syd Brown, who was enjoying a great innings there with Classic Mission and Triton. Brown, because things were going so well for him in Australia, decided to settle at Warwick Farm and for six months Eales was his foreman. That was the stepping stone to him returning to New Zealand and setting up shop again at Brown's former Woodville stables. During the 1982/83 season he relocated to Awapuni.

In nearly 50 years Eales trained 1352 winners, placing him fifth on the all-time list. On Australian forays he won the 1986 Caulfield Cup with Mr Lomondy, the 1993 Mackinnon Stakes with The Phantom and the 1987 O'Shea Stakes with Our Silver Elm. Quite incredibly he trained most winners on eight different tracks – Trentham, Hastings, Awapuni, Waipukurau, Waverley, Tauherenikau, Otaki and Hawera. He enjoyed 20 wins at group one level, but probably his favourite horse was Commissionaire, who didn't make that grade but racked up 21 wins. His vast contribution to racing was recognised in 2001 when he received the "Contribution to Racing Excellence" award at the Mercedes annual awards dinner.

SOME CONSOLATION

An unusual each-way bet paid off for Windsor Park Stud in Brisbane's famous $1 million Stradbroke Handicap. Windsor Park principal Nelson Schick had spent six months yearning for a group one win for exciting emerging star Falkirk. The first setback came when he went sore and had to be scratched from the Telegraph Handicap. Then after scraping into the Stradbroke field he raced erratically and finished out of the money. But that was of little consequence to Windsor Park. The winner was their newly acquired stallion Thorn Park, scoring the first group one win of an already high profile career.

WEDDING BELLS

Two high-profile racing personalities joined in wedlock on June 26 with the marriage of David Ellis and Karyn Fenton. Principal of the Te Akau racing empire and a director of New Zealand Thoroughbred Racing, Ellis hit the headlines in the summer when paying $1.1 million for the Danehill-Grand Echezeaux colt at the national yearling sales. Fenton is group communications manager for Tower Ltd, but thousands of racegoers know her much better as a longstanding Trackside presenter.

July

TRENTHAM ABANDONED

Disastrously heavy track conditions forced the Wellington Racing Club to cancel its major winter raceday, leaving no running of the Wellington Steeplechase, Wellington Hurdles, Parliamentary Handicap and Whyte Handicap. Club president Ron Dixon said the financially troubled club would lose $20,000 through not racing – but would have lost substantially more if it had proceeded then had to abandon the meeting partway through the card. Dixon also said the writing was on the wall for future winter meetings at Trentham. In future, he said, meetings at the track should be scheduled between October and May.

LISA CROPP

Lisa Cropp

Lisa Cropp made a winning return to race riding at Pukekohe, two years after suffering life-threatening injuries in a fall at Macau. The Cambridge-based rider, who rates as New Zealand's most travelled jockey, has more than 700 career wins. The last time she had appeared in public as a rider was in the role of assistant clerk of the course.

SINGAPORE CONTRACT

Talented apprentice Jason Waddell accepted a three-month contract to ride for Laurie Laxon in Singapore. At the time of the arrangement Laxon was leading in the Singapore trainers' premiership, with his closest rival the Australian John Meagher.

BRUNO CANNATELLI'S FOCUS ON KIWIS IN OZ

Action across the Tasman

By David Bradford
Photos by Bruno Cannatelli

A pair of three-year-old fillies salvaged what had been an ordinary season for Kiwi-trained gallopers in Australia when winning the South Australian and Queensland Oaks. They were the Murray Baker-trained Dowry, who starred in Adelaide, and Vouvray, who

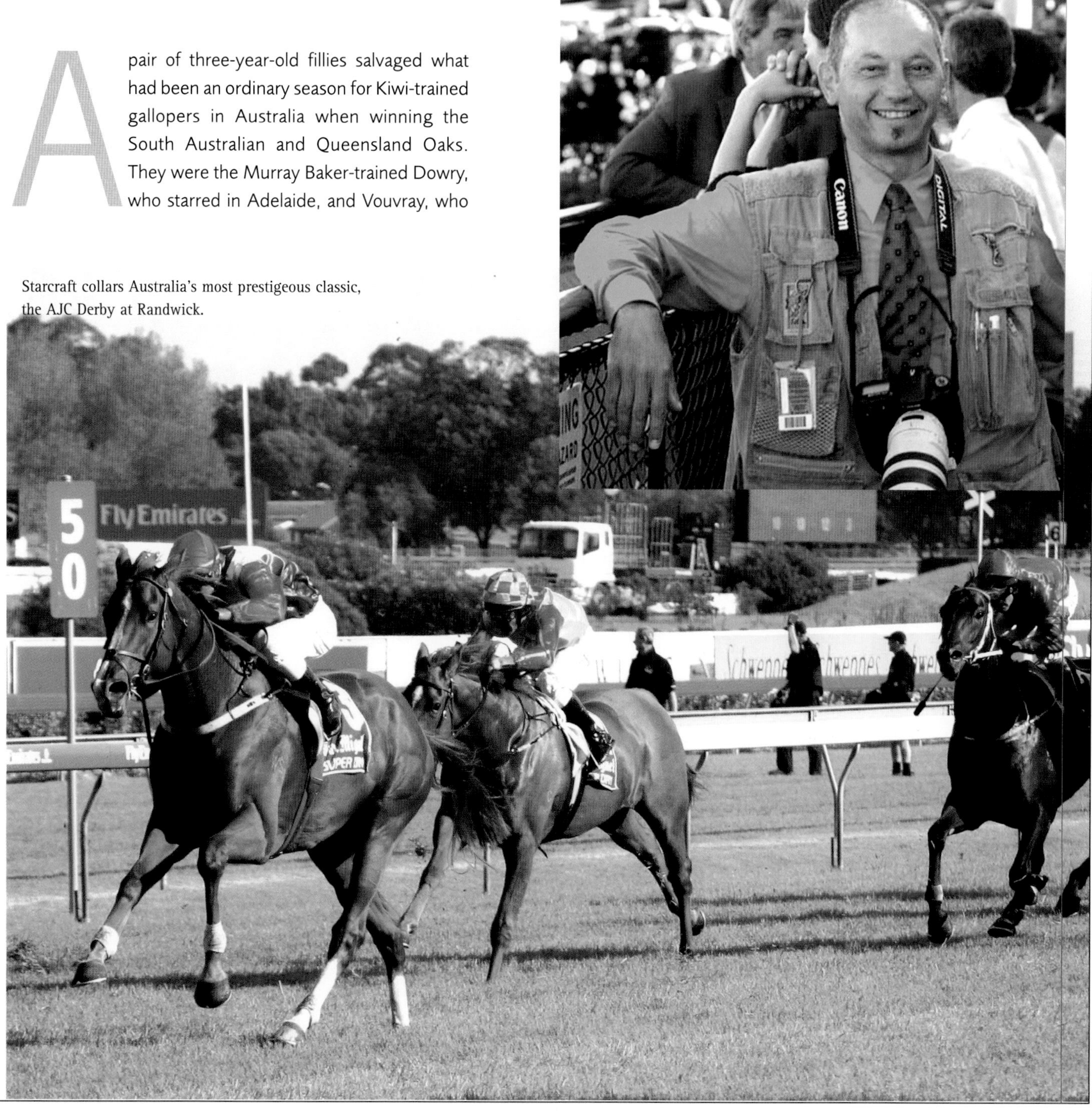

Starcraft collars Australia's most prestigeous classic, the AJC Derby at Randwick.

provided Paul O'Sullivan with his final group one winner before moving to Hong Kong when scoring in Brisbane.

Dowry's classic assault on Adelaide stemmed from a strong late run to win the Manawatu Classic over 2000 metres at Awapuni in early April. Luck was all against her in her first two Australian outings but she clearly outstayed her rivals over 2500 metres in the $A250,000 group one South Australian Oaks. She is a daughter of Bahhare, who was standing at Rich Hill Stud at the time of her conception, and the Noble Bijou mare Meant For Me, who has also left the good winners Richfield Destiny and Fatal. It was a good meeting for Rich Hill Stud as Pantani, a son of resident sire Pentire, won the Adelaide Cup for Australian trainer Robbie Laing.

The Queensland Oaks provided a trifecta for the New Zealand breeding industry when Vouvray won from former stablemate Zumanity and Winning Belle. Both Vouvray and Winning Belle are daughters of Zabeel, while Zumanity is by O'Reilly.

Paul O'Sullivan had taken Vouvray to Brisbane on a short preparation and the filly's great win was a tribute to his training skills, which did not go unnoticed in Hong Kong. The flow on for O'Sullivan was a wave of new clients.

Vouvray is the property of Trelawney Stud, who bred her in partnership with Philippines racing identity Orchie Santos. Whereas Dowry had made $53,000 at auction as a yearling, Vouvray fetched $300,000. Trelawney was able to buy her in for half that amount and she is already a bargain.

New Zealand stables scored other important wins in Melbourne, Queensland and Adelaide. Rosina Lad gave Levin trainer David Haworth his first Australian win in the Waterford Crystal Mile at Moonee Valley, while Paul O'Sullivan won the QTC Cup with Falkirk and Peter Walker, the Carlton Draught Stakes at Morphetville with Bel Air. Mostly, though, the pickings were lean for New Zealand-trained horses in the major Australian races and fortune seemed to desert them when it was most needed. With reasonable luck Distinctly Secret could have won both the Mackinnon Stakes and the Sandown Classic, while stablemate King's Chapel would have been much more competitive in the Stradbroke Handicap if he hadn't been buffeted out of the race.

But plenty of significant Australian races fell to Kiwi-breds. Among them were the AJC Derby (Starcraft), the VRC Turnbull Stakes (Studebaker), VRC Ascot Vale Stakes (Scaredee Cat), VRC Craiglee Stakes (Pentastic), MVRC Schweppes Strakes (Our Egyptian Raine), AJC Craven Plate (Shower of Roses), Sandown Classic (Legible), AJC Summer

Waikato Stud's Australian group winner Scaredee Cat.

New Zealand bred mare Legible just manages to hold out fellow kiwi Distinctly Secret in the Sandown Classic.

Pantani, a product of Rich Hill Stud, takes out the Adelaide Cup.

Reset wins the Cadbury Guineas before his sale for $18 million for stud duties.

Cup (Stadium), MVRC Sunline Stakes (Sylvana), Tulloch Stakes (Starcraft), Queensland Guineas (Winning Belle), QTC O'Shea Stakes (Pentastic), Doomben Classic (Drunken Joker), BTC Chairman's Handicap (So Assertive) and Ipswich Cup (Portland Singa).

But flying the flag higher for New Zealand than any of these wins was the unbeaten Zabeel three-year-old Reset, raced by high-profile Melbourne owner Lloyd Williams and trained by Graeme Rogerson. After coasting through the grades he stepped up to group company to win the Cadbury Guineas and the VATC Futurity Stakes. He was then bought by Darley Australia for $18 million and retired to stud at a fee of $33,000.

New Zealand's South Australian Oaks winner, Dowry.

Former star New Zealand jockey Michael Walker celebrates being an Australian resident by winning the Brisbane Cup on Danestorm.

BELOW: Vouvray (No. 18) home for another New Zealand win in the Queensland Oaks at the expense of former stablemate Zumanity.

ROSS STEVENSON

THE GLAD AND SAD TALE OF TAATLETAIL

Tragic end of top filly

By David Bradford

Racing folk have always been – probably always will be – suckers for Cinderella stories. That's why a legion of fans loved the small, once unwanted filly Taatletail as she blazed her way to fame and then mourned her death in a freak stable accident. Just how good she could have been is a question that even time will be unable to answer. But that in no way diminishes what she achieved.

When she won the group one New Zealand One Thousand Guineas Taatletail was recording her fifth successive win in as many starts. She was also completing a treble of wins in the New Zealand Bloodstock filly-of-the-year series after having already taken the Highview Stakes (formerly the Gold Trail Stakes) and the Lowland Stakes. Only two other fillies had previously accomplished that – Swell Time in 1971 and Phillipa Rush in 1989.

Going into the One Thousand Guineas there were some doubts as to how she would cope with the 1600 metres. That was taken care of when Michael Walker took her to an early lead, slackened the pace and then sprinted home to hold off another classy filly in Kainui Belle, who had been the longshot winner of the Wellington Guineas.

A champion and her classic decorations.

At her next outing Taatletail finished second, beaten a length and a quarter by Russian Pearl, in the group one Bayer Classic, with Two Thousand Guineas winner King's Chapel third. Back to racing against her own sex in the group two Eight Carat Classic at Ellerslie on Boxing Day, she turned in something of shocker when finishing midfield in a race won by Kainui Belle. It was the only time she tackled a right-handed track and the only time she finished out of the money.

Taatletail's final race was to come in the electric atmos-

A winning farewell... a handsome win in the Sir Tristram Fillies Classic.

phere of the Waikato Racing Club's February meeting at Te Rapa, featuring three group races and a million dollar jackpot. She was all magic when winning the group two Sir Tristram Fillies Classic when having her first start for six weeks and racing beyond 1600 metres for the first time. But she coped with the 2000 metres in resounding fashion to win from Anne Carina and Madame Shinko after Michael Walker had kept her in touch with the pace throughout. It was her sixth win from eight starts and took her earnings to $336,000, a solid return on the $30,000 paid for her as a yearling by Graeme Rogerson.

Owners Brian Foster, Peter Glover, Russell Just, Dan McLuckie and Paul Meo, who raced her in partnership with Rogerson, were rowdily ecstatic. The syndicate was put together by Cherry Taylor, wife of Trelawney Stud proprietor Brent Taylor, and as Taatletail won an almost cult-like following, so did her owners as racegoers gave their enthusiasm the sign of approval. In response to her great Te Rapa win there was immediate talk about an Australian autumn campaign with options such as the Doncaster Handicap and the AJC Oaks. But sadly the odyssey was at an end.

Before the month was through Taatletail was involved in a freakish accident in her stall and had to be put down. It was a devastating blow to those closest to her and especially co-trainer Stephen Autridge who had handled her brilliantly through a campaign which began in August. Though Graeme Rogerson has a reputation for being a fearless buyer at the top end of the yearling market, he is also prepared to take a punt on lesser lights that take his fancy. Grand Archway, the champion Australian filly of her era, cost less than $35,000 and so did his Golden Slipper winner Polar Success.

Taatletail, by Faltaat from the Defensive Play mare Defensive Lady, was bred by Deborah Ho of Macau who has dabbled in New Zealand bloodstock for around twenty years. Her father, Stanley Ho, was one of the founders of thoroughbred racing in Macau but is even more widely known as a casino owner.

GROUP RESULTS

2003-2004

By David Bradford

GROUP 1

Lashed.

MUDGWAY PARTSWORLD STAKES

G1, WFA 1340m, $100,000, Wanganui, August 30

1. MISS POTENTIAL
5 m, Dolphin Street – Richfield Rose (Crested Wave).
Owners A W Borrie.
Breeders B Borrie.
Trainer Bill Borrie.
Jockey Reese Jones.
2. Tit For Taat
6 g, Faltaat – Miss Kiwitea (Truly Vain).
Owners R I & Est Late W D Scott.
Breeders R I & Est late W D Scott.
Trainer Anne & Wayne Herbert.
3. Rosina Lad
5 g, Faltaat – Arctic Life (Arctic Tern).
Owners J M & Mrs K A Goodwin.
Breeders R M Warwick Ltd.
Trainer David Haworth.
MARGINS: Time: 01:18.02 Track: easy
Others: Irish Rover, Burglar, Lordship, Hail, Hello Dolly, Reg, Ernest William, Rodin, Sound The Alarm, Tuscany Warrior, Fritz, Special Call, Starbo

KELT CAPITAL STAKES

G1, WFA 2040m, $750,000, Hastings, September 27

1. DISTINCTLY SECRET
5 g, Distinctly North – Te Akau Secret (Lord Ballina).
Owners Messrs D C Ellis, K T O'Donnell, W R Schwamm & M A Shorter.
Breeders D C Ellis.
Trainer Mark Walker.
Jockey Opie Bosson.
2. Hail
6 g, Stark South – Valley Court (Pompeii Court).
Owners Messrs A J Cunningham & R B Marsh.
Breeders Fayette Park Stud Ltd.
Trainer Bruce & Stephen Marsh.
3. Irish Rover
6 g, Kenfair – Sterling Lea (One Pound Sterling).
Owners Messrs E Carson & B J McCahill Snr.
Breeders B J McCahill.
Trainer Eddie Carson.
MARGINS: Time: 02:03.64 Track: firm
Others: Ben Sparta, Hello Dolly, Kaapeon, Raspberry Ripple, St Reims, El Duce, Ernest William, Cent Home, Tit For Taat, Miss Potential, Tuscany Warrior, Penny Gem

AVERY FORD CAPTAIN COOK STAKES

G1, WFA 1600m, $100,000, Trentham, October 25

1. PENNY GEM
4 m, Pentire – Gemscay (Maizcay).
Owners A F & Mrs C I Abel, Messrs A K Bell, C W Cherrie, P A Moroney & B A Schroder.
Breeders A R Galbraith, J W Thompson & Waitaria Holdings Ltd.
Trainer Michael Moroney & Andrew Scott.
Jockey Michael Coleman.
2. Marie Claire
5 m, O'Reilly – Trotanoy (Lord Seymour).
Owners Messrs P J Vela ONZM & P M Vela.
Breeders P J & P M Vela.
Trainer Paul O'Sullivan.
3. Hustler
4 g, Al Akbar – Flush (Full On Aces).
Owners Messrs P W Jolly & J P Reid.
Breeders Mrs D Whittaker & Mrs J A Wilson.
Trainer Paul Harris.
MARGINS: Time: 01:34.57 Track: firm
Others: Irish Rover, Black Muscat, Millennium, Rodin, Miss Potential, Ernest William, Ben Sparta, Danzapride, Desert Bay, Fritz

NEW ZEALAND BLOODSTOCK 1000 GUINEAS

G1, 3YOF 1600m, $275,000, Riccarton Park, November 8

1. TAATLETAIL
3 f, Faltaat – Defensive Lady (Defensive Play).
Owners Messrs B J Foster, P C Glover, S R Just, D McLuckie, P L Meo & G A Rogerson.
Breeders Miss D Ho.
Trainer Graeme Rogerson & Stephen Autridge.
Jockey Michael Walker.
2. Kainui Belle
3 f, Kashani – Lady Ukiah (Straight Strike).
Owners Mrs J J & P W Rogers.
Breeders Mrs J J & P W Rogers.
Trainer Vanessa & Wayne Hillis.
3. Unearthed
3 f, Felix the Cat – Minsky (Western Symphony).
Owners D A Dollimore.
Breeders M J Brown.
Trainer Paul Harris.
MARGINS: Time: 01:37.64 Track: firm
Others: Personal Column, Classic Clare, Catscan, Her Hidden Talent, Eternal Melody, Eftee One, Rapid Kay, Sarah Little, Salsa, Danette, Spur Bird, Hot Elle, The Persuader

COUPLAND S BAKERIES NZ 2000GUINEAS

G1, 3YO 1600m, $300,000, Riccarton Park, November 12

1. KING'S CHAPEL
3 c, King Of Kings – Lower Chapel (Sharpo).
Owners Tauranga Racing Syndicate (Mgr D C Ellis).
Breeders Norelands Stud.
Trainer Mark Walker.
Jockey Opie Bosson.
2. Sarah Vee
3 f, End Sweep – Captivating (Canny Lad).
Owners R E Vernall.
Breeders G Fischl.
Trainer Michael Moroney & Andrew Scott.
3. Kainui Belle
3 f, Kashani – Lady Ukiah (Straight Strike).
Owners Mrs J J & P W Rogers.
Breeders Mrs J J & P W Rogers.
Trainer Vanessa & Wayne Hillis.
MARGINS: Time: 01:36.34 Track: firm
Others: Coup Timaru, Blood 'N' Bone, Spur Bird, Unearthed, Juicy Fruit Mambo, Catscan, J'Lo, Ocean Melodie, Lilakyn, Lord Asterix, Carlisle Bay

BAYER CLASSIC

G1, 3YO 1600m, $190,870, Otaki, November 27

1. RUSSIAN PEARL
3 c, Soviet Star – Velinda (Veloso).
Owners Pearl Racing Stables Ltd.
Breeders C P & Mrs M J A Howells & P Setchell.
Trainer Bruce & Stephen Marsh.
Jockey Hayden Tinsley.
2. Taatletail
3 f, Faltaat – Defensive Lady (Defensive Play).
Owners Messrs B J Foster, P C Glover, S R Just, D McLuckie, P L Meo & G A Rogerson.
Breeders Miss D Ho.
Trainer Graeme Rogerson & Stephen Autridge.
3. King's Chapel
3 c, King Of Kings – Lower Chapel (Sharpo).
Owners Tauranga Racing Syndicate (Mgr D C Ellis).
Breeders Norelands Stud.
Trainer Mark Walker.
MARGINS: _ HEAD, 1 1/4 LEN, 1 3/4 LEN
Time: 01:34.96 Track: firm
Others: Danbird, Brave Flyer, Tadan, Pride Of The Class, Magistra Delecta, Rockabubble, Heloise, Rat Tat, Waromar, Artemesia

NEW ZEALAND BLOODSTOCK AVONDALE CUP

G1, OPN HCP 2200m, $150,000, Avondale, December 3

1. REGAL KRONA
8 g, Krona – Regal Cent (Centaine).
Owners Messrs P L Keppel, H R McGlade & R M Norman.
Breeders H R & Est late A McGlade.
Trainer Sheryl & Roger McGlade.
Jockey Andrew Calder.
2. The Mighty Lions
5 m, Grosvenor – Maybe Yes (Last Tycoon).
Owners Gold and Blue Syndicate.
Breeders Trelawney Stud.
Trainer Michael Moroney & Andrew Scott.
3. Bel Air
7 g, Victory Dance – Hollywood Hotel (Nassipour).
Owners Messrs M J Surgenor & P J Walker.
Breeders Grande Vue Lodge Syndicate.
Trainer Peter Walker.
MARGINS: 2 LEN, SHORT HEAD, LONG HEAD
Time: 02:13.51 Track: firm
Others: Asgoodas, Penny Gem, El Duce, Memphis Blues, Millennium, Leica Guv, Lafleur, Ebony Honor, Betta Watch It, Nadir Shah, Mick Bailey, Pennies In Heaven, Rodin

MERCEDES DERBY

G1, 3YO 2400m, $484,000, Ellerslie, December 26

1. CUT THE CAKE
3 g, Yamanin Vital – Icing On The Cake (Straight Strike).
Owners Messrs N M Anderson, G W

Breingan, G J N Jaggaer, T T Manning P A Moroney & A P Ramsden.
Breeders P A Moroney.
Trainer Michael Moroney & Andrew Scott.
Jockey Michael Coleman.
2. Mount Street
3 g, Kilimanjaro – Real Trier (Turf Ruler).
Owners P B Newsom, A Wales, A M Whitehouse & B K S Woon.
Breeders P B Newsom.
Trainer Colin Jillings & Richard Yuill.
3. Masai
3 g, Kilimanjaro – Hat Trick (Deputy Governor).
Owners Messrs I O Cowley, R H Gregory, J W Keith & A Rapana.
Breeders Mrs B S & R H Gregory.
Trainer Graham Richardson & Mark Donoghuc.
MARGINS: LONG HEAD, LONG NECK, 3/4 LEN Time: 02:28.88 Track: firm
Others: Waitoki Dream, Terrain, Firewheel, Russian Pearl, The Market Man, Maroofity, Senorita Rosay, Philamor, Joyful Winner, Mr Sleeman, Tadan, Brillanti

LION RED AUCKLAND CUP

G1, OPN HCP 3200m, $350,000, Ellerslie, January 1
1. UPSETTHYM
5 m, Rhythm – Set Up (Zabeel).
Owners Pepsi Syndicate.
Breeders Mrs J A & P Hogan.
Trainer Karen Fursdon.
Jockey Gemma Sliz.
2. Galway Lass
5 m, Rhythm – Ballycairn (Zabeel).
Owners Augusta Bloodstock Ltd.
Breeders Mrs J A & P Hogan.
Trainer Paul O'Sullivan.
3. My Governess
5 m, Deputy Governor – Regal Orphan (Zamazaan).
Owners J E & Mrs J J Boon.
Breeders P J B Smith.
Trainer John Boon.
MARGINS: 1 1/4 LEN, 1 1/4 LEN, LEN Time: 03:23.61 Track: firm
Others: The Mighty Lions, Lord Belvedere, Asgoodas, Supa Belt, Singing Star, Sunray, Our Unicorn, Branson, Regal Krona, Ebony Honor, Cyclades, Ready To Rumble, Spit 'N' Polish, Leica Guv, Love Fly Her

SKY CITY RAILWAY STAKES

G1, OPN HCP 1200m, $250,000, Ellerslie, January 1
1. VINAKA
5 g, Volksraad – Shepherd's Delight (Famous Star).
Owners Mrs A & J A Gibbs.
Breeders Mrs A & J A Gibbs.
Trainer Paul O'Sullivan.
Jockey Opie Bosson.
2. Pay My Bail
3 f, Justice Prevails – Ebony Jane (Three Legs).
Owners Messrs T A Green & T J McKee ONZM.
Breeders G W de Gruchy.
Trainer Stephen & Trevor McKee.
3. Tully Dane
5 h, Danehill – Good Faith (Straight Strike).
Owners R McDonald.
Breeders .
Trainer Michael Moroney & Andrew Scott.
MARGINS: LONG NECK, LONG HEAD, 3/4 LEN Time: 01:08.66 Track: firm
Others: Miss Potential, Taimana, Travellin' Man, Sound The Alarm, Danroad, Sunlaw, El Nino, Dragon Tiger, Clean Bowled, Diamond Like, Danasar

ZABEEL CLASSIC

G1, WFA 2000m, $150,000, Ellerslie, January 2
1. LASHED
4 m, Encosta De Lago – Traffic Watch (Salieri).
Owners Lady & Sir Patrick Hogan.
Breeders Mrs C M Upjohn.
Trainer Graeme Rogerson & Stephen Autridge.
Jockey Opie Bosson.
2. Penny Gem
4 m, Pentire – Gemscay (Maizcay).
Owners A F & Mrs C I Abel, Messrs A K Bell, C W Cherrie, P A Moroney & B A Schroder.
Breeders A R Galbraith, J W Thompson & Waitaria Holdings Ltd.
Trainer Michael Moroney & Andrew Scott.
3. El Duce
8 g, Lord Ballina – El Fugaz (Sir Avon).
Owners D T Lee, Mrs D M Logan & Dr J L Sprague.
Breeders Mrs D M Logan.
Trainer Donna & Dean Logan.
MARGINS: 1 1/2 LEN, 3/4 LEN, 1 1/4 LEN Time: 02:02.62 Track: firm
Others: Hail, Ubiquitous, Philamor, Waitoki Dream, Doyle, St Reims, Surprize Surprize, Maze, Woburn

ING LIFE NEW ZEALAND OAKS

G1, 3YOF 2400m, $300,000, Trentham, January 17
1. WHARITE PRINCESS
3 f, His Royal Highness – Regal Visit (Vice Regal).
Owners N M Cantwell, M R Curd, T A Robinson, K J Tod, K R Williams & R J Wong.
Breeders Lambourn Stud Ltd.
Trainer Lisa Latta.
Jockey Bruce Herd.
2. Filante Etoile
3 f, Soviet Star – Georgiana (Nassipour).
Owners Messrs P J Vela ONZM & P M Vela.
Breeders P J & P M Vela.
Trainer Colin Jillings & Richard Yuill.
3. Midnight Kiss
3 f, Groom Dancer – Midnight Assembly (Night Shift).
Owners Forhomes Furnishers & Flooring Ltd & Ms D G Ryder.
Breeders Forhomes Furnishers & Flooring Ltd.
Trainer Karyn McQuade.
MARGINS: LEN, 1/2 LEN, 1 1/4 LEN Time: 02:26.88 Track: firm
Others: French Lady, Kind Return, Madame Shinko, Kainui Belle, Eternal Melody, Senorita Rosay, Glenview Lass, Calveen, Buckle My Shoe, Eftee One, Eternal Lee, Matches, Ocean Melodie, Grand Times, Justine Coup

ING TELEGRAPH HANDICAP

G1, OPN HCP 1200m, $100,000, Trentham, January 17
1. KING'S CHAPEL
3 c, King Of Kings – Lower Chapel (Sharpo).
Owners Tauranga Racing Syndicate (Mgr D C Ellis).
Breeders Norelands Stud.
Trainer Mark Walker.
Jockey Noel Harris.
2. Sunlaw
5 m, Desert Sun – Cereno Cloud (Terreno).
Owners L H Chan.
Breeders S Eagleton.
Trainer Graeme Sanders & Debbie Sweeney.
3. Sedecrem
5 g, Faltaat – Real Trier (Turf Ruler).
Owners Messrs C J Giltrap, W C McDonald, P J Walker & E H Ward.
Breeders P B Newsom.
Trainer Colin Jillings & Richard Yuill.
MARGINS: SHORT HEAD, 3/4 LEN, SHORT HEAD Time: 01:06.79 Track: firm
Others: Travellin' Man, Diamond Like, El Nino, Tully Dane, Sound The Alarm, Don't Tell Tom, Pay My Bail, Taimana, Danroad, Golden Harvest

HOLDEN THORNDON MILE

G1, OPN HCP 1600m, $130,000, Trentham, January 24
1. SIR KINLOCH
5 g, Rhythm – Ivory (Gold And Ivory).
Owners Messrs H S, H S & S S Dyke.
Breeders H S, H S & S S Dyke.
Trainer Colin Jillings & Richard Yuill.
Jockey Lee Rutherford.
2. Sedecrem
5 g, Faltaat – Real Trier (Turf Ruler).
Owners Messrs C J Giltrap, W C McDonald, P J Walker & E H Ward.
Breeders P B Newsom.
Trainer Colin Jillings & Richard Yuill.
3. Elendil
4 g, His Royal Highness – Just A Fallacy (Mr Illusion).
Owners Cops 'n' Robbers Syndicate.
Breeders J D E McKenzie.
Trainer Peter McKenzie.
MARGINS: NECK, HEAD, SHORT HEAD Time: 01:36.84 Track: easy
Others: Lashed, Travellin' Man, Surprize Surprize, Alyssum, Critic, Boycott, Portofino Bay, Coup Liner, Our Fuji, Shartiz, Kakaho, Tonic, Marie Claire, Silky Red Boxer

LION BROWN WELLINGTON CUP

G1, OPN HCP 3200m, $250,000, Trentham, January 24
1. CLUDEN CREEK
5 g, Yamanin Vital – Fort Girl (Beaufort Sea).
Owners B A Barber, Mrs Ali Macdonald & N A Purvis.
Breeders B A Barber & N A Purvis.
Trainer John Boon.
Jockey Andrew Calder.
2. Bel Air
7 g, Victory Dance – Hollywood Hotel (Nassipour).
Owners Messrs M J Surgenor & P J Walker.
Breeders Grande Vue Lodge Syndicate.
Trainer Peter Walker.
3. Ebony Honor
7 g, Honor Grades – Only Love (Wollow).
Owners Mrs J M & M T Harriman.
Breeders Haunui Farm Ltd.
Trainer Stephen & Trevor McKee.
MARGINS: 3/4 LEN, 3 3/4 LEN, SHORT HEAD Time: 03:26.49 Track: easy
Others: Hail, Cabella, The Mighty Lions, Sensuous, Carrera, Tunzi, Princess Oregon, Corrupted, Hoof'n It, Cyclades, Torlesse, Semper Fidelis, Baloney, Rising Heights, Galway Lass

WHAKANUI STUD INTERNATIONAL STAKES

G1, WFA 2000m, $100,000, Te Rapa, February 7
1. LASHED
4 m, Encosta De Lago – Traffic Watch (Salieri).
Owners Lady & Sir Patrick Hogan.
Breeders Mrs C M Upjohn.
Trainer Graeme Rogerson & Stephen Autridge.
Jockey Opie Bosson.
2. Penny Gem
4 m, Pentire – Gemscay (Maizcay).
Owners A F & Mrs C I Abel, Messrs A K Bell, C W Cherrie, P A Moroney & B A Schroder.
Breeders A R Galbraith, J W Thompson & Waitaria Holdings Ltd.
Trainer Michael Moroney & Andrew Scott.
3. Kaapstad Way
8 g, Kaapstad – Crysell Way (Star Way).
Owners The Chatsworth Trust.
Breeders A Snellex, G R K Taylor & Windsor Park Stud Ltd.
Trainer Chris & Colleen Wood.
MARGINS: _ HEAD, 1 1/4 LEN, NECK Time: 02:03.71 Track: firm
Others: Hail, Scarlet Rose, Singing Star, Sir Kinloch, El Duce, For Love, Greene Street, Danzaman

WAIKATO DRAUGHT SPRINT

G1, WFA 1400m, $100,000, Te Rapa, February 7
1. SEDECREM
5 g, Faltaat – Real Trier (Turf Ruler).
Owners Messrs C J Giltrap, W C McDonald, P J Walker & E H Ward.
Breeders P B Newsom.
Trainer Colin Jillings & Richard Yuill.
Jockey Grant Cooksley.
2. Zvezda
5 g, His Royal Highness – Carnival Girl (Roughcast).
Owners Mrs K D H Lane.
Breeders Mrs K D Lane.
Trainer Kay Lane.
3. Rapid Kay
3 f, Towkay – Racing Waters (Racing Is Fun).
Owners Bleap Syndicate.
Breeders Little Avondale Trust.
Trainer Mark Walker.
MARGINS: 1 1/4 LEN, 3/4 LEN, 3/4 LEN Time: 01:22.53 Track: firm
Others: King's Chapel, Vinaka, Sunlaw, Danbird, Mr Robert, Pay My Bail, Penitentiary, Silvaraad, Pure Theatre, Diamond Like, Tully Dane

FAMILY HOTEL WFA

G1, WFA 1400m, $100,000, Hastings, February 19
1. KING'S CHAPEL
3 c, King Of Kings – Lower Chapel (Sharpo).
Owners Tauranga Racing Syndicate (Mgr D C Ellis).
Breeders Norelands Stud.
Trainer Mark Walker.
Jockey Rhys McLeod.
2. Vinaka
5 g, Volksraad – Shepherd's Delight (Famous

Star).
Owners Mrs A & J A Gibbs.
Breeders Mrs A & J A Gibbs.
Trainer Paul O'Sullivan.
3. Sedecrem
5 g, Faltaat – Real Trier (Turf Ruler).
Owners Messrs C J Giltrap, W C McDonald, P J Walker & E H Ward.
Breeders P B Newsom.
Trainer Colin Jillings & Richard Yuill.
MARGINS: 3 1/4 LEN, LONG HEAD, 1/2 LEN Time: 01:20.32 Track: firm
Others: Zvezda, Doyle, Ernest William, Travellin' Man, Danbird, Penitentiary, Magistra Delecta, Irish Rover

FORD ELLERSLIE SIRES PRODUCE STAKES

G1, 2YO 1200m, $120,000, Ellerslie, February 28
1. IFLOOXCOULDKILL
2 f, Daggers Drawn – Hear's Hoping (Dahar).
Owners M & Mrs N Carroll, Mrs K Devine, A J & Mrs C Sutherland.
Breeders Curraghmore Stud Ltd.
Trainer Paul O'Sullivan.
Jockey Leith Innes.
2. Egyptian Ra
2 g, Woodborough – Egyptian Queen (Karioi Lad).
Owners C A Ball, R J Barton, Mrs L M Rae, Mrs P E Sapich, Mrs M K Scott, B W & Mrs E K Wootton.
Breeders C A Ball & M L Barratt.
Trainer Kenny Rae.
3. Velasco
2 f, Flying Spur – Vital Curves (McGinty).
Owners Mrs J F Andrews & J K Sullivan.
Breeders J K Sullivan & Ms J Andrews.
Trainer Bryce Tankard.
MARGINS: 3/4 LEN, 1 3/4 LEN, LEN Time: 01:14.06 Track: soft
Others: Atapi, Keeninsky, Clean Sweep, Can't Hackit, Eloa, Lotzatow, Alinsky, Kapsdan, Florilegium, Sharka Zulu, Sandboy

NEW ZEALAND STAKES

G1, WFA 2000m, $100,000, Ellerslie, February 28
1. LASHED
4 m, Encosta De Lago – Traffic Watch (Salieri).
Owners Lady & Sir Patrick Hogan.
Breeders Mrs C M Upjohn.
Trainer Graeme Rogerson & Stephen Autridge.
Jockey Opie Bosson.
2. Deebee Belle
6 m, Bin Ajwaad – Deebee Lady (Brilliant Invader).
Owners Deebee Belle Syndicate.
Breeders D A & Mrs N H Bell.
Trainer Tony & Pam Gillies.
3. Hail
6 g, Stark South – Valley Court (Pompeii Court).
Owners A J Cunningham & R B Marsh.
Breeders Fayette Park Stud Ltd.
Trainer Bruce & Stephen Marsh.
MARGINS: 1/2 LEN, 1 1/4 LEN, 7 LEN Time: 02:13.17 Track: heavy
Others: Quick Lip, Danzaman, Singing Star, Greene Street

NEW ZEALAND BLOODSTOCK BREEDERS STAKES

G1, WFA F&M 1600m, $120,000, Te Aroha, March 13
1. SURPRIZE SURPRIZE
6 m, Prized – Impossible Dream (Imposing).
Owners Mrs C A & G E Vazey.
Breeders Mrs J M Wilding.
Trainer Kevin Hughes.
Jockey Grant Cooksley.
2. Diamond Like
4 m, Danehill – Tristalove (Sir Tristram).
Owners Ms E L, Sir Patrick & Lady Hogan, Mrs N K & P Hunt.
Breeders Cambridge Stud.
Trainer Paul O'Sullivan.
3. Penny Gem
4 m, Pentire – Gemscay (Maizcay).
Owners A F & Mrs C I Abel, A K Bell, C W Cherrie, P A Moroney & B A Schroder.
Breeders A R Galbraith, J W Thompson & Waitaria Holdings Ltd.
Trainer Michael Moroney & Andrew Scott.
MARGINS: NECK, 3/4 LEN, SHORT HEAD Time: 01:34.87 Track: firm
Others: Belle Femme, Kainui Belle, Sunlaw, Rodrigo Rose, Tina Temple, Amah Dramas, Sokool, Scarlet Rose, Alyssum, Foxy Blonde, Deebee Belle

FORD MANAWATU SIRES PRODUCE STAKES

G1, 2YO 1400m, $120,000, Awapuni, April 3
1. KEENINSKY
2 c, Stravinsky – So Keen (Jade Hunter).
Owners Mrs D & J Carter, B T Hall & G A Rogerson.
Breeders B T Hall & J A Rowan.
Trainer Graeme Rogerson & Stephen Autridge.
Jockey Allan Peard.
2. Manten
2 c, Encosta De Lago – Dazzling Belle (Desert Sun).
Owners Aitetu Company Ltd.
Breeders Monovale Holdings Ltd, G A Rogerson & Westbury Stud Ltd.
Trainer Graeme Rogerson & Stephen Autridge.
3. Egyptian Ra
2 g, Woodborough – Egyptian Queen (Karioi Lad).
Owners C A Ball, R J Barton, Mrs L M Rae, Mrs P E Sapich, Mrs M K Scott, B W & Mrs E K Wootton.
Breeders C A Ball & M L Barratt.
Trainer Kenny Rae.
MARGINS: 1 1/4 LEN, LEN, LONG NECK Time: 01:23.37 Track: firm
Others: Atapi, Kapsdan, Velasco, Shastri, Sir Woody, Clean Sweep, Mucho, Volk Dancer, Iflooxcouldkill, Majestic Sweep

EASTER HANDICAP

G1, OPN HCP 1600m, $150,000, Ellerslie, April 10
1. POMP AND GLORY
5 g, Pompeii Court – Aptitude (Brauner).
Owners J M Clydesdale & T W Crommelin.
Breeders Cromco Thoroughbreds (NZ) Ltd.
Trainer Alan Jones & Brett McDonald.
Jockey Opie Bosson.
2. Rodrigo Rose
5 m, Rodrigo de Triano – Rosebrook (Vain).
Owners Lady & Sir Patrick Hogan, Mr P J & Mrs S G Walker.
Breeders T O Harrison.
Trainer Graham Richardson & Mark Donoghue.
3. Jetski
6 g, Jetball – Making Waves (Bakharoff).
Owners B J Cooper, B V Guy, Mrs D M Logan & H B Norcross.
Breeders D G & R B McLaren Ltd.
Trainer Donna & Dean Logan.
MARGINS: 1/2 LEN, SHORT HEAD, 1 3/4 LEN Time: 01:32.29 Track: firm
Others: Travellin' Man, Diamond Like, Irish Rover, Regal Krona, Millennium, Marie Claire, Surprize Surprize, Sokool, Danceinthesun, Upsetthym, Mr Robert, Akela, Sir Kinloch, Ubiquitous, Let's Planet

2. Montreal Gold
3 f, Gold Brose – Lady Ballina (Lord Ballina).
Owners Monty Syndicate.
Breeders N C Lockyer Family Trust.
Trainer Frank & Craig Ritchie.
3. Wee Winkle
3 g, Tuscany Flyer – La Resuelto (Show King).
Owners G J Blackmore, Mrs E J Deans, Messrs R D & S P Irvin & G N Johnson.
Breeders G W Grammer & W J Harris.

AUCKLAND RACING CLUB

Taimana.

GROUP 2

GLENMORGAN GENEROUS STAKES

G2, WFA 1600m, $120,000, Otaki, September 13
1. IRISH ROVER
6 g, Kenfair – Sterling Lea (One Pound Sterling).
Owners Messrs E Carson & B J McCahill Snr.
Breeders B J McCahill.
Trainer Eddie Carson.
Jockey David Walker.
2. Miss Potential
5 m, Dolphin Street – Richfield Rose (Crested Wave).
Owners A W Borrie.
Breeders B Borrie.
Trainer Bill Borrie.
3. Tit For Taat
6 g, Faltaat – Miss Kiwitea (Truly Vain).
Owners R I & Est Late W D Scott.
Breeders R I & Est late W D Scott.
Trainer Anne & Wayne Herbert.
MARGINS: Time: 001:36.1 Track: easy
Others: El Duce, Ernest William, Rodin, Jetski, Conquistar, Hail, Hello Dolly, Starbo, Deebee Belle, Real Vision, Lordship

LINDAUER GUINEAS

G2, 3YO 1600m, $60,000, Ellerslie, October 4
1. BRIDIE BELLE
3 f, Al Akbar – Golinda (Crested Wave).
Owners L D & Mrs M Pettifer.
Breeders J D Corcoran.
Trainer Chris & Colleen Wood.
Jockey Lucas Camilleri.

Trainer Evan & J J Rayner.
MARGINS: Time: 01:49.55 Track: heavy
Others: James Blond, Governare, Kauri King, Elferon, Pay The Believers, Shereigns, Ensuave

WELLINGTON THOROUGHBRED BREEDERS GUINEAS

G2, 3YO 1500m, $60,000, Trentham, October 25
1. KAINUI BELLE
3 f, Kashani – Lady Ukiah (Straight Strike).
Owners Mrs J J & P W Rogers.
Breeders Mrs J J & P W Rogers.
Trainer Vanessa & Wayne Hillis.
Jockey Noel Harris.
2. Rat Tat
3 g, Slavic – Picnic in the Park (Bel Bolide).
Owners R N Cunningham.
Breeders Clear Valley Stables & R G Lithgow.
Trainer Ron Cunningham.
3. Magistra Delecta
3 f, Al Akbar – Grosvenor's Girl (Grosvenor).
Owners Mrs M A, Est Late P E & Mr T R Faith.
Breeders Mrs M A & Est late P E Faith.
Trainer Marie Faith.
MARGINS: Time: 01:28.82 Track: firm
Others: Mount Street, Clifton, Russian Pearl, Waromar, Governare, Wee Winkle, Carlisle Bay, Wise Master, Dealmaker, Mr Bojangles, Madame Shinko, Meggido

CANTERBURY DRAUGHT NEW ZEALAND CUP

G2, OPN HCP 3200m, $180,000, Riccarton Park, November 15
1. TORLESSE
6 g, Volksraad – Seamist (Beaufort Sea).

Owners Ngapuke Stables Syndicate.
Breeders Mrs B J & Est late A G Wigley.
Trainer Mandy Brown.
Jockey Terry Moseley.
2. Cabella
5 m, Senor Pete – Miss Fiesta (Fiesta Star).
Owners Thomas Cooker No 1 Syndicate.
Breeders B A Collins & K M Rowe.
Trainer Kevin Hughes.
3. Galway Lass
5 m, Rhythm – Ballycairn (Zabeel).
Owners Augusta Bloodstock Ltd.
Breeders Mrs J A & P Hogan.
Trainer Paul O'Sullivan.
MARGINS: Time: 003:20.8 Track: firm
Others: Soldier Blue, Sam McClay, Andy, Baloney, Lough Rinn, Our Shiraz, Aeropraise, Galahad, Dantessa, Reality Check, Deegan, Stevie Wood, Coup South, Mike

NRM/AUCKLAND THOROUGHBRED BREEDERS STAKES

G2, WFA F&M 1400m, $60,000, Pukekohe Park, November 22
1. PAY MY BAIL
3 f, Justice Prevails – Ebony Jane (Three Legs).
Owners Messrs T A Green & T J McKee ONZM.
Breeders G W de Gruchy.
Trainer Stephen & Trevor McKee.
Jockey Lee Rutherford.
2. Miss Potential
5 m, Dolphin Street – Richfield Rose (Crested Wave).
Owners A W Borrie.
Breeders B Borrie.
Trainer Bill Borrie.
3. Amah Dramas
6 m, Barathea – Enchilada (Alydar).
Owners D A Hayes.
Breeders D P R Esplin & S J Rush.
Trainer Don Sellwood.
MARGINS: LONG NECK, 1/2 LEN, 3 LEN
Time: 01:22.37 Track: firm
Others: Foxy Blonde, Rodrigo Rose, Sierra Dane, Critic, Swallow, Scarlet Rose, Glitzy, Caballos, Surprize Surprize, Like The Wind, Ascending, Ginzapearl, Hidden Factor

EAGLE TECHNOLOGY COUNTIES CUP

G2, OPN HCP 2100m, $100,000, Pukekohe Park, November 22
1=. LEICA GUV
5 g, Deputy Governor – Leica Or Not (Kendor).
Owners R A & Mrs R J Scarborough.
Breeders R A Scarborough.
Trainer Jeff & Emma-Lee McVean.
Jockey Eddie De Klerk.
1=. PENNY GEM
4 m, Pentire – Gemscay (Maizcay).
Owners A F & Mrs C I Abel, Messrs A K Bell, C W Cherrie, P A Moroney & B A Schroder.
Breeders A R Galbraith, J W Thompson & Waitaria Holdings Ltd.
Trainer Michael Moroney & Andrew Scott.
Jockey Michael Coleman.
3. Memphis Blues
5 m, Blues Traveller – Otoia Belle (War Hawk II).
Owners B J & Mrs J P Coleman, Messrs A & N H Young.
Breeders R J Knight.
Trainer Martin Dunlop.
MARGINS: DEAD HEAT, DEAD HEAT, 2 LEN
Time: 02:13.22 Track: firm
Others: Lafleur, Singing Star, Regal Krona, Sunray, Something Majic, Black Muscat, Quick Lip, Raspberry Ripple, Betta Watch It, Ebony Honor, Crown Prince, Cyclades, My Governess

MATUA VALLEY WINES CONCORDE

G2, OPN HCP 1200m, $60,000, Avondale, December 3
1. TAIMANA
5 m, Woodman – Abbaye (Ahonoora).
Owners T J Bodle.
Breeders Mrs J A & P Hogan.
Trainer Michael Moroney & Andrew Scott.
Jockey Michael Coleman.
2. Sunlaw
5 m, Desert Sun – Cereno Cloud (Terreno).
Owners L H Chan.
Breeders S Eagleton.
Trainer Graeme Sanders & Debbie Sweeney.
3. Scutarius
9 g, Esquire – Peg's Joy (Le Monarc).
Owners J S & Mrs M Dyke.
Breeders Mrs P J, Miss S P & Miss V S Kaye.
Trainer Bernard Dyke.
MARGINS: 1/2 LEN, 3/4 LEN, SHORT NECK
Time: 01:08.49 Track: firm
Others: Dragon Tiger, Delargo, Double Ar Be, Miss Potential, Silver Sister, Sound The Alarm, Danceinthesun, Bankonit, Time Warp, Travellin' Man, Blu Rapture, Danasar, Warmark

SKY CITY AVONDALE GUINEAS

G2, 3YO 2000m, $60,000, Avondale, December 6
1. PHILAMOR
3 g, Generous – Plaid (Morcon).
Owners Archer Corporation Ltd.
Breeders Archer Corporation Ltd.
Trainer Tony Cole.
Jockey Reese Jones.
2. Mount Street
3 g, Kilimanjaro – Real Trier (Turf Ruler).
Owners Messrs P B Newson, A Wales, A M Whitehouse & B K S Woon.
Breeders P B Newsom.
Trainer Colin Jillings & Richard Yuill.
3. Maroofity
3 g, Maroof – Howkudai (Don't Forget Me).
Owners Tauranga Racing Syndicate (Mgr D C Ellis).
Breeders Mrs J A A & J D Todd.
Trainer Mark Walker.
MARGINS: 1 1/2 LEN, 3/4 LEN, 2 1/4 LEN
Time: 02:02.97 Track: firm
Others: Tadan, Firewheel, Terrain, Oscatello, Sayyida, Brillanti, Dickiedooda, Hot Elle, Pay The Believers, Eastern Lodge

WAIKATO TIMES GOLD CUP

G2, OPN HCP 2400m, $100,000, Te Rapa, December 13
1. EL DUCE
8 g, Lord Ballina – El Fugaz (Sir Avon).
Owners D T Lee, Mrs D M Logan & Dr J L Sprague.
Breeders Mrs D M Logan.
Trainer Donna & Dean Logan.
Jockey Rhys McLeod.
2. My Governess
5 m, Deputy Governor – Regal Orphan (Zamazaan).
Owners J E & Mrs J J Boon.
Breeders P J B Smith.
Trainer John Boon.
3. Bel Air
7 g, Victory Dance – Hollywood Hotel (Nassipour).
Owners Messrs M J Surgenor & P J Walker.
Breeders Grande Vue Lodge Syndicate.
Trainer Peter Walker.
MARGINS: 4 LEN, 3/4 LEN, 1 3/4 LEN Time: 02:31.95 Track: soft
Others: Singing Star, Lord Belvedere, Regal Krona, Athens, Our Unicorn, Lord Mighty Mellay, Imperial Brief, Devious, Benchmark, Cut The Pack, Lafleur, Sunray, Asgoodas

EIGHT CARAT CLASSIC

G2, 3YOF 1600m, $100,000, Ellerslie, December 26
1. KAINUI BELLE
3 f, Kashani – Lady Ukiah (Straight Strike).
Owners Mrs J J & P W Rogers.
Breeders Mrs J J & P W Rogers.
Trainer Vanessa & Wayne Hillis.
Jockey Noel Harris.
2. Eftee One
3 f, Volksraad – Bashful Lady (Imperial Guard).
Owners Mrs F Torrance.
Breeders B W & Mrs R A Wilson.
Trainer Richard Dee & Matthew Dixon.
3. Danette
3 f, Danske – Amynette (Amyntor).
Owners Messrs J R Collinson, M W Freeman, P N Jacobsen, A J & P B Mora.
Breeders Cambridge Hunt Ltd.
Trainer Dick & Chris Bothwell.
MARGINS: 1 1/4 LEN, 1/2 LEN, 1 1/4 LEN
Time: 01:33.87 Track: firm
Others: Luca, Sarah Vee, Mohawk, Taatletail, Miss Tea Rose, Minza Diamond, Hot Elle, Marlena, Ocean Melodie, Rockabubble, Pride Of The Class

NZ HERALD QUEEN ELIZABETH HANDICAP

G2, OPN HCP 2400m, $100,000, Ellerslie, December 26
1. UPSETTHYM
5 m, Rhythm – Set Up (Zabeel).
Owners Pepsi Syndicate.
Breeders Mrs J A & P Hogan.
Trainer Karen Fursdon.
Jockey Gemma Sliz.
2. Lafleur
4 m, Zabeel – Desert Lily (Green Desert).
Owners Messrs P J Vela ONZM & P M Vela.
Breeders P J & P M Vela.
Trainer Jim Gibbs.
3. Leica Guv
5 g, Deputy Governor – Leica Or Not (Kendor).
Owners R A & Mrs R J Scarborough.
Breeders R A Scarborough.
Trainer Jeff & Emma-Lee McVean.
MARGINS: 1 1/4 LEN, LONG HEAD, _ HEAD
Time: 02:33.55 Track: firm
Others: Asgoodas, Ready To Rumble, Love Fly Her, My Governess, Sunray, Regal Krona, Ebony Honor, Cyclades, Classy's Magic, Bel Air, Catchmeifyoucan, Tunzi

NEW ZEALAND BLOODSTOCK ROYAL STAKES

G2, 3YOF 2000m, $120,000, Ellerslie, January 2
1. BUCKLE MY SHOE
3 f, Rory's Jester – Rose Of Marizza (Nassipour).
Owners Mrs B R O'Sullivan.
Breeders B T Agnew.
Trainer Paul O'Sullivan.
Jockey Leith Innes.
2. Kainui Belle
3 f, Kashani – Lady Ukiah (Straight Strike).
Owners Mrs J J & P W Rogers.
Breeders Mrs J J & P W Rogers.
Trainer Vanessa & Wayne Hillis.
3. Eftee One
3 f, Volksraad – Bashful Lady (Imperial Guard).
Owners Mrs F Torrance.
Breeders B W & Mrs R A Wilson.
Trainer Richard Dee & Matthew Dixon.
MARGINS. 3/4 LEN, SHORT HEAD, 3/4 LEN
Time: 02:04.52 Track: firm
Others: Luca, Ocean Melodie, Calveen, Classy Belle, Eternal Lee, Glenview Lass, Champagne Heights, Filante Etoile, Identity, Heads Or Tales, The Bell Ringer

JERRY CLAYTON BMW TROPHY

G2, OPN HCP 1600m, $100,000, Ellerslie, January 2
1. POMP AND GLORY
5 g, Pompeii Court – Aptitude (Brauner).
Owners Messrs J M Clydesdale & T W Crommelin.
Breeders Cromco Thoroughbreds (NZ) Ltd.
Trainer Alan Jones & Brett McDonald.
Jockey Lynsey Hofmann.
2. Our Fuji
4 g, Fuji Kiseki – Feisty Kate (Marscay).
Owners Messrs T J Burn, G H Mander & R P Rosenberg.
Breeders Stratheden Stud Pty Ltd.
Trainer Peter & Nikki Hurdle.
3. Danceinthesun
4 m, Desert Sun – Miss Tripper (Vice Regal).
Owners Mrs A M & S B Phillips.
Breeders Mrs A M & S B Phillips.
Trainer Graeme Sanders & Debbie Sweeney.
MARGINS: HEAD, 1 1/2 LEN, NECK Time: 01:34.66 Track: firm
Others: Kakaho, Amah Dramas, Sir Kinloch, Desperate, Fire In The Hole, Double Ar Be, Carlton Bru, Zahdeal

FORD WAKEFIELD CHALLENGE STAKES

G2, 2YO 1200m, $100,000, Trentham, January 17
1. KAPSDAN
2 f, Kaapstad – Danaselvam (Danehill).
Owners Mandalay Bay Syndicate (Mgr D C Ellis).
Breeders Mrs J & T M Henderson.
Trainer Mark Walker.
Jockey Opie Bosson.
2. Egyptian Ra
2 g, Woodborough – Egyptian Queen (Karioi Lad).
Owners Messrs C A Ball & R J Barton, Mesdames L M Rae, P E Sapich, M K Scott & E K Wootton.
Breeders C A Ball & M L Barratt.
Trainer Kenny Rae.
3. Prickle
2 f, Pins – Snobbish (Centaine).
Owners B Anderson, R Dalley, G Shaw, G R & K T Stanley & Turk's No 3 Syndicate.
Breeders G J Chittick.

Trainer Paul O'Sullivan.
MARGINS: 1 1/2 LEN, 3 3/4 LEN, NOSE
Time: 01:07.24 Track: firm
Others: Florilegium, Lotzatow, Platinum Slipper, Atapi, Summer Nymph, Sheka, Towkahn, Dominica, Go Our Breeze, Sir Woody

CAMBRIDGE STUD SIR TRISTRAM FILLIES CLASSIC

G2, 3YOF 2000m, $100,000, Te Rapa, February 7
1. TAATLETAIL
3 f, Faltaat – Defensive Lady (Defensive Play).
Owners Messrs B J Foster, P C Glover, S R Just, D McLuckie, P L Meo & G A Rogerson.
Breeders Miss D Ho.
Trainer Graeme Rogerson & Stephen Autridge.
Jockey Michael Walker.
2. Anne Carina
3 f, Danske – Lidahya (Dahar).
Owners Llanhennock Trust.
Breeders Llanhennock Trust.
Trainer Graeme Sanders & Debbie Sweeney.
3. Madame Shinko
3 f, Shinko King – Madame Mac (Lanfranco).
Owners Mad Mac Syndicate.
Breeders R J Knight & N F O'Styke.
Trainer Jim Wallace.
MARGINS: LONG NECK, 1 1/2 LEN, SHORT NECK Time: 02:04.16 Track: firm
Others: Justine Coup, Highflying, Haylee Baylee, Danette, Mohawk, Filante Etoile, Kind Return, Ashkala, Saveke, Glenview Lass, Native Song, Montreal Gold, Boulevardofdreams

ROBIN, DUKE OF BEDFORD MATAMATA BREEDERS STAKES

G2, 2YOF 1200m, $70,000, Matamata, February 14
1. VELASCO
2 f, Flying Spur – Vital Curves (McGinty).
Owners Mrs J F Andrews & J K Sullivan.
Breeders J K Sullivan & Ms J Andrews.
Trainer Bryce Tankard.
Jockey Andrew Calder.
2. Acupuncture
2 f, Pins – Quack (Magic Ring).
Owners Mrs C & W L Bolton.
Breeders T J Bodle.
Trainer Mark Walker.
3. Can't Hackit
2 f, Fasliyev – Close Your Eyes (Geiger Counter).
Owners D B Gardner.
Breeders Chatham Lodge Thoroughbred Ltd.
Trainer Kevin Cullen.
MARGINS: NOSE, 3/4 LEN, LONG NECK
Time: 01:12.25 Track: easy
Others: Volk Dancer, Prickle, Majestic Sweep, Florilegium, Queenza, Platinum Slipper, Steffi, Madamanz

CHAMPIONSHIP STAKES

G2, 3YOF 2100m, $100,000, Ellerslie, February 28
1. BOULEVARDOFDREAMS
3 f, Daggers Drawn – Faustina (Sackford).
Owners T Van Beurden.
Breeders G R Cunningham & N W Nicholson.
Trainer Vanessa & Wayne Hillis.
Jockey Gary Grylls.
2. Partee
3 f, Sandtrap – Te Akau Jo (Sir Tristram).
Owners C J Bothwell, J M Mccarvill & Est late L McCarvill.
Breeders B S Mullane, P Setchell & L Williams.
Trainer Dick & Chris Bothwell.
3. Haylee Baylee
3 f, Oregon – Mac's Gold (Le Belvedere).
Owners J C Morell.
Breeders J C Morell.
Trainer John Morell.
MARGINS: 3 LEN, 1 1/2 LEN, 8 1/2 LEN
Time: 02:18.04 Track: soft
Others: Madame Shinko, Saveke, Azapak, Buckle My Shoe, Glenview Lass, Richter Pass, Anne Carina, Highflying, Our Sunny Joy

WESTERNBAY FINANCE JAPAN/NZ TROPHY

G2, OPN HCP 1600m, $100,000, The Tauranga Racecourse, March 27
1. SILKY RED BOXER
4 g, Casual Lies – Soleil Etoile (Star Way).
Owners Not Enough Taro Syndicate.
Breeders Mrs H G & W G Bax.
Trainer Heather Weller.
Jockey Noel Harris.
2. Pomp And Glory
5 g, Pompeii Court – Aptitude (Brauner).
Owners J M Clydesdale & T W Crommelin.
Breeders Cromco Thoroughbreds (NZ) Ltd.
Trainer Alan Jones & Brett McDonald.
3. Marie Claire
5 m, O'Reilly – Trotanoy (Lord Seymour).
Owners P J Vela ONZM & P M Vela.
Breeders P J & P M Vela.
Trainer Paul O'Sullivan.
MARGINS: 1 1/4 LEN, _ HEAD, HEAD Time: 01:33.90 Track: firm
Others: Danceinthesun, Surprize Surprize, Royal Secret, Fire In The Hole, Boycott, Regal Krona, Jetski, Desert Flight, Upsetthym, Sir Kinloch, Zvezda

LAWNMASTER AWAPUNI GOLD CUP

G2, WFA 2000m, $80,000, Awapuni, April 3
1. IRISH ROVER
6 g, Kenfair – Sterling Lea (One Pound Sterling).
Owners E Carson & B J McCahill Snr.
Breeders B J McCahill.
Trainer Eddie Carson.
Jockey David Walker.
1. DISTINCTLY SECRET
5 g, Distinctly North – Te Akau Secret (Lord Ballina).
Owners D C Ellis, K T O'Donnell, W R Schwamm & M A Shorter.
Breeders D C Ellis.
Trainer Mark Walker.
Jockey Opie Bosson.
3. Lough Rinn
5 g, Jahafil – Lough Allen (Omnicorp).
Owners Mrs J L & R P Nolan, Mrs B M & T A Smith.
Breeders Mrs J L & R P Nolan & Mrs B M & T A Smith.
Trainer Ron Nolan.
MARGINS: DEAD HEAT, 4 1/2 LEN, 1 1/4 LEN Time: 02:02.52 Track: firm
Others: Greene Street, Kaapstad Way, Boycott, Princess Oregon, Doyle, Ambush

HAWKE S BAY CUP GOLD CUP IN ASSOCIATION WITH DAVMET NZ LTD

G2, OPN HCP 2200m, $77,600, Hastings, April 17
1. ROYAL SECRET
4 m, His Royal Highness – Premium Star (Super Gray).
Owners W M Brausch, P F Dawson, G B & J A Thomson.
Breeders W M Brausch, G B & J A Thomson.
Trainer Peter Harris.
Jockey Noel Harris.
2. Regal Krona
8 g, Krona – Regal Cent (Centaine).
Owners P L Keppel, H R McGlade & R M Norman.
Breeders H R & Est late A McGlade.
Trainer Sheryl & Roger McGlade.
3. Baloney
7 g, St Hilarion – Kim's Doll (Dolly's Alydar).
Owners J G & Mrs M A Wellington.
Breeders J G & Mrs M A Wellington.
Trainer Dick & Chris Bothwell.
MARGINS: LONG HEAD, LEN, 2 3/4 LEN
Time: 02:14.10 Track: firm
Others: Bel Air, Baywatch Babe, Sensuous, Tina Temple, Madison Gray, Singing Star, Sideto Emdeca, Alcatraz, Just Honor, Greene Street, Rotang, Scusa Mi

TRAVIS STAKES

G2, WFA F&M 1600m, $80,000, Te Rapa, April 24
1. BRIDIE BELLE
3 f, Al Akbar – Golinda (Crested Wave).
Owners L D & Mrs M Pettifer.
Breeders J D Corcoran.
Trainer Chris & Colleen Wood.
Jockey Allan Peard.
2. Belle Femme
4 m, Zeditave – Cast Your Fate (Bletchingly).
Owners Mrs J L Egan & Ms M E Kent.
Breeders Chantilly Partnership.
Trainer Stephen & Trevor McKee.
3. Rodrigo Rose
5 m, Rodrigo de Triano – Rosebrook (Vain).
Owners Lady & Sir Patrick Hogan, Mr P J & Mrs S G Walker.
Breeders T O Harrison.
Trainer Graham Richardson & Mark Donoghue.
MARGINS: SHORT NECK, 3/4 LEN, HEAD
Time: 01:34.95 Track: firm
Others: Marie Claire, Diamond Like, Surprize Surprize, Elegant Emerald, Kapsjoy, Danceinthesun, Volksini, Rapid Kay, Akela, Pride Of The Class, Amah Dramas, Gristle, Sokool

GROUP 3

CANTERBURY RACING WINTER CUP

G3, OPN HCP 1600m, $60,000, Riccarton Park, August 2
1. TUSCANY WARRIOR
5 h, Tuscany Flyer – Blue Ruffles (Piperhill).
Owners J F & Mrs S L Street.
Breeders Miss K M Banks & Mrs C A Rouse.
Trainer Lisa Latta.
Jockey Robert Hannam.
2. Decent Girl
6 m, Centaine – Fidelity (Fiesta Star).
Owners D & Mrs V I Bowen, P D Inglis, J M & Mrs M P Stuart & G K Taylor.
Breeders G J Chittick & M R Ormond.
Trainer Paul Harris.
3. Joseph
6 g, Starjo – Black Mist (Sound Reason).
Owners Mrs S Simson.
Breeders Mrs S Simson.
Trainer Kevin Gray.
MARGINS: Time: 01:37.16 Track: soft
Others: Danzapride, Albacora, The Cheek, Bodie, Irish Rover, Ghostly Smile, Moore's Hall, Real Vision, Pont Aven, Burton, Perceptible, Global Charmer, Missy, Regal Night, Zen

MERIAL METRIC MILE

G3, OPN HCP 1600m, $45,000, Awapuni, September 6
1. DUNMORE BOY
5 g, Tinryland Lad – Lindo Chaval (Brauner).
Owners E & Mrs R M Carson.
Breeders E & Mrs R M Carson.
Trainer Eddie Carson.
Jockey Leanne Isherwood.
2. Joseph
6 g, Starjo – Black Mist (Sound Reason).
Owners Mrs S Simson.
Breeders Mrs S Simson.
Trainer Kevin Gray.
3. Starbo
6 g, Starjo – Sarton (Marceau).
Owners Messrs A E & A H James.
Breeders D H Cudby & A E James.
Trainer Allan James.
MARGINS: Time: 01:43.32 Track: heavy
Others: Danzapride, Tuscany Warrior, Andy, Reg, Sweet Dancer, Lady Of The House, Van Winkle, Danzaman, Decent Girl, War Dancer, Galahad

HIGHVIEW STAKES

G3, 3YOF 1200m, $50,000, Otaki, September 13
1. TAATLETAIL
3 f, Faltaat – Defensive Lady (Defensive Play).
Owners Messrs B J Foster, P C Glover, S R Just, D McLuckie, P L Meo & G A Rogerson.
Breeders Miss D Ho.
Trainer Graeme Rogerson & Stephen Autridge.
Jockey Michael Walker.
2. Rapid Kay
3 f, Towkay – Racing Waters (Racing Is Fun).
Owners Bleap Syndicate.
Breeders Little Avondale Trust.
Trainer Mark Walker.
3. Pay My Bail
3 f, Justice Prevails – Ebony Jane (Three Legs).
Owners Messrs T A Green & T J McKee ONZM.
Breeders G W de Gruchy.
Trainer Stephen & Trevor McKee.
MARGINS: Time: 01:10.16 Track: easy
Others: Catscan, J'Lo, Kalamata, Look At Moiye, Scene Steeler, The Bell Ringer, Magistra Delecta, Dragon Maiden, Bless, Eminem, Quivira, Sarah Vee

WINDSOR PARK GOLAN HAWKE S BAY GUINEAS

G3, 3YO 1400m, $100,000, Hastings, September 27
1. STARDANE

AUCKLAND RACING CLUB

Pay My Bail.

3 g, Soviet Star – Astradane (Danehill).
Owners B J & Mrs M A Harvey, B L & Mrs M M Jenkins.
Breeders Trelawney Stud.
Trainer Brian Jenkins.
Jockey Rhys McLeod.
2. Penitentiary
3 g, Pentire – Strangeways (Veloso).
Owners J C & Mrs M A Thompson.
Breeders Mrs V M Langsford.
Trainer Richard Otto & Stephen Fache.
3. Eftee One
3 f, Volksraad – Bashful Lady (Imperial Guard).
Owners Mrs F Torrance.
Breeders B W & Mrs R A Wilson.
Trainer Richard Dee & Matthew Dixon.
MARGINS: Time: 001:20.7 Track: firm
Others: Magistra Delecta, Green Machine, Rat Tat, J'Lo, Rockabubble, Danboss, Tadan, Parliament, Waromar, Brillanti, Clifton, Wee Winkle, Shadowfax Babe

INDIAN DANEHILL LOWLAND STAKES

G3, 3YOF 1400m, $45,000, Trentham, October 11
1. TAATLETAIL
3 f, Faltaat – Defensive Lady (Defensive Play).
Owners Messrs B J Foster, P C Glover, S R Just, D McLuckie, P L Meo & G A Rogerson.
Breeders Miss D Ho.
Trainer Graeme Rogerson & Stephen Autridge.
Jockey Michael Walker.
2. Danette
3 f, Danske – Amynette (Amyntor).
Owners Messrs J R Collinson, M W Freeman, P N Jacobsen, A J & P B Mora.
Breeders Cambridge Hunt Ltd.
Trainer Dick & Chris Bothwell.
3. Clifton
3 f, Bahhare – Instantly (Spectacular Love).
Owners P M Merton & Rich Hill Thoroughbreds Ltd.
Breeders Ms S S Elias, H A Fletcher & A R Galbraith.
Trainer J G Sargent & K L Allpress.
MARGINS: Time: 01:28.68 Track: heavy
Others: Magistra Delecta, Her Hidden Talent, Rutland Lass, Whatronnielikes, Turtle Creek, Bev's Choice, Eternal Melody, J'Lo

FAYETTE PARK STAKES

G3, WFA F&M 1400m, $40,000, Hawera, October 18
1. ASCENDING
5 m, Bigstone – Ascendo (Conquistarose).
Owners D S & Mrs A B Alderslade, M L & Mrs M J Murdoch.
Breeders G J Clatworthy, Haunui Farm Ltd & G H Madill.
Trainer Moira Murdoch.
Jockey Brian Hibberd.
2. Akela
6 m, Al Akbar – Zephana (Zephyr Bay).
Owners B F & Miss K C Avery, Mesdames J M Brown & P E Stott & C J Wood.
Breeders B F Avery & C J Wood.
Trainer Chris & Colleen Wood.
3. Critic
5 m, Centaine – Benazir (Vice Regal).
Owners Messrs M C Acklin & G J Chittick.
Breeders G J Chittick.
Trainer Jeanann Hercock.
MARGINS: Time: 01:23.42 Track: firm
Others: Sierra Dane, Luscilla, Rodrigo Rose, Minnie Belt, Blessed Sun, Blackrock College, Surprize Surprize, Mae Bee, Tina Temple, Hurricane Strike, Fair Padoza, Ain't All Trumps

LION RED PLATE

G3, WFA 1200m, $40,000, Arawa Park, October 18
1. PAY MY BAIL
3 f, Justice Prevails – Ebony Jane (Three Legs).
Owners Messrs T A Green & T J McKee ONZM.
Breeders G W de Gruchy.
Trainer Stephen & Trevor McKee.
Jockey Lee Rutherford.
2. Diamond Like
4 m, Danehill – Tristalove (Sir Tristram).
Owners Ms E L, Sir Patrick & Lady Hogan, Mrs N K & P Hunt.
Breeders Cambridge Stud.
Trainer Paul O'Sullivan.
3. Sedecrem
5 g, Faltaat – Real Trier (Turf Ruler).
Owners Messrs C J Giltrap, W C McDonald, P J Walker & E H Ward.
Breeders P B Newsom.
Trainer Colin Jillings & Richard Yuill.
MARGINS: Time: 01:10.14 Track: firm
Others: Glitzy, Danzapride, Vinaka, Travellin' Man, Shady Devil, Fritz, Palliser Bay

CENTRA ROTORUA CHALLENGE PLATE

G3, OPN HCP 1900m, $40,000, Arawa Park, October 18
1. SUNRAY
4 h, Zabeel – Lambert Miss (Danzatore).
Owners Mualim Hasnan Ltd.
Breeders Mrs J A & P Hogan.
Trainer Paul O'Sullivan.
Jockey Michael Coleman.
2. Ben Sparta
7 g, Stark South – Cilla Red (Sky Chase).
Owners Mrs G J King & G Merkulov.
Breeders Mrs M A Kelly & M J Quest.
Trainer George Merkulov.
3. Asgoodas
6 g, Honor Grades – Oso Sasha (Veloso).
Owners Kinross No 3 Syndicate.
Breeders Kinross No 3 Syndicate.
Trainer Donna Fleming.
MARGINS: Time: 01:58.23 Track: firm
Others: Tansorka, Supa Belt, Lord Silver Dale, Deebee Belle, Galahad, Being Supreme, Titian, Atta Glance, Mick Bailey, Raspberry Ripple

LINDAUER GRANDEUR STAKES

G3, WFA 2000m, $35,000, Ellerslie, November 4
1. EL DUCE
8 g, Lord Ballina – El Fugaz (Sir Avon).
Owners D T Lee, Mrs D M Logan & Dr J L Sprague.
Breeders Mrs D M Logan.
Trainer Donna & Dean Logan.
Jockey Lisa Allpress.
2. St Reims
4 h, Zabeel – L'Quiz (L'Enjoleur).
Owners February Syndicate.
Breeders Mrs J A & P Hogan.
Trainer Chris McNab.
3. Millennium
6 g, Prized – Royal Med (Medieval Man).
Owners D G & R B McLaren Ltd, Messrs J B Ede, L L Stevens & W M Wilson.
Breeders D G & R B McLaren Ltd.
Trainer Stephen & Trevor McKee.
MARGINS: Time: 002:07.5 Track: easy
Others: Lafleur, Singing Star, No Fibs, Deebee Belle, Clemenger, Sweet Dancer, Leica Guv, Ready To Rumble

INTERCONTINENTAL WELLINGTON CUDDLE STAKES

G3, F&M 1600m, $40,000, Trentham, November 4
1. RODRIGO ROSE
5 m, Rodrigo de Triano – Rosebrook (Vain).
Owners Lady & Sir Patrick Hogan, Mr P J & Mrs S G Walker.
Breeders T O Harrison.
Trainer Graham Richardson & Mark Donoghue.
Jockey Jason Waddell.
2. Sweet Revenge
5 m, Justice Prevails – Sal Tarrago (Tarrago).
Owners C M & Mesdames R F Arnold & M F Childs, Messrs L E Kenny, N D Misseldine & P J McVicker.
Breeders Mrs H E & S F Kelly.
Trainer Gary Vile.
3. Creil
4 m, Frenchpark – Fortiare (Shearwalk).
Owners J D Georgetti & Mrs G E Kenny.
Breeders Cambridge Hunt Ltd.
Trainer Geoff Georgetti.
MARGINS: Time: 01:35.42 Track: firm
Others: Akela, Mae Bee, Luscilla, Blackrock College, Sursum Corda, Blessed Sun, Touch Of Defiance, Uisce Beagh, City Of Dreams, Deciding Stride

GOLD CLUB METROPOLITAN TROPHY HANDICAP

G3, OPN HCP 2500m, $40,000, Riccarton Park, November 8
1. TORLESSE
6 g, Volksraad – Seamist (Beaufort Sea).
Owners Ngapuke Stables Syndicate.
Breeders Mrs B J & Est late A G Wigley.
Trainer Mandy Brown.
Jockey Terry Moseley.
2. Our Shiraz
6 m, Nediym – Kotobuki (Vice Regal).
Owners Dr H M & Dr W J Bishop, P J & Mrs S L Kay.
Breeders P J & Mrs S L Kay.
Trainer Michael Pitman.
3. Cabella
5 m, Senor Pete – Miss Fiesta (Fiesta Star).
Owners Thomas Cooker No 1 Syndicate.
Breeders B A Collins & K M Rowe.
Trainer Kevin Hughes.
MARGINS: Time: 02:44.32 Track: firm
Others: Baloney, Soldier Blue, Stevie Wood, Joseph, Aeropraise, Galadriel, Vatican Heights, Ayrgo, Danzaman

SKYCITY HAMILTON GUINEAS

G3, 3YO 1600m, $50,000, Te Rapa, November 8
1. PHILAMOR
3 g, Generous – Plaid (Morcon).
Owners Archer Corporation Ltd.
Breeders Archer Corporation Ltd.
Trainer Tony Cole.
Jockey Reese Jones.
2. Waitoki Dream
3 g, Pentire – Calm Lover (Spectacular Love).
Owners Mrs K L & M J Shallue.
Breeders Mrs J G Sclater, C C E & J W Thompson.
Trainer Kevin Cullen.
3. Mount Street
3 g, Kilimanjaro – Real Trier (Turf Ruler).
Owners Messrs P B Newson, A Wales, A M Whitehouse & B K S Woon.
Breeders P B Newsom.
Trainer Colin Jillings & Richard Yuill.
MARGINS: Time: 01:37.15 Track: firm
Others: Oscatello, Maroofity, Tadan, Artemesia, Brilliant Flash, The Bell Ringer, Clifton, Rat Tat, Ioneday, Il Generale

CHRISTCHURCH CASINO CHURCHILL STAKES HANDICAP

G3, OPN HCP 1600m, $40,000, Riccarton Park, November 15
1. JACK BE NIMBLE
5 g, Exploding Prospect – Picea (McGinty).
Owners B J Cottle & Miss J D Hillis.
Breeders Ancroft Stud Ltd.
Trainer Joanne Hillis.
Jockey Andrew Calder.
2. Portofino Bay
6 g, McGinty – Deutzia (Chem).
Owners Messrs W R Campbell, B Roitero & K J Sowman.
Breeders B Roitero.
Trainer John & Karen Parsons.
3. Ima Royal
5 m, His Royal Highness – I'm A Roughie (Roughcast).

Owners J M W Curran & Mrs S A Phillips.
Breeders Galaxy Exports Ltd.
Trainer Kelly Thompson.
MARGINS: Time: 01:36.78 Track: firm
Others: Minnie Belt, Chestpeak, Doyle, Rising Heights, Oxborough Castle, Pledge, Global Charmer

LINDAUER STEWARDS STAKES HANDICAP

G3, OPN HCP 1200m, $50,000, Riccarton Park, November 15
1. FINGALBUNT
4 g, Miesque's Son – Kooeloah (Royal Academy).
Owners Fingal Figures Syndicate.
Breeders Dojona Nominees Pty Ltd & E Lomas.
Trainer Les Didham.
Jockey Lance Robinson.
2. Delargo
5 g, Encosta De Lago – Slippery Auri (Willingly).
Owners Messrs S L Cranfield, A C Fuller, K W Green & R J Miller.
Breeders G D Smith.
Trainer Robert Priscott.
3. Golden Harvest
4 g, Carolingian – Irish Mist (Shannon).
Owners Messrs M P Breslin & W J Gleeson, Mrs S A Mason & M J Morton.
Breeders Mrs S M Harty.
Trainer Mike Breslin.
MARGINS: Time: 01:09.49 Track: firm
Others: Dominatrix, Mareeba, Go Thenaki, Wild Planet, Million Stars, The Green Man, Yorkminster, Life Of Riley, Slinky Planet

TAURANGA STAKES

G3, WFA 1600m, $40,000, The Tauranga Racecourse, November 15
1. JUST AQUA
8 g, Justice Prevails – Aquilac (Crested Wave).
Owners Mrs D & P L Wong.
Breeders Mrs E, R & W Alexander & Mrs J & R Cleary.
Trainer Graeme Sanders & Debbie Sweeney.
Jockey Lee Rutherford.
2. Ben Sparta
7 g, Stark South – Cilla Red (Sky Chase).
Owners Mrs G J King & G Merkulov.
Breeders Mrs M A Kelly & M J Quest.
Trainer George Merkulov.
3. Sir Kinloch
5 g, Rhythm – Ivory (Gold And Ivory).
Owners Messrs H S, H S & S S Dyke.
Breeders H S, H S & S S Dyke.
Trainer Colin Jillings & Richard Yuill.
MARGINS: Time: 01:36.62 Track: firm
Others: Marie Claire, Spring Seasons, Millennium, Victory Smile, Icey Red, Lafleur, Atta Glance, Tansorka

ROBERTSON HOLDEN EULOGY STAKES

G3, 3YOF 1600m, $50,000, Awapuni, December 13
1. KAINUI BELLE
3 f, Kashani – Lady Ukiah (Straight Strike).
Owners Mrs J J & P W Rogers.
Breeders Mrs J J & P W Rogers.
Trainer Vanessa & Wayne Hillis.
Jockey Noel Harris.
2. Classic Clare
3 f, Gold Brose – Funny Features (Archway).
Owners Kotuku Investments Ltd.
Breeders Goldbro Services Pty Ltd.
Trainer Shane Kennedy.
3. Wharite Princess
3 f, His Royal Highness – Regal Visit (Vice Regal).
Owners N M Cantwell, M R Curd, T A Robinson, K J Tod, K R Williams & R J Wong.
Breeders Lambourn Stud Ltd.
Trainer Lisa Latta.
MARGINS: LONG NECK, LEN, 2 LEN Time: 01:36.30 Track: easy
Others: Dowry, Supa Strike, Life Time, Unearthed, Vel Canto, Goodgollymissmolly, Our Kitty, Kashilldo, Danette, Azapak

GASMATE STAKES

G3, WFA F&M 1600m, $40,000, Te Rapa, December 13
1. SOKOOL
5 m, Bin Ajwaad – Dancing Mill (Kala Dancer).
Owners G J F Castle, Miss R Clubb, Messrs D G Dent, R A Hedges, S A Ironside & J G McLintock.
Breeders Mrs G & G M Levick.
Trainer Frank & Craig Ritchie.
Jockey Eddie De Klerk.
2. Surprize Surprize
6 m, Prized – Impossible Dream (Imposing).
Owners Mrs C A & G E Vazey.
Breeders Mrs J M Wilding.
Trainer Kevin Hughes.
3. Rodrigo Rose
5 m, Rodrigo de Triano – Rosebrook (Vain).
Owners Lady & Sir Patrick Hogan, Mr P J & Mrs S G Walker.
Breeders T O Harrison.
Trainer Graham Richardson & Mark Donoghue.
MARGINS: 1 1/4 LEN, LEN, 2 1/4 LEN Time: 01:39.08 Track: easy
Others: Rapid Kay, Ascending, For Love, Belle Femme, Volksini, Hidden Factor, Mary Seton, Visique, Amah Dramas, Foxy Blonde

Z-ONE MOTORING MANAWATU CUP

G3, OPN HCP 2300m, $60,000, Awapuni, December 20
1. RISING HEIGHTS
6 g, Stark South – Fairy Heights (Tristrams Heritage).
Owners Mrs N E & P E Izett.
Breeders Mrs J M & W J Ewen.
Trainer Howie & Lorraine Mathews.
Jockey Darryl Bradley.
2. Corrupted
6 g, British Banker – Zanzibar Lady (Nassipour).
Owners T Sargent.
Breeders R G Lithgow.
Trainer Peter Lock.
3. Galway Lass
5 m, Rhythm – Ballycairn (Zabeel).
Owners Augusta Bloodstock Ltd.
Breeders Mrs J A & P Hogan.
Trainer Paul O'Sullivan.
MARGINS: LONG NECK, LONG NECK, NECK Time: 02:21.49 Track: firm
Others: Mae Bee, Supa Belt, Branson, Crown Control, Princess Oregon, Life's A Gamble, Mudgee's Gold, Cluden Creek, Eagarpence, Bejayjay, Semper Fidelis, Lord Mighty Mellay, Baywatch Babe, Teearcy

HIGGINS CHALLENGE STAKES

G3, WFA 1400m, $50,000, Awapuni, December 20
1. DOYLE
8 g, Dance Floor – Shelley Lack (Prince Echo).
Owners Mrs N E & P E Izett.
Breeders Mrs J Broome.
Trainer Howie & Lorraine Mathews.
Jockey Jason Waddell.
2=. Hail
6 g, Stark South – Valley Court (Pompeii Court).
Owners Messrs A J Cunningham & R B Marsh.
Breeders Fayette Park Stud Ltd.
Trainer Bruce & Stephen Marsh.
2=. Burglar
5 g, Housebuster – Centre Isle (Centaine).
Owners D S & Mrs A B Alderslade, M L & Mrs M J Murdoch.
Breeders Roberts Holdings Ltd.
Trainer Moira Murdoch.
MARGINS: 3/4 LEN, DEAD HEAT, DEAD HEAT Time: 01:24.12 Track: firm
Others: Silky Red Boxer, On Spec, Bunker, Oui Brigitte, Silver Sister, Anson Bay, Greene Street

ARC LIFE MEMBERS KING S PLATE

G3, WFA 1600m, $50,000, Ellerslie, December 26
1. UBIQUITOUS
3 g, Tale of the Cat – Zahra (Zabeel).
Owners G G Syndicate Ltd & O G Glenn.
Breeders R W E Moore.
Trainer Michael Moroney & Andrew Scott.
Jockey Rhys McLeod.
2. Doyle
8 g, Dance Floor – Shelley Lack (Prince Echo).
Owners Mrs N E & P E Izett.
Breeders Mrs J Broome.
Trainer Howie & Lorraine Mathews.
3. Surprize Surprize
6 m, Prized – Impossible Dream (Imposing).
Owners Mrs C A & G E Vazey.
Breeders Mrs J M Wilding.
Trainer Kevin Hughes.
MARGINS: 2 3/4 LEN, 3/4 LEN, LEN Time: 01:34.13 Track: firm
Others: Bon Ace, Amah Dramas, Icey Red, St Reims, Zeconquer, Sokool, Clemenger

WESTBURY STUD ECLIPSE STAKES

G3, 2YO 1200m, $50,000, Ellerslie, January 2
1. ALINSKY
2 g, Stravinsky – Alynda (Nassau).
Owners A L & Miss C A Jones & Mrs L C Jones MBE.
Breeders A L Jones.
Trainer Alan Jones & Brett McDonald.
Jockey Lynsey Hofmann.
2. Florilegium
2 f, Cape Cross – Gardenia (Danehill).
Owners Messrs B Reid & G A Rogerson.
Breeders Sir Patrick & Lady Hogan.
Trainer Graeme Rogerson & Stephen Autridge.
3. Atapi
2 c, Last Tycoon – Pride Of Ingenue (Proud Knight).
Owners J C & Mrs M A Thompson.
Breeders Blue Gum Farm Pty Ltd & Ingenue Breeding Syndicate.
Trainer Richard Otto & Stephen Fache.
MARGINS: 3/4 LEN, LONG HEAD, 3 1/4 LEN Time: 01:10.64 Track: firm
Others: Royal Babe, Senorita Ivory, Tri Star, Victory Strike, Sheka, Eloa, Velasco, Midnight Dip, Dominica

TOTARA LODGE COMMUNITY TRUST TRENTHAM STAKES

G3, WFA 2400m, $50,000, Trentham, January 19
1. SEMPER FIDELIS
7 m, Grosvenor – Miss Alfie (Alvaro).
Owners M K & Mrs P M Oulaghan.
Breeders M K & Mrs P M Oulaghan.
Trainer Mark Oulaghan.
Jockey Tony Allan.
2. Quick Lip
6 m, Casual Lies – Straight Lip (Straight Strike).
Owners Mrs L A & Messrs W E Lincoln, J S Moody & R A Verry.
Breeders Mrs A P & J H Lincoln.
Trainer Roger Verry.
3. Bel Air
7 g, Victory Dance – Hollywood Hotel (Nassipour).
Owners Messrs M J Surgenor & P J Walker.
Breeders Grande Vue Lodge Syndicate.
Trainer Peter Walker.
MARGINS: 2 LEN, LONG HEAD, NOSE Time: 02:33.94 Track: soft
Others: For Love, Torlesse, Mudgee's Gold, The Market Man, Our Unicorn, Wolf Creek, Supa Belt, Absolut Peace

MONTJEU WELLINGTON STAKES

G3, 3YO 1600m, $45,000, Trentham, January 24
1. NATIVE SONG
3 f, Mellifont – Enhanced (Caro).
Owners N A Pollard.
Breeders N A Pollard.
Trainer Paddy Kauri.
Jockey Opie Bosson.
2. Danette
3 f, Danske – Amynette (Amyntor).
Owners Messrs J R Collinson, M W Freeman, P N Jacobsen, A J & P B Mora.
Breeders Cambridge Hunt Ltd.
Trainer Dick & Chris Bothwell.
3. Bhandara
3 f, Zabeel – Vedodara (Kreisler).
Owners Barlow Thoroughbred Ltd.
Breeders Barlow Thoroughbred Ltd.
Trainer J G Sargent & K L Allpress.
MARGINS: NECK, NECK, 4 3/4 LEN Time: 01:37.16 Track: easy
Others: Depuessence, De La Costa, Dickiedooda, Penny Hill, Il Generale, The Cat's Whiskers, Energetic Star

WHITE ROBE LODGE HANDICAP

G3, OPN HCP 1600m, $35,000, Wingatui, February 14
1. VOLRONAMO
4 g, Volksraad – Conquisate (Conquistarose).
Owners Messrs C J Black, W N Cameron, R W Gibson, K A Heckler, E L Olsen & J R Vessey.
Breeders C J Black, W N Cameron, R W

Gibson, K A Heckler, E L Olsen & J R Vessey.
Trainer Steven Prince.
Jockey Jamie Bullard.
2. Say Magic
7 g, Magic Ring – Play Safe (Marscay).
Owners Ms C Franich.
Breeders Tristan Antico Thoroughbreds.
Trainer K N Fleming.
3. Burton
7 g, Personal Escort – Minshu (Tom's Shu).
Owners Mrs D M & T K Sidey.
Breeders Mrs D M & T K Sidey.
Trainer Brian & Shane Anderton.
MARGINS: 4 1/2 LEN, 1/2 LEN, NECK Time: 01:37.09 Track: easy
Others: Foxy Blonde, Personalize, Hauriri Boy, Coup Liner, Ima Royal, Jan Valachi, Mareeba, Tapildanz

THE ANGUS INN DESERT GOLD STAKES

G3, 3YOF 1500m, $40,000, Trentham, March 6
1. PRIDE OF THE CLASS
3 f, Volksraad – Grosvenor's Pride (Grosvenor).

OWNERS CLASS OF 2002 SYNDICATE.

Breeders P A Smithies.
Trainer Michael Moroney & Andrew Scott.
Jockey Mark Barnsley.
2. Rapid Kay
3 f, Towkay – Racing Waters (Racing Is Fun).
Owners Bleap Syndicate.
Breeders Little Avondale Trust.
Trainer Mark Walker.
3. Vision
3 f, Entrepreneur – Eye Full (Palatable).
Owners Est Late G H & Mrs M I D Murfitt.
Breeders Mrs M I D & Est late G H Murfitt.
Trainer Roger James & Leanne Bertling.
MARGINS: 1 1/4 LEN, _ HEAD, NECK Time: 01:31.89 Track: easy
Others: Scene Steeler, Catscan, Bhandara, Native Song, Mytrice, Danette, Ever After, Mixty Motion, Lilakyn, Rough Crossing, Grand Legacy, Cent A Misse, Clifton, Shadowfax Babe, Starkay

THOMPSON HANDICAP

G3, OPN HCP 1600m, $35,000, Otaki, March 13
1. DOYLE
8 g, Dance Floor – Shelley Lack (Prince Echo).
Owners Mrs N E & P E Izett.
Breeders Mrs J Broome.
Trainer Howie & Lorraine Mathews.
Jockey Jason Waddell.
2. Silky Red Boxer
4 g, Casual Lies – Soleil Etoile (Star Way).
Owners Not Enough Taro Syndicate.
Breeders Mrs H G & W G Bax.
Trainer Heather Weller.
3. Minnie Belt
4 m, Oregon – Lady Di (Star Of Luskin).
Owners K & Mrs K A Gray.
Breeders K & Mrs K A Gray.
Trainer Kevin Gray.
MARGINS: 1/2 LEN, 3/4 LEN, NOSE Time: 01:34.11 Track: firm
Others: Irish Rover, Madison Gray, Tonic, Hoopla, Boycott, Ernest William, Baileys On Ice, Argegno, Sierra Dane, Say Magic, Blackrock College, Miss Is Brash

FORD 2YO CLASSIC

G3, 2YO 1200m, $45,000, Pukekura Raceway, March 20
1. KEENINSKY
2 c, Stravinsky – So Keen (Jade Hunter).
Owners Mrs D & J Carter, B T Hall & G A Rogerson.
Breeders B T Hall & J A Rowan.
Trainer Graeme Rogerson & Stephen Autridge.
Jockey Allan Peard.
2. Alinsky
2 g, Stravinsky – Alynda (Nassau).
Owners Mrs C A Hawkes, A L Jones & Mrs L C Jones MBE.
Breeders A L Jones.
Trainer Alan Jones & Brett McDonald.
3. Kapsdan
2 f, Kaapstad – Danaselvam (Danehill).
Owners Mandalay Bay Syndicate (Mgr D C Ellis).
Breeders Mrs J & T M Henderson.
Trainer Mark Walker.
MARGINS: HEAD, 1 1/2 LEN, NOSE Time: 01:09.36 Track: firm
Others: Clifton Prince, Viennetta, Clean Sweep, Atapi, How Fantastique, Can't Hackit, La Sizeranne, Lotzatow, Sir Woody, Master Blaster, Summer Nymph, Steely King

HOOKER PACIFIC TARANAKI CUP

G3, OPN HCP 2000m, $50,000, Pukekura Raceway, March 20
1. I'M FIGHTIN
5 g, Prized – Kaapstine (Kaapstad).
Owners Mrs E E & S F Browne, Mrs L C Jones MBE & T Millar.
Breeders Mrs E E & S F Browne, Mrs L C Jones & T Millar.
Trainer Alan Jones & Brett McDonald.
Jockey Lynsey Hofmann.
2. Lough Rinn
5 g, Jahafil – Lough Allen (Omnicorp).
Owners Mrs J L & R P Nolan, Mrs B M & T A Smith.
Breeders Mrs J L & R P Nolan & Mrs B M & T A Smith.
Trainer Ron Nolan.
3. Kaapstad Way
8 g, Kaapstad – Crysell Way (Star Way).
Owners The Chatsworth Trust.
Breeders A Snellex, G R K Taylor & Windsor Park Stud Ltd.
Trainer Chris & Colleen Wood.
MARGINS: 1/2 LEN, LEN, HEAD Time: 02:01.74 Track: firm
Others: Bodie, Baloney, Madison Gray, Princess Oregon, Burton, Baywatch Babe, Thatsacurlyone, Ernest William, Greene Street, Alpine Delight

THE OAKS STUD MANAWATU CLASSIC

G3, 3YO 2000m, $60,000, Awapuni, April 3
1. DOWRY
3 f, Bahhare – Meant For Me (Noble Bijou).
Owners A R Lawrence, S C Montgomery & J A Rattray.
Breeders Miss J L Smith, D A Thomas & L Williams.
Trainer Murray Baker.
Jockey Darryl Bradley.
2. Terrain
3 g, Kilimanjaro – Tweed View (Imposing).
Owners G A Rogerson & Westbury Stud Ltd (Mgr E J Watson).
Breeders Mrs L A Warwick.
Trainer Graeme Rogerson & Stephen Autridge.
3. Gorgeous George
3 g, Turtle Island – Red Briar (Amalgam).
Owners Mrs M E Burns, Mrs J E & J R Coltman, T A D McFadden, S J Penney & Miss H L Volz.
Breeders Mrs J E & J R Coltman & T A D McFadden.
Trainer Frank & Craig Ritchie.
MARGINS: 3/4 LEN, 1 3/4 LEN, 3/4 LEN Time: 02:03.84 Track: firm
Others: Sea Of Jewels, Grace And Favour, Partee, Vouvray, Vision, Turtle Creek, Scene Steeler, Native Song, Azapak, Light Majesty, Dangerous Day, Lion

CHRISTCHURCH CASINO EASTER CUP STAKES

G3, OPN HCP 1600m, $40,000, Riccarton Park, April 17
1. BALMUSE
4 g, Lord Ballina – Musing (Music Maestro).
Owners P M Connor & K T Myers.
Breeders J N Wallace.
Trainer Kevin Myers.
Jockey Jamie Bullard.
2. Baileys On Ice
4 m, O'Reilly – Creme Anglaise (Crested Wave).
Owners P J Blackwell, O K Booth, G C Cotterill, Ms L E Lawton, G A J McLeod, P A Moroney & B A Schroder.
Breeders G J Chittick.
Trainer Michael Moroney & Andrew Scott.
3. Nat Nat
4 g, Faltaat – Cuddly (Bakharoff).
Owners B Hohaia, N Pilcher, M & Mrs V Purdon.
Breeders R M Warwick Ltd.
Trainer Peter & Dawn Williams.
MARGINS: 1 3/4 LEN, NECK, HEAD Time: 01:35.59 Track: firm
Others: Branson, Amico, Jan Valachi, Cabella, Danzaman, Wild Planet, Jack Be Nimble, Ima Royal, Hustler, The Green Man, Burton

WESTBURY STUD SUNLINE STAKES

G3, 3YO 1200m, $60,000, Te Rapa, April 24
1. FALKIRK
3 c, Tale of the Cat – Madam Valeta (Palace Music).
Owners Windsor Park Stud Ltd.
Breeders J A Burnet & Windsor Park Stud Ltd.
Trainer Paul O'Sullivan.
Jockey Leith Innes.
2. Brave Flyer
3 g, Danasinga – Jelignite Jen (Crested Wave).
Owners M J Stedman.
Breeders G E S Lowe.
Trainer Lance Noble.
3. Pay My Bail
3 f, Justice Prevails – Ebony Jane (Three Legs).
Owners T A Green & T J McKee ONZM.
Breeders G W de Gruchy.
Trainer Stephen & Trevor McKee.
MARGINS: 1 1/2 LEN, 1 1/4 LEN, SHORT NECK Time: 01:09.29 Track: firm
Others: Joyful Winner, Sarajay, Glamour Puss, Green Machine, Blood 'N' Bone, Grace De Soir, Boxer Fluffies, Torrey Pines

COCA-COLA CANTERBURY GOLD CUP

G3, WFA 2000m, $60,000, Riccarton Park, May 1
1. BRANSON
5 g, Personal Flag – Chasing The Habit (Sky Chase).
Owners Six Sigma Racing Ltd.
Breeders J H & Mrs M C Loveridge & Mrs I M Roddick.
Trainer Paul Harris.
Jockey Lance Robinson.
2. Cabolla
5 m, Senor Pete – Miss Fiesta (Fiesta Star).
Owners Thomas Cooker No 1 Syndicate.
Breeders B A Collins & K M Rowe.
Trainer Kevin Hughes.
3. Danzaman
8 g, Danzalion – Thika (Holy Smoke II).
Owners J K Mason.
Breeders F J & Mrs P M Ramsay.
Trainer John Mason.
MARGINS: 2 LEN, LEN, 3/4 LEN Time: 02:03.26 Track: easy
Others: Irish Rover, O'Ella, Ima Royal, Border Callant, Baileys On Ice, Jack Be Nimble, Jan Valachi, Society Beau, Greene Street, Our Shiraz, Il Tenore, Hustler

FIRST SOVEREIGN TRUST ROTORUA CUP

G3, OPN HCP 2300m, $80,000, Arawa Park, May 8
1. NO FIBS
8 m, Casual Lies – Madam's Choice (Dealers Choice).
Owners E J Wood.
Breeders E J Wood.
Trainer Sheryl & Roger McGlade.
Jockey Lynsey Hofmann.
2. Memphis Blues
5 m, Blues Traveller – Otoia Belle (War Hawk II).
Owners B J & Mrs J P Coleman, A & N H Young.
Breeders R J Knight.
Trainer Martin Dunlop.
3. Danzaman
8 g, Danzalion – Thika (Holy Smoke II).
Owners J K Mason.
Breeders F J & Mrs P M Ramsay.
Trainer John Mason.
MARGINS: NOSE, 1 1/4 LEN, _ HEAD Time: 02:29.39 Track: easy
Others: Escobar, Cut 'N' Dry, Bejayjay, Sensuous, Diamond Hill, Titian, Regal Krona, Vettori Tycoon, Baywatch Babe, Shady Devil, Ambush, Just Honor, Challenge

CROMBLE LOCKWOOD CORNWALL HANDICAP

G3, OPN HCP 2200m, $50,000, Ellerslie, June 7
1. BEJAYJAY
6 g, Coral Reef – Galaxy Light (Balios).
Owners P L McKenzie.
Breeders Galaxy Exports Ltd.
Trainer Peter McKenzie.
Jockey Lee Rutherford.
2. Blown Away
8 g, Exploding Prospect – We Greta (Bold And Able).
Owners A D & Mrs L R Murray.

Breeders A D Murray.
Trainer David Murray.
3. Crown Prince
6 g, Vice Regal – Green Queen (King Delamere).
Owners D H & H Watson.
Breeders J J Allan.
Trainer Jim Pender.
MARGINS: 1 1/2 LEN, SHORT HEAD, HEAD
Time: 02:29.56 Track: heavy
Others: No Fibs, Tantalic, Ebony Boy, Trout'll Do, Stark Inn, Just Not Cricket, Darth Vader, Live The Reality, Gristle, Clever Devil

PREMIER JUMPS

HANZ 114TH GRAND NATIONAL HURDLES

OPN HDL 4200m, $40,000, Riccarton Park, August 6
1. COOL WATER
9 g, Tanker Port – Irene Adair (Balmerino).
Owners Messrs M A & N & Mesdames P M & S L Treweek.
Breeders Willow Park Motor Hotel Ltd.
Trainer Joanne Moss.
Jockey Rochelle Lockett.
2. Willywince
9 g, Gaius – Ingresea (Beaufort Sea).
Owners W E & Mrs K N Calder.
Breeders W E Calder & W W Day.
Trainer John & Karen Parsons.
3. Classic Spirit
12 g, Beldale Lear – Madam's Choice (Dealers Choice).
Owners E J Wood.
Breeders E J Wood.
Trainer Sheryl & Roger McGlade.
MARGINS: Time: 04:43.05 Track: easy
Others: Foreign Seas, Eye Chance, Bushland, Al Burkan, Boy Oh Boy, Honestly, Oneway Street

PYNE GOULD GUINNESS 129TH GRAND NATIONAL STEEPLECHASE

OPN STP 5600m, $50,000, Riccarton Park, August 9
1. CUCHULAINN
11 g, Pat's Victory – Paid For (Commoner).
Owners G G Robb.
Breeders P Neilson.
Trainer Bob Autridge.
Jockey Finbarr Leahy.
2. Eric The Bee
12 g, St Hilarion – Brazen Princess (Zamazaan).
Owners M Watt.
Breeders S C Montgomery, J A Rattray & G B Sargent.
Trainer Kevin Hughes.
3. No Sweat
9 g, Kyoei Dapper – Miss Lincoln (Makor).
Owners P S & Mrs C Nelson.
Breeders Mrs C & P S Nelson.
Trainer Paul Nelson.
MARGINS: Time: 06:50.16 Track: easy
Others: Sir Avion, Gold Story, Highlander, Herne

THE MAD BUTCHER PAKURANGA HUNT CUP

OPN STP 4900m, $30,000, Ellerslie, August 23
1. WANDERLUST
11 g, Globetrotter – Hauma (So Sharp).
Owners Mrs A Browne & K S Browne MBE.
Breeders K N Shearer.
Trainer Ann & Ken Browne.
Jockey Michelle Hopkins.
2. Smart Hunter
12 g, Ivory Hunter – Jeanne's Jest (Red Jester).
Owners Mrs A Browne & K S Browne MBE.
Breeders Mrs C & P S Nelson.
Trainer Ann & Ken Browne.
3. Boon's Boy
11 g, Babarooom – Hasty's Girl (Hastings Road).
Owners Mrs A Browne & K S Browne MBE.
Breeders Mrs A & K S Browne.
Trainer Ann & Ken Browne.
MARGINS: Time: 06:54.35 Track: heavy
Others: Gold Story, Royal Ways, Golden Flare, Impressive King, Titus

DUNSTAN FEEDS WAIKATO HURDLES

OPN HDL 3200m, $40,000, Te Rapa, May 15
1. FONTERA
5 g, Kingsttenham – Garter Star (Diamante D).
Owners D M, H T, M J & S C O'Leary.
Breeders Mrs Y J Cavanagh.
Trainer Kevin Myers.
Jockey Issac Lupton.
2. Rabbit
5 g, Lowell – Purple Vixen (In the Purple).
Owners M S & R M Connors.
Breeders Mrs S A Broughton.
Trainer Raymond Connors.
3. My Willie Montague
9 g, Markella – Belle Du Nord (Arctic Tern).
Owners Mrs D M Cowling, A M Gatt & D A M Williams.
Breeders D A M, Mrs K M & Miss Z M Williams.
Trainer Craig Thornton.
MARGINS: 5 3/4 LEN, NECK, 1 3/4 LEN
Time: 03:39.92 Track: soft
Others: Al Burkan, Honestly, Willywince, Krona's Lead, Deceit, Ultimate Game, Patronage, Lucky Tip, Profiler, Danz

ECOLAB WAIKATO STEEPLECHASE

OPN STP 4900m, $50,000, Te Rapa, May 15
1. GOLD JET
7 g, Jetball – Rhine Goddess (Rheingold).
Owners Mrs H C & M I McCone, G J & Mrs I M Roddick.
Breeders Mrs I M Roddick.
Trainer Brian & Shane Anderton.
Jockey Tom Hazlett.
2. Doctor Heights
7 g, Doctor David – Victory Heights (Sir Tristram).
Owners M S & R M Connors.
Breeders D B & Mrs M P Jones.
Trainer Raymond Connors.
3. Wanderlust
11 g, Globetrotter – Hauma (So Sharp).
Owners Mrs A Browne & K S Browne MBE.
Breeders K N Shearer.
Trainer Ann & Ken Browne.
MARGINS: LONG HEAD, 14 LEN, LONG HEAD Time: 05:57.96 Track: soft
Others: Impressive King, Crojack, Prince William, Bit Of A Myth, Gold Story, Sir Avion, Cool Conductor

Fontera.
TRISH DUNELL

FRIDAY FLASH GREAT NORTHERN HURDLES

OPN HDL 4190m, $70,000, Ellerslie, June 5
1. CUCHULAINN
11 g, Pat's Victory – Paid For (Commoner).
Owners G G Robb.
Breeders P Neilson.
Trainer Bob Autridge.
Jockey Finbarr Leahy.
2. Al Burkan
10 g, Aliyoun – Petite Dawn (Never Til Dawn).
Owners Mrs M G & N W Candy.
Breeders Mrs M G & N W Candy.
Trainer Gary Vile.
3. Challenge
6 g, Yachtie – Marinos (Moss Trooper).
Owners Mrs E R Myers.
Breeders Lambourn Stud Ltd.
Trainer Kevin Myers.
MARGINS: 4 1/2 LEN, 2 3/4 LEN, 3 3/4 LEN
Time: 05:10.31 Track: heavy
Others: Patronage, Nasser, Lucky Tip, Honestly, Ultimate Game, My Willie Montague, Doctor Heights

MERCEDES GREAT NORTHERN STEEPLECHASE

OPN STP 6400m, $100,000, Ellerslie, June 7
1. WANDERLUST
11 g, Globetrotter – Hauma (So Sharp).
Owners Mrs A Browne & K S Browne MBE.
Breeders K N Shearer.
Trainer Ann & Ken Browne.
Jockey Michelle Hopkins.
2. Aquaria Dancer
8 g, Zabeel – Balmereve (Balmerino).
Owners D V Baker, Ms H E Flinn & Mrs R J Owen.
Breeders Mrs J A & P Hogan.
Trainer Heather Flinn.
3. Golden Flare
12 g, Touching Wood – Golden Glow (Lucifer II).
Owners C W Foote & G N Sharp.
Breeders T F Harvey.
Trainer Raylene Whiteside.
MARGINS: 14 LEN, LONG HEAD, 15 LEN
Time: 08:18.30 Track: heavy
Others: Cool Conductor, Bart, Bit Of A Myth, Gold Story, Ilika Dance

DILMAH EARL GREY MCGREGOR GRANT STEEPLECHASE

OPN STP 4900m, $25,000, Ellerslie, June 19
1. KIA KING
7 g, Kingsttenham – Glory Phantasy (Musical Phantasy).
Owners Mrs A Browne & K S Browne MBE.
Breeders R L Allen.
Trainer Ann & Ken Browne.
Jockey Michelle Hopkins.
2. Cool Conductor
10 g, Icelandic – Orchestration (Zamazaan).
Owners Jump At The Chance Syndicate.
Breeders Mrs M J & M S Wallis.
Trainer Tony Cole.
3. Impressive King
8 g, Omnicorp – Identified (So Called).
Owners Mrs A Browne & K S Browne MBE.
Breeders Fayette Park Stud Ltd.
Trainer Ann & Ken Browne.
MARGINS: 13 LEN, 5 LEN, 5 1/2 LEN Time: 06:33.94 Track: heavy
Others: Cardiac, Titus, Montacute, Golden Flare, Bit Of A Myth, Single Minded, Aquaria Dance

ASHWELL FARM HAWKE'S BAY STEEPLECHASE

OPN STP 4800m, $40,000, Hastings, July 3
1. GOLD JET
7 g, Jetball – Rhine Goddess (Rheingold).
Owners Mrs H C & M I McCone, G J & Mrs I M Roddick.
Breeders Mrs I M Roddick.
Trainer Brian & Shane Anderton.
Jockey Tom Hazlett.
2. Cuchulainn
11 g, Pat's Victory – Paid For (Commoner).
Owners G G Robb.
Breeders P Neilson.
Trainer Bob Autridge.
3. Doctor Heights
7 g, Doctor David – Victory Heights (Sir Tristram).
Owners M S & R M Connors.
Breeders D B & Mrs M P Jones.
Trainer Raymond Connors.
MARGINS: 2 1/4 LEN, 10 LEN, 2 LEN Time: 06:25.77 Track: heavy
Others: Impressive King, Imperial Warrior, Willie Tee, Cardiac

Leith Innes.

JOCKEYS PREMIERSHIP

First title for Leith Innes

Jockey	Starts	Wins	2nd	3rd	4th	Stakes
Innes L G	725	114	85	89	73	$1558050
Walker M J	634	107	78	63	79	$1561244
Bradley D G	683	106	101	92	94	$1156331
Busson O P	442	01	50	50	47	$2188686
Bullard J S	517	79	63	64	44	$667536
* Waddell J L	687	79	86	77	61	$852796
Calder A J	679	78	63	61	74	$1098771
Walker D J	584	67	44	61	60	$861598
Coleman M T	579	57	73	49	73	$1281692
Hannam R J	592	56	52	46	42	$579329
* Hercock K R	551	56	53	54	53	$565313
Tinsley H S	392	56	53	54	45	$930516
* Lammas C E	668	55	63	53	57	$708442
Sweeney M C	612	51	54	50	57	$640697
Hampton M L	453	50	53	49	33	$388447
Johnson P D	418	48	56	45	33	$695410
Harris N G	398	46	29	47	35	$944765
Herd B S	450	46	42	48	46	$669265
Moseley T R	494	46	44	39	51	$512019
Taylor P A	676	44	63	56	66	$532060
Lawson J S	390	43	39	39	36	$328899
Rutherford L C	640	43	65	58	60	$843840
Bates J C	407	42	28	45	44	$403953
Laking J D	284	42	33	26	22	$324745
Allpress L J	436	40	41	45	34	$444860
Young L K	411	39	35	36	41	$302011
Cooksley G L	181	34	28	15	17	$795845
Hofmann L H	525	34	35	37	43	$579067
Peard A C	359	34	39	28	27	$544685
Robinson L M	413	33	44	42	39	$326824
Grylls G J	396	32	30	41	27	$629799
Allan T K	372	31	37	33	33	$366737
Russell T J	365	31	26	28	29	$344236
* Sliz G K	370	31	21	31	31	$594187
Williams K	420	31	33	29	44	$206565
Colgan V A	266	30	34	32	28	$327102
Smith K A	345	29	23	32	38	$255901
* Holmes P T	354	28	25	35	21	$316105
Williamson M J	373	28	22	31	36	$292155
Du Plessis M R	223	26	38	21	16	$298180
* Johnston V D	298	24	26	25	25	$274888
Barnsley M	345	22	19	34	34	$211286
* Cheshire L G D	206	22	17	13	15	$180966
Collins S L	332	22	24	25	26	$189087
Jones B R	244	22	25	22	22	$424908
Richards P S	211	22	20	25	24	$165245

Jockey	Starts	Wins	2nd	3rd	4th	Stakes
Innes M B	452	21	32	39	32	$279258
Thornton T D	407	21	31	29	46	$303830
Hopkins M R	96	20	11	11	12	$272190
* Anderson C I	346	19	25	21	36	$246685
Davidson Kelly	404	19	17	28	39	$256458
* Lockie S W K	325	19	27	31	17	$177333
McLeod R	162	19	19	13	12	$744410
* Newton T C	203	19	24	7	23	$137426
Riddell J K B	129	19	23	16	15	$203540
* Collins K N	247	18	20	24	16	$136026
* Fraser R K	147	18	15	10	4	$159901
* Kelly S	227	18	17	15	23	$208885
Hibberd B	237	17	27	15	26	$181109
De Klerk E	274	16	15	20	27	$245097
McCann S	249	15	26	21	25	$162645
Rogers J E M	168	14	14	16	13	$141725
Lupton I A	71	13	12	11	5	$148198
* Stam R	129	13	4	12	9	$119413
* Todd J R	261	13	20	18	17	$98126
Birkett J	157	12	11	13	6	$78537
* Bothamley D R	312	12	24	18	19	$123080
Lockett R J	46	12	7	2	4	$98087
McNab M J	167	12	12	21	14	$115423
Norvall R M B	355	12	25	25	24	$202728
* Cameron M	189	11	19	17	8	$82588
Leahy T F	65	11	9	10	6	$189050
Chipperfield C M	76	10	9	10	5	$126940
Lamb E D	93	10	11	8	13	$100713
* Waters K L	172	10	9	7	10	$87001
Hazlett T J	66	9	7	12	5	$152800
McGregor L D	109	8	6	10	8	$50190
* Ropiha B	91	8	7	10	9	$63940
* Te Maari C I	117	8	2	13	10	$48098
Montague C J	69	7	5	3	8	$56200
* Parker L K	83	7	5	9	6	$43961
Spratt S C	95	7	9	7	8	$58263
Belsham T M	25	6	3	4	5	$50400
* Houston S S	86	6	5	6	8	$42660
* Mason R S	92	6	14	8	9	$84040
Tunbridge J V	112	6	9	3	5	$51898
Carmine C L	156	5	8	14	15	$54747
* Hoek M J	69	5	7	8	8	$54940
* Payne M E	35	5	3	5	1	$35025
Taggart A B	192	5	10	12	16	$57750

* Denotes apprentice rider

TRAINERS PREMIERSHIP

Mark Walker by three

Mark Walker.

Trainer	Starts	Wins	2nd	3rd	4th	Stakes
Walker M W	409	76	53	53	39	$1555717
Rogerson G A & S R Autridge	578	73	57	53	60	$1375577
O'Sullivan P D	382	63	48	47	45	$1369993
McKee T J & S J	499	55	54	50	52	$832878
Moroney M D & A D Scott	441	55	54	39	50	$1340198
Pitman M R	511	49	65	52	56	$462222
Myers K T	224	45	33	26	13	$444302
Marsh R B & S B	292	39	35	38	41	$678429
Harris P D	413	37	33	30	33	$419546
James R A & Ms L Bertling	205	37	34	26	18	$336035
Sharrock S A	226	35	35	31	20	$405462
Williams P J & Mrs D M	163	35	15	22	20	$238512
Wheeler J R	475	34	34	45	48	$310485
Anderton B J & S C	306	30	27	25	30	$253440
Baker M P	260	30	28	37	25	$318188
Parsons J F & Mrs K G	266	30	25	25	25	$298313
Zimmerman K A	234	30	29	21	38	$290137
Hughes K H	235	27	24	29	25	$332425
Ritchie C E B & F T	214	27	13	22	20	$357417
Gray K	320	26	24	33	33	$390850
Jillings C M & R A Yuill	207	25	22	24	17	$677883
Sargent J G & K L Allpress	165	24	29	18	13	$546878
Browne Mrs A & K S	275	23	17	27	28	$400950
Wood Mrs C L & C J	215	23	21	20	25	$361690
Collett R D	141	22	21	17	8	$252430
Hurdle P J & Mrs N A	119	22	16	8	16	$203937
Vile G R	233	22	21	24	19	$260090
Logan Mrs D M & G D	235	21	26	21	27	$302735
Mathews H W & Mrs L A	170	21	30	23	9	$293802
Gibbs J A	90	20	11	6	10	$239032
Jones A L & B McDonald	203	20	20	19	29	$436953
Breslin M P	188	19	20	23	26	$209147
Latta L M	244	19	17	18	19	$394532
Richardson G N & M J Donoghue	146	19	8	14	13	$275400
Sanders G K & Mrs D A Sweeney	236	19	19	22	26	$272108
Hay J T	127	18	14	19	11	$142410
Lock P W	177	18	14	16	15	$135192
Beckett L R	115	17	5	14	14	$97517
Cole T W	140	17	15	17	14	$338585
Herbert Mrs A L & I W	124	17	11	15	17	$161968
Oulaghan M K	172	17	8	18	10	$212025
Anderton H T & S J	107	15	15	10	15	$119729
Boon J E	112	15	14	17	7	$389845
Brosnan M H	136	15	17	13	11	$166095
Pender J C	187	15	12	15	13	$191594

Trainer	Starts	Wins	2nd	3rd	4th	Stakes
Priscott R B	163	15	19	18	19	$191845
Rayner E W & Miss J J	120	15	17	9	11	$194179
Wallace J V	102	15	8	13	9	$99878
Lynds J R	121	14	12	12	12	$153296
Manning R R	135	14	18	14	14	$125775
Searle G L	161	14	15	18	10	$149033
Waddell D L	215	14	12	12	13	$187930
Eales N D & M N J	144	13	23	13	9	$141298
Fleming K N	134	13	17	18	11	$99238
George I L	141	13	8	8	10	$74125
McNeilly L A	98	13	19	10	12	$82902
Alexander K J	84	12	10	9	7	$120863
Autridge R	127	12	17	11	12	$189875
Gibson G	110	12	11	12	8	$69388
Gillies T R & Mrs P J	93	12	9	9	9	$105375
Haworth D R & Mrs S C	136	12	13	20	11	$95787
McCarroll C R	84	12	8	16	9	$115347
McQuade K L	81	12	15	5	7	$171425
Noble L R	95	12	15	14	5	$118090
Otto R A & S J Fache	140	12	7	12	8	$162253
Prendergast Mrs L R & A W	109	12	7	14	11	$109978
Clotworthy K F & W S	125	11	13	15	7	$134875
Hillis Mrs V D & W P	71	11	6	5	5	$379010
Hrstich B C	51	11	4	10	3	$103085
McKay P N	102	11	8	10	10	$201850
Prince S J	65	11	4	5	4	$88815
Wallace B J	107	11	14	6	6	$142962
Auret N J	46	10	10	5	8	$112812
Connors R M	61	10	11	7	6	$101653
Fursdon K	65	10	4	7	5	$346711
McGlade H R & Mrs S A	155	10	15	13	14	$270050
Searle G L & H J	73	10	3	5	4	$83312
Bergerson R J	66	9	4	3	8	$59925
Bothwell R J & C J	124	9	15	11	7	$190272
Brown A J	31	9	5	3	3	$211150
Cameron S L	74	9	5	11	3	$75003
Dee R J & M T Dixon	89	9	9	8	10	$151430
Didham L G	103	9	8	10	5	$84687
Gulliver S W	113	9	4	5	6	$89075
Jenkins P P	75	9	6	2	9	$80825
McKay J D & Mrs T	89	9	8	6	14	$81315
McKenzie P L	58	9	6	6	9	$192940
Roberts D B	111	9	6	11	6	$99175
Sellwood D G	136	9	9	22	12	$135238
Todd CBE M J Todd	128	9	16	17	13	$75950